*C*ᵃᵖᵗ· Nat Herreshoff

THE WIZARD OF BRISTOL

C*apt.* Nat Herreshoff

THE WIZARD OF BRISTOL

The life and achievements of
Nathanael Greene Herreshoff,
together with an account of some of
the yachts he designed

BY L. FRANCIS HERRESHOFF

ILLUSTRATED

Sheridan House

First paperback edition
published 1996 by
Sheridan House, Inc.
145 Palisade Street
Dobbs Ferry, NY 10522

First published 1953 by Sheridan House, Inc.

Library of Congress Cataloging-in-Publication Data

Herreshoff, Lewis Francis, 1890-1972
  Capt. Nat Herreshoff, the wizard of Bristol

   Includes index.
   1. Herreshoff, Nathanael Greene, 1848-1938.
   2. Ship-building—Rhode Island—Bristol—History.
   3. Naval architects—Rhode Island—Bristol—Biography
   4. Bristol, R.I.—Biography. I. Title.
   VM140.H4H4 1981
   623.8'1223'0924 [B]   80-28519

Printed in the United States of America

ISBN 1-57409-004-6

To the Memory
of My Father

Contents

$C^{apt.}$ Nat Herreshoff

THE WIZARD OF BRISTOL

CHAPTER ONE

The Time and the Place

Mᴏsᴛ biographies and many books start off with a preface, then an introduction follows, and sometimes even an inaugural chapter, but, Gentle Reader, if you are like myself you will often skip these parts in your rush to get to the real substance of the thing. "We Americans are busy people," you will say, "so never mind the fanfare and build up, just give us the real *pièce de resistance* without any extra dressing."

There is another reason also for my abruptness, and that is that our subject, Mr. Herreshoff, was very direct, straightforward and, at times, even blunt in his manner. He used no fanfare or mannerisms; in fact I think we may say his most outstanding characteristics were his direct acting mind and his love for the naked truth. He certainly had no patience with the shams, deceits, and confusions which prevent most of us from seeing clearly or thinking logically.

I believe he would say of this book, or any other for that matter: "Why have an introduction? If you have anything to say, say it. There is no need of explaining why we are writing it. The text, if it is any good, will make that obvious." I am sure he would say: "Never mind about telling what a wonderful book this is to be, for the reader will decide that for himself after he has turned the last page."

But, Gentle Reader, I am entirely inadequate as a writer to take you directly to the crux of the matter. So, unfortunately, I must make some of the excuses generally found in an introduc-

11

tion, and I want to state quite clearly that this is no writing to be judged by the gentlemen who have studied the art of composition at either of the Cambridges. No, surely this will be no sublime composition where, for the form of the thing, its perfect balance of sentence—its cadence, if you like—the author has sacrificed the subject matter to achieve some accepted style. Instead, it is a simple writing intended only to describe the life work of Mr. Herreshoff, and, if possible, to correct several myths and falsehoods which have sprung up around his life.

While I am quite aware that such a prosaic attempt will not meet with the popular opinion of what a biography should be, still on the whole it may in this form be of more use to the student than some writing intended to amuse rather than to instruct, though at the present time it seems the custom of the biographer to dig out all the dirt, sordidness, and eccentricity of his subject and lay it before the reader.

For instance, each biography of Thoreau, as it comes out, makes him out to be more and more of a wild Indian instead of the original thinker that he was. But in the case of our subject, Mr. Herreshoff, I believe we can find enough of interest to talk about without departing much from his life's work.

As the time at which an individual is born, or rather educated, has nearly as much effect on his character as environment itself, we have called this first chapter, "The Time and the Place," and while this writer, like many others, believes that inheritance dominates all other factors in forming character, he has chosen the time and the place as the best medium of introducing Mr. Herreshoff and has taken later chapters to describe his inheritance and education.

As for the time, Nathanael Greene Herreshoff was born in 1848, and to be more exact on March 18 of that year which, strange to say, is a little over one hundred years ago from this writing. To those interested in yachting, it might be mentioned that this was three years before the "America" went to England to race for the Queen's Cup. It was a period about half way between the Mexican and Civil wars, and a time in this country when the various industries were employing many more people than previously in the manufacture of textile machinery, agricultural implements, fire arms; and the clock makers were setting up large factories and working out the technique of mass production. This certainly was a time when the stars were in a propitious position for accomplishment—a time quite different from the present when each man's arm seems turned against the other man.

Perhaps the time at which a person is educated is of more importance in forming his character, and that Mr. Herreshoff was between thirteen and seventeen years old during the Civil War no doubt had an effect on his convictions, for this great struggle of conscience and humanity against vested interests had rocked the whole country in a deadly argument. Those who were boys during this period were fed up with argument and as a class were short spoken; they were courageous, practical, and sometimes hard, and this is clearly shown in the portraits and daguerreotypes of the men of Mr. Herreshoff's age. Perhaps they had to be hard to face conditions after the Civil War, but at any rate these portraits show a quite different type of man from those of a decade before or a generation after.

Before the Civil War this country had produced some really good writers and, several years before, some notable painters, but after the war the arts and literature were at their lowest ebb. At this time the steam engine was the reigning god, for no one then knew how to make dollars by electricity or gasoline. Commodore Vanderbilt in New York had made several million dollars with his steamships, which ran in most every direction, and he was beginning to take an interest in the iron horse or at least was buying up the rails the iron horse ran on in and out of New York. The steam engine was pumping water to most of the cities; it was running all factories not located near water power; it was sawing lumber and pumping out mines.

During the eighteen forties and fifties fast ship-rigged vessels, generally called "clipper ships," were developed both for carrying passengers to California during the gold rush and for shipping tea from China. To quote from A. H. Clark's book, *The Clipper Ship Era,* "The building of clipper ships in the United States reached its zenith in 1853. In that year forty-eight clippers were added to the California fleet and the wild excitement of building, owning, and racing these splendid ships was at its height."

After the Civil War, however, the steamship was so successfully taking the place of the clipper that practically no more clipper ships were built in this country. The steamer passage across the Atlantic was being spoken of as the Atlantic Ferry, and although for several years to come the sailing ships held the records for crossings, particularly running to the eastward, the steamer with sail as auxiliary power was making by far the most regularly scheduled passages.

It is little wonder that a youth brought up in a seaport in those times should have had thoughts mostly about sail and steam, and as many boys of a later generation were to dream of electricity, the internal combustion engine, and the airplane, young N. G. Herreshoff was dreaming about sail and steam.

Now that we have considered the time of Mr. Herreshoff's boyhood we should look at the place, for there is no doubt that boyhood associations, and the traditions of one's home town, have a marked effect on one's later career or course of action.

The place, Bristol, Rhode Island, where our subject was born, was one of our old seaports before vessels became so large that they required more draft, and although the old town had not been founded until about 1680 it soon went into shipping, for by 1690 it seems to have had fifteen of its vessels engaged in foreign trade. Bristol had originally been a part of the Plymouth colonies, made up of the three counties of Plymouth, Barnstable and Bristol, but the Bristol lands were inhabited mostly by Indians. At first Massasoit was the Indian chief of this district, and until his death in 1662 he remained friendly and faithful to the Plymouth Colony. He was succeeded by his son, Wamsutta, who reigned but a short time when Massasoit's second son, Philip, became chief of the Wampanoag tribe. Philip, although he was said to be partly of white blood, hated the English and started to war against them in 1675, but he was driven to a retreat at Mount Hope within the present township of Bristol, where he was shot and killed in 1676.

After King Philip's War it became practical to settle this region, so four wealthy Englishmen, temporarily residing in Boston, purchased about seven thousand acres of that part of Bristol County that borders on Narragansett Bay which had previously been called the Mount Hope Lands. These four original settlers or proprietors were men of means and apparently had good educations, for they laid the town out in a grand way with broad parallel streets as if planning a city. So far as I know, Bristol is one of the oldest New England towns that originally had straight streets for, as they say, most other towns built their streets along cowpaths. It is said that the founders laid the town out to be a seaport and that they hoped Bristol would be the shipping point for southern Massachusetts, as old Bristol in England was the shipping port for the western part of that country. But I fear one of the reasons the Bristolians took so suddenly to the water was that the soil of Bristol was not particularly fertile; its dry lands were stony and its low lands boggy, but I have no intention to write a history of the town and only want to explain the reason for its nautical inclination. I cannot refrain, however, from saying something about the people of Rhode Island, for in many ways they were quite different from the Puritans at Plymouth. And while it has been said that Bristol originally was a part of the Plymouth Colony, this was before it was settled. After it was settled it belonged to the Massachusetts Bay Colony until 1747 when it became a part of more liberal-minded Rhode Island.

But the early Bristol people were intimately connected with those of Boston during the first seventy years of Bristol's settlement, and the trail, or road, between the two places was called— at least for part of its way—the Anawan Trail for it went by Anawan Rock where the friendly Indian, Anawan, lived. Many of the early Rhode Islanders came from Boston and, as some said, left it for conscience sake, not liking the narrow Puritans or the witch-burning Salemites. However, many of the settlers around Newport and Kingston in South County were well-to-do English gentlemen who set up large farms and country estates with handsome manor houses. History relates that several of these families came over to raise horses and at a very early date they developed a famous breed of horses called a Narragansett Pacer. By 1686 Bristol was shipping these horses to South America and the West Indies.

These Rhode Islanders were not religious fanatics or fugitives from persecution; very few of them were connected with the renegades who had murdered Charles I and foisted the Commonwealth and Cromwell on the people. Free thought and religious freedom were allowed in the state, and although the Church of England, or what was spoken of as the Episcopalian faith during the Revolution, was the most respected church in the state, almost all other religions were represented, including numerous Quakers, and one of the proofs of this religious tolerance is that the first synagogue in America was located at Newport. So the people as a whole were more worldly than those of Massachusetts. They lived, dressed, ate, and I might say drank, like the European gentlemen of that time. There was no danger in Rhode Island of being burned as a witch if someone did not like your religion or coveted your property.

So with their worldliness they soon went into commerce, shipping, privateering, and running slave ships. The latter two activities called for fast vessels, and it is my opinion that the Rhode Islanders developed the world's fastest topsail schooners and brigs around 1800. Many of the slavers hailed from Bristol and between 1700 and 1800 there was no stigma associated with running slave ships. But the vessels had to be fast simply to transfer their living cargo from Africa with as little loss as possible, for only a slave in good condition brought a good price at the market. While it is true that Bristol ships landed slaves at Charleston, South Carolina, until about 1812 most of the slave running was done before that. Of the ships landing slaves in Charleston between 1804 and 1807—two hundred and two in all—seven hailed from Great Britain, three from France, one from Sweden, sixty-one from Charleston, and fifty-nine from Rhode Island; all other American ports accounted for but eight.

An ancestor of the writer is credited with owning ten slavers at Bristol in 1806 and having interest in four others. The Bristol slave ships sailed from their home port with a cargo of rum which they traded on the coast of Africa for slaves; then they ran to

Cuba where the slaves were traded for a cargo of molasses, which in turn was taken to Bristol on the third leg of their triangular cruise. At Bristol there were quite extensive rum distilleries which are said to have distilled two hundred gallons a day in 1800.

However, it was not until after about 1820, when English and American men-of-war were suppressing the slave trade, that the horrors of the middle passage became notorious. At that time it is believed some slave ships disgorged, or threw overboard, their whole cargo of slaves so as not to be caught with this contraband on board. It is said that at times the whole shipment of slaves were shackled to an anchor chain and heaved overboard at once. This was done so none could be found floating by the overtaking revenue cutters. Although after the War of 1812 slave running was very profitable, it was looked on as a form of piracy and the crew of the slave ships were subject to capital punishment if caught. I believe few, if any, slavers sailed out of Narragansett Bay after 1812.

The slave ships that sailed from Bristol were quite small, probably mostly under a hundred tons; they were of light build and carried large sail area. Their rig was mostly topsail schooner and brig, and they were undoubtedly remarkably fast.

But there was another type of fast sailer being built in the Bay and this was the Colonial Privateer. Rhode Island produced more of these ships, which sailed and fought under the British flag, than any other of the colonies, and it is said that between 1700 and the Revolution one hundred eighty privateers were built or fitted out in the Bay. The author's great-great-uncle was the captain of one named "Prince Charles of Lorraine" which was particularly active in the war of her time between France and England and among other activities, in 1744, ransacked and plundered the French settlements along the coast of French Guiana much to the profit of his owner and himself.

These privateers of Narragansett Bay were lightly built and depended on their speed for escape or capture. Their usual mode of attack, even if it was a considerably larger vessel, was to lay to windward of their intended prize and with a long-range long gun drop a shot on her every quarter of an hour or so, all the time keeping just out of range of their antagonist's guns. In this way they made many captures without themselves being damaged, but this technique is only possible with a very fast and weatherly ship.

So, together with the practice of building slave ships and privateers for some hundred years, the art of designing and building fast sailing ships had been developed to a remarkably high degree in Narragansett Bay.

In the War of 1812 Bristol sent out several privateers and one of them, the "Yankee," was the most successful of all American privateers. It is estimated she destroyed more than five million dollars of English shipping and no doubt brought to the old town of Bristol several fortunes for the profits of one cruise were divided as follows: owners, $223,313.10; captain, $15,789.69, and so on down to Jack Jibsheet and Cuffee Cockroach, the two colored cabin boys who shared respectively $738.19 and $1,121.88. These were large sums of money in those days.

The "Yankee" was at sea less than three years as a privateer and made six cruises in that time; she undoubtedly brought more than a million dollars into the town, including some ships that her owners subsequently employed with profit as cargo vessels and whalers. Although there are practically no authentic plans, models, or lines of the Narragansett Bay privateers, I have had the "Yankee" described to me by a man whose father had seen her. She was said to have had a great deal of dead rise to her sections, and was fine on the waterline at both ends, and was said to have carried a large but very neat and light rig. Her best point of sailing, compared to other vessels of her time, was close hauled and, while we have no record of her speed under full sail in a chase, she did make a passage from Ascension to Cape St. Augustine, a distance of 1,200 miles, in seven and one half days. Another time she ran 3,500 miles in twenty-seven days. Most likely her speed when driven hard was in the neighborhood of fourteen miles an hour, or twelve knots.

Another privateer that hailed from Bristol was the "Macdonough"; she was larger than the "Yankee" and considered faster. While she took many prizes in the last year of the war, they all, I believe, were retaken by the many English cruisers along our coast so that as a privateer she was not profitable. She is said to have made a passage between Havana and Bristol in six days although becalmed one day of the passage. The "Macdonough" was later sold to Cuban owners and became a slaver.

After the War of 1812 Bristol went in for whaling as well as general commerce, and in 1837 its whaling fleet numbered nineteen ships. Bristol continued building ships until about 1850, and between 1830 and 1856 sixty vessels were built and rigged there.

And this brings us up to N. G. Herreshoff's boyhood, and I must say he often spoke with great respect of the ship carpenters, boatbuilders, riggers, block makers, and sail makers who were still working in the old town and many of whom, as a matter of fact, were the first employees in his brother John's boat yard which was started about 1856. All of his life Mr. Herreshoff bewailed the fact that he could never get their equals in his later employees, and as Herreshoff yachts were considered of the highest quality in the world, it would appear that the native Bristol workmen at the time of his boyhood were real artists.

I have devoted all this space to the history of the town and the type of vessels built there because I believe that the traditions of Bristol and the craftsmen who lived there had a profound influence on Mr. Herreshoff's character. I know definitely he was one of the most skillful workers I have ever seen with the light shipbuilding tools, and I believe he acquired many of these skills in his childhood from his father and other native Bristolians. To me, a knowledge of how things are made seems the most important enlightenment a designer can have, for only then can he design things that are practical to make and only then will he have the complete confidence and respect of his workmen. There is no doubt that Mr. Herreshoff was a skilful mechanic at a very early age, perhaps fifteen or sixteen, and all during his life he could direct his workmen, or explain to them in a very few words, the most practical method for accomplishing their particular tasks. One of the most remarkable features of all his designs was that the work could be made with the commercial materials available at the time and with simple tools and equipment. Perhaps no one knew better than he all of the tricks and techniques of pattern making, casting, forging, machining, sheet metal work, and general wood construction; and I refer here to these arts as practiced

or performed by hand or with hand tools. While his later education, which we will speak of in a later chapter, increased his
knowledge in all these arts, I cannot help but think it was mostly
started with his early contact with Bristol mechanics, for time
and again he would say to me in describing some technique or
showing me how to do something: "This is the way so-and-so
used to do it," naming some Bristol blacksmith, block maker, rigger, boatbuilder or sail maker of his boyhood. And while we have
no space in this book to go into the history of cabinetmaking,
clockmaking and ropemaking in Rhode Island, it is well known
that these endeavors had reached a high state of perfection there
in colonial times.

Even some of the Rhode Island gentlemen of leisure were
mechanically minded and used small lathes for ivory turning and
other ornamental turning, as many of the gentlemen of Europe
had during the preceding century. All of these things had an
effect on the traditions of the place and must have had a
profound influence on molding the intellect of a boy of the time.
In other words, this was a region that could mold a Yankee
mechanic with greater perfection than places slightly to the westward where commercialism was the first consideration, and their
famous product was the wooden nutmeg; while off to the eastward the finer arts had been looked down on by the descendants
of the Puritans.

But we should now look at the geography of the place for perhaps the principal influences of environment are geographical,
that is, climate, location, etc. The town of Bristol is located on
a peninsula which, as it protrudes southward, approaches the
center of Narragansett Bay. This neck of land in some ways is
shaped like a lobster claw, with Bristol harbor the space between
the jaws, and as the land narrows in toward the north, at what
might be called the wrist of the claw, the town is nearly
surrounded by water. While it cannot be said that there is any
high land in the neighborhood, still this region is of a rolling
nature as if leveled off and slightly gouged out in the glacial
period. From the slightly elevated land back of the town one can
command a panorama of some interest for, if not grand or inspir-
ing, it at least has a certain fascination for a sailor—before him

are several islands, points and bays so arranged that one overlaps another in a way that awakens the imagination and forms a visual pull that cannot be resisted by the young Anglo-Saxon. Thus, for centuries the boys of the town have been drawn to the waters of the Bay by this ever present picture.

Off to the south lies the island of Rhode Island only separated from Bristol by a sheet of water half a mile wide. In former times there were several windmills on the island of Rhode Island and from Bristol they gave the scene a rather foreign aspect, but to a lover of Rhode Island johnnycakes the slowly revolving sails of these mills brought pleasant thoughts for the mills were grinding meal from Rhode Island white cap and Rhode Island golden cap corn. And if there is anything better than that for a steady diet this writer has never tasted it, for it can be consumed with pleasure in one form or another three times a day for three hundred and sixty-five days of the year. Johnnycakes, corn bread, brown bread, Indian pudding, scallops rolled in corn meal and fried in bacon fat in a skillet—yes, bless the Narragansett Indians who gave us this corn. It might be interesting to note here that our Mr. Herreshoff ate these johnnycakes seven eighths of the mornings of his life. I suppose I should apologize to the patient reader, but he would readily excuse me if he had been brought up in sight of those windmills.

Just to the westward of the island of Rhode Island is a fairly straight, sparkling strip of the Bay running in a compass course nearly south by west, clear to Newport, but this magnificent sheet of water is somewhat obscured from view by Hog Island which partly encloses the southern side of Bristol Harbor: otherwise Bristol Harbor would be quite exposed to southerly winds. Then more to the westward, and perhaps bearing southwest, lies Prudence Island—an island six miles long—and while Prudence cuts off much of the view farther to the southwest, still in places over its lower lands the more distant country shows up in blues, greens, and browns depending on the season. Surely, on a clear day after a snowstorm the distant colors are lovely.

On the west side of Bristol Harbor lies Popasquash Neck, and this was the birthplace of Nathanael Greene Herreshoff. But we must locate Bristol more clearly in the mind of the reader and

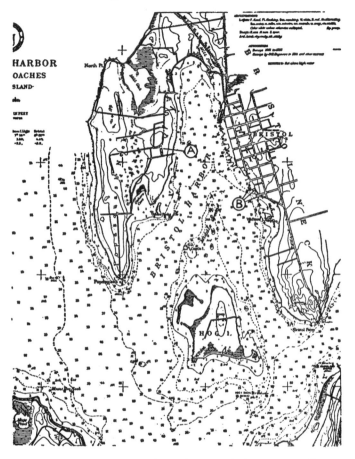

Figure 1. Bristol Harbor, showing (A) Popasquash Neck where Captain Nat was born and (B) the location of The Herreshoff Manufacturing Company where his famous yachts were designed and built.

perhaps partly account for its becoming so successful as a yacht-building locality. Bristol is ten miles north of Newport, and Newport is one of the best yacht-racing locations in the world. Bristol, you might say, is midway between New York and Boston. Boston is much nearer overland, but before the Cape Cod Canal was cut New York was not only closer by water but also much of the run to New York was in somewhat sheltered waters. So Bristol may have been quite near the center of yachting between 1850 and 1900 when yachting, to quite an extent, was confined to the region between Maine and the Chesapeake. Bristol in these times had excellent communications both by water and rail with our eastern cities, and at times coal, lumber and other yacht-building necessities were landed from schooners right onto the wharf of the Herreshoff Manufacturing Company. Even in the writer's youth several varieties of excellent oak were felled within fifty miles of the town.

Bristol enjoys a mild climate compared to most New England towns. The northeast winter gales that rake the coast north of Cape Cod are rather tempered when they reach Bristol, and while the snowfall there is perhaps more than in places right on the ocean the snow is apt to be level and not drifted. Although the northwest gales roar across Bristol with the same velocity as other eastern towns, she never feels the icy blasts that come down the Hudson. The water in Narragansett Bay is some ten degrees warmer than that north of Cape Cod, and this seems to make the falls later and prolong the Indian summer at times almost to Christmas. In fact the pleasant weather of autumn in Bristol is only surpassed by that of Newport, Nantucket, and Provincetown which are even closer to the Gulf Stream.

The prevailing wind in Narragansett Bay is decidedly southwest, and in the spring it often blows a good breeze from that quarter day after day with tiring monotony. Though the temperature is not low, this chilly, damp breeze from the Atlantic keeps one in thick clothes until June. In the summer, however, this breeze, which blows nearly every afternoon, keeps Bristol delightfully cool, and when the breeze dies down at sunset and the heat of the day has passed, a quiet restfulness permeates the air. This was the time, in days gone by, when the good people of the town made their calls, for it was delightful in the balminess of the evenings to walk through the streets of the old town which in many places were a continuous bower or arbor formed by the branches of gigantic elms that met overhead some fifty feet above the street. These evening calls were in no way social engagements, but were simply the spontaneous desire of friends and relations to commune with one another, for throughout the town a genuine friendliness prevailed.

Perhaps the peculiar tranquility of the place was partly due to the subduing effect of the southwest wind and perhaps partly as a result of the good Bishop Griswold having long resided there, for his famous revivals of the eighteen twenties had changed the thoughts of many people from the worldliness of slave ship and privateering days to a thoughtful piety—a piety that not only called for an effort to prepare one's self for a future life, but more particularly to help one another in this life—for which he set the example in both his acts of kindness and his lessons in refined conversation. Even in my childhood the conversations of a summer evening were entirely devoid of sarcasm, contradiction, and boastfulness. Perhaps some of my readers will think this a stupid sort of conversation, but you will find that when people rich in experience and skillful in conversation get together there is never a moment of boredom. In these evening talks or visits the person speaking was never interrupted, and no one would have thought of contradiction. Thus the speaker could speak slowly with well-chosen words. He knew his listeners would wait for the full meaning of his sentences, and that each word would be carefully considered. The subject may have been the speaker's travels in Europe, or one of the ladies may have described her life in Latin America: perhaps a book of some significance was reviewed, but more often than not one of the older persons would tell anecdotes of past times. The men spoke in a kindly voice and the response of the ladies was in a low, soft and melodious tone. Even if the conversation took a genealogical turn, the ladies remained tranquil for they knew that Grandma at the end of the veranda could settle all questions without controversy, and as the moon rose above the eaves of the house and shone down on the old lady's face, as she sat in her cap and cashmere shawl, you could see that she had enjoyed the evening as well as anyone.

Refreshments were seldom served during these evening calls, and stimulants quite unnecessary for the fragrance of the flower gardens, at it permeated the summer night, was in itself slightly intoxicating. No doubt, if called for, a decanter of old Madeira could be found on the sideboard but even that could not have increased the natural feeling of well-being inherent in a Bristol summer evening.

On account of its mild summer weather Bristol had been a summer retreat for Bostonians since colonial times, and later some New Yorkers, who preferred rest and quiet to the gayer society of Newport, visited the town annually. The matrons of Bristol had no little reputation for hospitality, and, as managers of the kitchen, perhaps could not be excelled by any north of the Mason and Dixon line. For generations they had been collecting receipts of, and perfecting, the local dishes. In colonial times some of the larger houses of the town had expert colored cooks who may have been trained in Cuba during the slave running days. The early matrons of Bristol must have made many gastronomical experiments: they must have had a highly perfected sense of taste together with some originality for they have handed down to posterity several dishes not generally known outside of the town. To me, even a quahaug pie made by a Bristol cook of the old school seems far ahead of the best that English cooks can offer and far superior to the complicated concoctions of the French school.

Each season of the year brought forth its appropriate viands, one after the other, so that the menus of no two weeks of the year were alike. The Bristol housewife had Rhode Island greenings for her pies and apple slumps, Rhode Island Red poultry for roasting and for chicken pies, Rhode Island corn meal for at least a dozen dishes and, as a last resort, she could always fall back on a Rhode Island clam chowder with complete confidence. The fish of the Bay allowed a pleasant variety to the Friday meals, for hardly anything is nicer than a broiled squitegue or a baked tautog while scup in its season was as delightful to the palate as it was fun to catch. As for the shellfish that grew in the deep blue clam mud of the Bay, well, there is nothing like them anywhere else except in Buzzards Bay and that may be one reason that a clam chowder, a clam bake, or a clam pie cannot be made out of these regions. The scallops, quahaugs, and oysters used to be plentiful and particularly tasty.

But the fall of the year was when a Bristol kitchen gave off its most enticing odors, for one after another there were special field days for "putting up," as they used to say, pickles from green tomatoes, making grape jellies and grape jam from the large, fragrant wild grapes of the district. Then the quince jelly and quince preserves were put up; and after cold weather had set in and the pigs were killed, sausage meat was made, and the long and complicated process of making mince meat was undertaken, which at times took the best part of a week before the large crocks in the cellar were filled with this aromatic mixture which would make the filling of mince pies until springtime, and, by the way, kept getting better and better. Most every Bristol home of any consequence had its own vegetable garden, and the warm, damp summer nights of the place produced luscious vegetables. Particularly, the lima beans and sweet corn grew with a perfection of quality and richness of taste. Many of these gardens had a row of herbs so the Bristol matron usually was well supplied with thyme, sweet marjoram, summer savory, and sage; also peppers of various kinds which generations of practice had taught them to use so skillfully that the odor alone of Bristol cooking was not the least of its charm.

I would like the reader to understand that I have not told these things about Bristol in a boastful way simply because it happened to be the writer's birthplace, but I have tried to show that Bristol during Mr. Herreshoff's life was an ideal place for undisturbed work and rest, and that the people of the place had a certain refinement. But most of all I have tried to bring out why it was possible for our subject to have the best of food, and this last in itself no doubt had a most important effect on his great energy and long life.

This is the best description of the time and the place that the writer can make, and in the next chapter we will describe Mr. Herreshoff's ancestors and from now on refer to him as Captain Nat for that will help to distinguish him from other Herreshoffs that will be mentioned. Also Captain Nat was what he was called most of his life.

CHAPTER TWO

Captain Nat's Ancestors

IN FORMER TIMES genealogy was looked upon almost entirely as an exact chronological listing of births, marriages, and deaths, but today many people are more interested in what is commonly called eugenics, so in this chapter if there is some slight discrepancy in dates, or in the spelling of someone's name, I believe it will be of little consequence for it is the character or peculiarities of Captain Nat's forebears that are the most important. One of the complications is that his ancestors can be traced back many generations, and that in itself makes a multiplicity of things, so for the sake of the reader I will only describe those ancestors who I believe threw strong characteristics. And all the time I am quite conscious that anyone who writes on genealogical matters will be contradicted by some of the relatives of his subject. Yes, I can plainly hear some female relation saying in a high tone of voice, "I never heard of such a thing! She wasn't his great-aunt at all, for she was nothing but his grandfather's sister." And, as experience has shown, it is best not to answer these outbursts; the writer will continue that policy.

The first Herreshoff that we know about was a member of the famous bodyguards of Frederick the Great of Prussia who were famous for being large and handsome men. This must have been in about 1750. His name was Carl Friederich Herrschhoff (original spelling). In about 1760 he married Agnes Muller who was said to have been lovely in person and well equipped mentally. They had a son born in the year 1763 who was also named Carl

Friederich Herrschhoff although he later changed the spelling of the name to Charles Frederick Herreshoff. Agnes Muller died soon after the birth of her son, and the father became melancholy and wandered away into Northern Italy and was never again heard from. The young Carl Friederich was cared for as a baby by two aunts, but later, when about eight years of age, was given into the full charge of a professor who lived in Potsdam. Frederick the Great often went to consult with this professor and there met the boy in whom he took a great interest for some reason or other, perhaps because he had known the parents. At any rate the king made arrangements to have him educated in a then famous school in Dessau where he studied for eight years and then came to this country in 1787 where he entered the importing business in New York City.

About 1793 he went to Providence, Rhode Island to confer on business matters with John Brown who was one of the leading merchants and shipowners of Providence. John Brown was impressed with the personal and mental attractions of young Herreshoff and took him to his home, the then new house on Power Street, which is now occupied by the Rhode Island Historical Society. Young Herreshoff, besides being a man of personal attraction, was a musician who sang as well as played on the flute. Sarah, the second daughter of John Brown, was also a musician so they sang and played together and became mutually attached. Their engagement at first was opposed by John Brown, which is not at all surprising, for young Herreshoff had no fortune other than a remarkably good education. But later, persuaded by his other daughter, Abby Francis, he consented to the marriage which was performed in the drawing room of the Power Street house on July 2, 1801.

The newly married pair, after living in several places, finally settled on one of the several country estates owned by John Brown. The one chosen was the Point Pleasant Farm on Popasquash Neck, Bristol, R.I. This piece of property and its colonial house had been owned by one Vassall who remained a Tory in the Revolutionary War so that the property was confiscated by the Rhode Island Assembly. During the Revolution it was occupied as a hospital for Rochambeau's soldiers, some of whom are buried on the property. In 1781 John Brown took this and other parcels of land in payment for money he had furnished to finance the Revolution. The house had been built in 1680 by Nathaniel Byfield, one of the original settlers of the town and a man of means. The house had more the style of a manor house than the usual colonial residence. There was a two-story hall running through the central part of the house terminating in large doors at each end. Near the house was a fair-sized brick building for the slaves and servants, and around the house there were several exotic trees which must have been planted at an early date. Some of these trees were varieties unknown to me, but the tulip trees had grown to the largest size I have ever seen. On the south side of the house was a well-sheltered flower garden, while on the east side a veranda looked out over Bristol Harbor and the town of Bristol beyond.

The original Carl Frederick, with what might be said to be a court education, was not adapted to life in America around 1800: he was said to have been a man of polished address, highly educated, an accomplished linguist in seven languages, and a good musician. He was variously employed by John Brown and died in 1819 while endeavoring to start an iron-smelting enterprise for him on his tract of land in Herkimer County, New York.

I have spoken at some length about the first American Herreshoff because several writers have said that Captain Nat was the son of a German engineer, and one said he was the son of a German mechanic, but the truth of the matter is that he belonged to the third generation of Herreshoffs in this country, and the first Herreshoff came over here before Germany was formed.

There were six children born to Carl Frederick and Sarah Brown Herreshoff between 1802 and 1812 and only one of them left descendants. This was Charles Frederick born in 1809 of whom we shall tell about later, but in the meantime perhaps we should review the Brown side of the family.

The first generation of Browns in America was Chad Brown and his wife, Elizabeth, who came over on the ship "Martin," which arrived at Boston in July, 1638. It is possible that his religious views were not in harmony with the Massachusetts settlers for he soon went to Providence, Rhode Island, and there with twelve others signed the original compact and thus became a colleague of Roger Williams. Chad was the first surveyor of the town of Providence and the first ordained Baptist pastor. At other times, I suppose, he was farming, trading, or hunting like other pioneers. Roger Williams, in speaking of the dissensions that disrupted the peace of the early colonies, speaks of Chad Brown in this wise: "The truth is that Chad Brown, that Holy man, now with God, and myself, brought the remaining after-comers and the first twelve to a one-ness by arbitration." This perhaps was no little feat in those days of strong conscience, when the best of friends, brothers, sisters, or sons might suddenly become enemies for conscience sake. However, Rhode Island seems to have been settled without burning a martyr or dipping a witch.

Somehow or other the Brown family in later years became prosperous and several of them were ship captains and shipowners until we get to the fifth generation of Browns in America, one of which was John Brown, born in 1736, and the great grandfather of Captain Nat. John Brown is said to have been "a man of magnificent projects and extraordinary enterprise." Though a wealthy merchant, and having larger interests at stake than most men, he was a patriotic leader in the struggle for American independence. He contributed substantial aid to the cause, which seems to have been appreciated by George Washington, for he presented John Brown with portraits of himself and Martha, portraits which were in Captain Nat's home. John Brown had made most of his fortune in shipping and ran a line of sailing ships directly to China and the East Indies. He was one of the principal owners of the Hope Furnace in Cranston, Rhode Island, which manufactured cannon for the Continental Army. He had the foresight to order his many ship captains to bring in gunpowder on their return voyages so that he was able to supply Washington's army at Cambridge, Massachusetts with this necessity when their supply was exhausted. He was the leader of the party that destroyed the British armed schooner "Gaspée" in Naragansett Bay on the tenth of June, 1772. Mr. A. DeWolf Howe, the New England historian, says that the first English blood of the Revolution was spilled in this affair, and while the Bostonians think their tea party was the first bold act of the war, the Rhode Islanders are proud of the burning of the "Gaspée," so I will give the reader a first-hand account of this action written by one Ephraim Bowen.

AN ACCOUNT
Of the Capture and Burning of the British Schooner
"GASPÉE"

In the year 1772, the British government had stationed at Newport, Rhode-Island, a sloop of war, with her tender, the schooner called the Gaspée, of eight guns, commanded by William Duddingston, a Lieutenant in the British Navy, for the purpose of preventing the clandestine landing of articles subject to the payment of duty. The Captain of this schooner made it his practice to stop and board all vessels entering or leaving the ports of Rhode-Island, or leaving Newport for Providence.

On the 10th day of June, 1772, Captain Thomas Lindsey left Newport in his packet for Providence, about noon, with the wind at north; and soon after the Gaspée was under sail, in pursuit of Lindsey, and continued the chase as far as Namcut Point (Now called Gaspée Point), which runs off from the farm in Warwick, about seven miles below Providence, and is now owned by Mr. John B. Francis, our late Governor. (Now a part of the Spring Green Farm, owned by Mrs. Frank Hale Brown). Lindsey was standing easterly, with the tide on ebb about two hours, when he hove about at the end of Namcut Point, and stood to the westward, and Duddingston in close chase, changed his course and ran on the Point near its end, and grounded. Lindsey continued in his course up the river, and arrived at Providence about sunset, when he immediately informed Mr. John Brown, one of our first and most respectable merchants, of the situation of the Gaspée. He immediately concluded that she would remain immovable until after midnight, and that now an opportunity offered of putting an end to the trouble and vexation she daily caused. Mr. Brown immediately resolved on her destruction; and he forthwith directed one of his trusty ship-masters to collect eight of the largest long-boats in the harbor, with five oars to each, to have the oars and rowlocks well muffled, to prevent noise, and to place them at Fenner's Wharf, directly opposite the dwelling of Mr. James Sabin, who kept a house of board and entertainment for gentlemen, being the same house purchased a few years after by the late Welcome Arnold; is now owned by, and is the residence of Colonel Richard J. Arnold, his son.

About the time of the shutting of the shops, soon after sunset, a man passed along the Main-street, beating a drum and informing the inhabitants of the fact that the Gaspée was aground on Namcut Point, and would not float off until 3 o'clock the next morning, and inviting those persons who felt a disposition to go and destroy that troublesome vessel, to repair in the evening to Mr. James Sabin's house. About 9 o'clock, I took my father's gun, and my powder-horn and bullets, and went to Mr. Sabin's, and found the southeast room full of people, where I loaded my gun; and all remained there till about 10 o'clock, some casting bullets in the kitchen, and others making arrangements for departure; when orders were given to cross the street to Fenner's Wharf, and embark, which soon took place, and a sea Captain acted as steerman of each boat, of which I recollect Captain Abraham Whipple, Captain John B. Hopkins, (with whom I embarked,) and Captain Benjamin Dunn. A line from right to left was soon formed, with Captain Whipple on the right, and Captain Hopkins on the right of the left wing.

The party thus proceeded till within about sixty yards of the Gaspée, when a sentinel hailed, "Who comes there?" No answer. He hailed again, and no answer. In about a minute, Duddingston mounted the starboard gunwale in his shirt, and hailed—"Who comes there?" No answer. He hailed again, when Captain Whipple answered as follows:—"I am the sheriff of the county of Kent, God Damn you; I have got a warrant to apprehend you, God Damn you; so surrender, God Damn you."

I took my seat on the main thwart near the larboard rowlocks, with my gun by my right side, and facing forwards. As soon as Duddingston began to hail, Joseph Bucklin, who was standing on the main thwart by my side, said to me, "Ephe, reach me your gun, and I can kill that fellow." I reached it to him accordingly, when during Captain Whipple's replying, Bucklin fired and Duddingston fell; and Bucklin exclaimed, "I have killed the rascal." In less time than a minute after Captain Whipple's answer, the boats were alongside of the Gaspée, and boarded without opposition. The men on deck retreated below as Duddingston entered the cabin.

As it was discovered that he was wounded, John Mawney, who had for two or three years been studying physic and surgery, was ordered to go into the cabin and dress Duddingston's wound, and I was directed to assist him. On examination, it was found the ball took effect about five inches directly below the navel. Duddingston called for Mr. Dickinson to produce bandages and other necessaries for the dressing of the wound, and when finished, orders were given to the schooner's company to collect their clothing and every thing belonging to them, and put them into their boats, as all of them were to be sent on shore. All were soon collected and put on board of the boats, including one of our boats.

They departed and landed Duddingston at the old still-house wharf, at Pawtuxet, and put the chief into the house of Joseph Rhodes. Soon after, all the party were ordered to depart, leaving one boat for the leaders of the expedition, who soon set the vessel on fire, which consumed her to the water's edge.

The names of the most conspicuous actors are as follows, viz.:— Mr. John Brown, Captain Abraham Whipple, John B. Hopkins, Benjamin Dunn, and five others, whose names I have forgotten, and John Mawney, Benjamin Page, Joseph Bucklin, and Turpin Smith, my youthful companions; all of whom are dead—I believe every man of the party, excepting myself; and my age is eighty-six years this twenty-ninth day of August, eighteen hundred and thirty-nine.—1839.

EPHRAIM BOWEN

After the burning of the "Gaspée," John Brown and several others of the expedition were in danger of being taken prisoners for the crown government or English naval authorities at Newport had offered substantial rewards for the capture or identification of persons connected with the affair, so it is said that John Brown for a while never slept more than a night or two in any one place but kept moving about. In his case this was easy to do for, besides his city residence, he had country seats in Cranston, Gloucester, Rhode Island, north Providence, Point Pleasant in Bristol, and the Spring Green estate in Warwick. However, Captain Abraham Whipple, who was afterward a commodore in the Continental Navy, commanded the flotilla of rowing boats at the burning of the "Gaspée" and seems to have been known to the English naval forces at Newport, commanded by Sir James Wallace, for they had written communications with each other which have been preserved. As the language used by both sides is so typical of that used in the seventeen seventies I quote it here:

Wallace to Whipple.

You, Abraham Whipple, on the 10th of June, 1772, burned his Majesty's vessel, the Gaspée, and I will hang you at the yard arm.

JAMES WALLACE

Whipple to Wallace:

To Sir James Wallace; Sir; Always catch a man before you hang him.   ABRAHAM WHIPPLE

Perhaps John Brown and his brother, Moses Brown, are best known as early educators in America. Their first attempt to introduce free schools in Providence was made in 1767. The Brown brothers were influential, particularly financially, in removing the College of Rhode Island from Warren to Providence where it was renamed Brown University. John Brown was one of the largest contributors to the institution of which he was the treasurer for twenty years. On May 14, 1770 he laid the corner stone of its first building now known as University Hall, which was erected on the original home lot of his ancestor, Chad Brown.

Before 1787 John Brown's city residence was at 37 South Main Street (later torn down for the erection of the Mechanics Bank) and here he gave his famous dinner to General Nathanael Greene, which was said to have been the largest dinner ever given in Rhode Island. In 1787 he built his Power Street mansion, at that time the finest house in the city. It was designed by his brother, Joseph Brown, who, besides being a professor of Experimental Philosophy at Brown University was a talented architect and, I believe, designed the First Baptist Church of that city and some of the buildings of Brown University as well as other Providence residences. He is the great uncle of Captain Nat, I believe, who, before 1800, first tried outside ballast on a sailboat.

Moses Brown, the youngest of the brothers, was a Quaker and, although he joined with his brother, John, in most enterprises, he kept aloof from the Revolutionary struggle. Moses was a successful business man and banker. Among other things, he financed and encouraged Samuel Slater, an English mechanic, to employ his skill in working out the first water-driven frames in America. Up to this time no spinning machinery had been successfully driven by water power. All obstacles were at length overcome and the great industry of spinning cotton by water power was inaugurated. Moses Brown lived to be ninety-eight years old and became quite wealthy, but his principal interests were charitable and educational. Among other things, he started the Friends' New England Boarding School, now called the Moses Brown School. An engraving of him was included in a brochure of early American educators among whom were Franklin, Rittenhouse, and others.

After this slight review of the Brown family which brings us down to Sarah Brown, the daughter of John Brown who married Carl Frederick Herreshoff and was of the sixth generation of Browns in America, we get back again to the Herreshoffs. Carl Frederick, as we have said before, died in 1819 leaving Sarah on the Point Pleasant Farm at Bristol with five children, all of whom had been born in Providence between 1802 and 1809. Both she and her children spent the rest of their lives either on the Point Pleasant Farm at Bristol or in visiting relations in Providence. John Brown had given this daughter the best education available at the time and she was especially proficient in music and mathematics, deriving consolation and giving pleasure to others by her skill on the piano which she played in a remarkably correct and brilliant manner. Her knowledge of astronomy also afforded her pleasure during many periods of quiet life spent in the country during the long years of her widowhood. She was delicate in constitution, austere in presence, and exact and methodical in her daily vocations. She read much and led a life of ease, indulging in her love of music and literature to her last days. Sally Brown Herreshoff must have inherited some fortune from her father, for both she and her children led the life of country ladies and gentlemen for almost two generations. She also inherited from her father a quantity of very fine furniture, china, silver, and portraits. There is no doubt that Captain Nat inherited some of his strong characteristics from this remarkable woman, his grandmother, but I must add that Sally Herreshoff was reputed to have been somewhat of a shrew and was quarrelsome. One of Captain Nat's brothers always said the later Herreshoffs inherited their love of rowing with one another from Sally Brown. She finally died at Bristol in 1846 in her seventy-third year.

Only one of the children of Sally Brown and Charles Frederick married; this child was also named Charles Frederick Herreshoff and was born in Providence in 1809. He graduated from Brown University in 1828 and afterwards lived on the Point Pleasant Farm with his brother and sisters. He seemed to have tried to run the farm as a gentleman farmer though all the time his thoughts were mostly on the water, for on one side of the farm was Bristol Harbor and on the other side Narragansett Bay. He was particularly interested in mechanics and was a skillful and finished woodworker. He delighted in making swinging gates for the farm, frames for harrows, and occasionally built a small boat just for amusement. But there was a young lady named Julia Ann Lewis from Boston who visited Bristol in the summers, coming over the road with her harpsichord by horse, wagon, and carriage, and this Charles Frederick, like his father before him, seems to have won his wife through a common interest in music, for Charles Frederick married Julia Ann Lewis on May 15, 1833. Julia Ann was descended from the famous Massachusetts families of Winslow and Lewis who, I believe, have two or more Mayflower antecedents. Her father was Joseph Warren Lewis of Boston, a captain of packet ships running between England and Boston who made eighty voyages over the ocean in that capacity and later became a Boston merchant. Lewis Wharf in Boston is named for the family.

In her youth Julia Ann lived on Charles Street, then (about 1820) a stylish outskirt of the city of Boston, which looked out over the Charles River only a short distance west of the State House. Just before this time Boston had produced some remarkable painters and was shortly to produce a string of talented literary men. At that time Boston could truthfully be called the hub of education and Julia Ann seems to have taken full advantage of the opportunities thus available for in later years she was able to teach her children in almost all subjects. She had been abroad with her father, and one of the things long cherished in the family was a fine French clock her father had purchased for her when in Europe.

Charles Frederick and Julia Ann had nine children, all born on the Point Pleasant Farm at Bristol between 1834 and 1854, all of whom lived to a ripe old age, which certainly was a remarkable feat in those days of high child mortality. So Julia Ann must have been a wonderful mother. Our subject, Captain Nat, was the seventh child and the fifth son and I will now quote almost verbatim from some writing of Captain Nat describing his early life on the Point Pleasant Farm in about 1855.

The house had a great kitchen with its brick oven of very ample proportions which was fired up every Saturday to do the week's baking of pies and cakes. In my younger days there was a stove with rotary top, a big affair in which there were six or eight holes for kettles, and by revolving the top any one or two of the kettles could be brought over the fire, the gasses passed under the others. This stove was replaced in about 1855 by one similar to the hard coal stove of later days.

Next to the kitchen and on the other side of the great chimney was the dining room which was also our living room. This had a very large fireplace kept burning and I remember very well the baking of johnny cakes on the hearth. The Indian meal and water dough was plastered on a board and propped up close in front of a hot fire, in a quite similar manner to the way the Indians did their cooking.

Our dining room had a long black walnut table which was necessary as there were nine children of us besides our parents and usually an aunt or uncle. The room also had my mother's Chickering piano, her work table, book shelves, and a beautiful French clock that was on a shelf in the corner. Of course there were many chairs and some of them very fine old mahogany which had belonged to great-grandfather John Brown.

In winter, after Christmas, a "fire-board" was placed in the throat of the fireplace and a coal burning stove was set just outside the hearth. This stove was a vertical sheet iron cylinder with fire brick lining at grate; the usual doors for fire box and ash pit. Just back of the stove my father had arranged a sheet iron drum of about the same size as the stove into which the flue ran. This drum had a baffle plate inside to compel the hot gasses to heat it all over; a pipe from this drum went up into the chamber above and into another drum, then to the chimney flue. With these drum heaters the heating of the living room and chamber was most efficient.

In those days my sleeping quarters were with my next younger brother in a "trundle bed" which when not in use rolled in under the parents' bed. It was mounted in wooden wheels four or five inches in diameter set in slots in the short legs of the bed. I well remember the fun we had after awakening mornings in putting our legs under the bed as far as our little bent up legs would allow, then giving a great push trying to reach the other side of the room.

I can very well remember the first mowing machine father had, and the trial of it, and think it was in 1855. Before that all mowing was done by scythes, and extra men were hired for it. Hay rakes were in use before that time, also cultivators and harrows, and I remember Father making the wooden part of some of these farm tools, also some very nice swinging gates to be put in driveways about the farm, for he was very fond of carpenter work and of doing it well. He had also built several very nice small boats—just for the fun of it.

In 1856 the Point Pleasant Farm was given over to Charles Frederick's elder brother, John Brown Herreshoff, so Charles Frederick and his family moved across the harbor to the town of Bristol and took a house at the lower end of the town, overlooking the harbor. Evidently the old homestead on the Point Pleasant Farm was no longer large enough for Charles Frederick and his large family besides his brothers and sisters who often spent some of the year there.

No doubt some of my readers will say about now: "Well, when are you going to tell about the sailboats?" To which I will reply: "Very soon now, but many people nowadays enjoy hearing about New England life in former times and it has been necessary to describe Captain Nat's principal ancestors to give one an idea of his inherited characteristics."

At the time the family moved over to the town side Charles Frederick was forty-seven years old and he must have inherited some means from his mother for I do not think he had any regular employment after the move to Bristol. This allowed him leisure for his principal pleasure, which was sailing, and I understand he visited every cove and island in Narragansett Bay annually and knew the exact location of many rocks.

Charles Frederick had built and owned sailboats while still liv-

Figure 2. The first Julia, built in about 1833 by Charles Frederick Herreshoff.

ing on the Point Pleasant Farm and one of them was the first "Julia." She was probably built about 1833, was about twenty-three feet long, and was quite similar in model and rig to other boats of the bay at that time and even before. This first "Julia" was a roomy boat with large cockpit, and besides taking many of

the family sailing all over the bay, she was used to take the family
visiting at other country estates around the bay where friends
and relations lived. One of the places she visited often was
Greensdale, the estate of General Nathanael Greene about half
way down the island of Rhode Island, and perhaps six miles by
water from Bristol. General Greene had been next in command
to Washington in the Revolution and was a friend of Charles
Frederick's grandfather, John Brown, so the families had been
very intimate. In those days Greensdale was occupied by a son of
the general, Dr. Nathanael Greene, who was a particular life-long
friend of Charles Frederick's, and that is the reason our subject
was named Nathanael Greene Herreshoff. At any rate these visits
to Greensdale were a particular delight to young Nat for apparently Mr. Greene made a great deal of his namesake.

Racing small sailboats had been popular in Narragansett Bay
since Colonial times, and the general type of craft used was
developed at Newport. It was a single-masted craft with the
rudder hung on the stern and was heavily ballasted with cobble
stones. These boats were called Point boats for they were mostly
built on a point of land extending out into Newport Harbor where
there was a colony of small boatbuilders. This type of boat was
later called a catboat when it became popular around New York,
and after one named "Una" was taken to England all Europe
spoke of them as Una boats for the next hundred years. Some of
these early Narragansett Bay boats were owned and sailed by
retired sea captains. No doubt some of them had been captains of
slavers and privateers and were great characters.

By 1850 Bristol, which is midway between Providence and
Newport, became a favorite meeting ground for the boats from
the several harbors in the bay. Bristol also had a most skillful sail
maker named Jonathan Alger who owned and sailed one of these
single-masted boats, so that altogether the men and boys of Bristol became very boat-minded. I must note that most of these
small sailboats of Narragansett Bay had a removable bowsprit
which fitted over the stemhead and was held down by a removable rod bobstay shaped like a long hook with the eye or link at
the forward end of the bowsprit while the hook hooked into a
staple driven into the side of the stem near the water line. These

boats never carried a jib in racing but only in making long passages in light or medium weather. The whole bowsprit and its gear could be quickly removed and stowed below, the jib, of course, set flying.

By about 1855 Charles Frederick built "Julia II" for the keen racing in the bay, and after 1864, when she was fitted with a shifting ballast box running athwartships and carrying a weight of

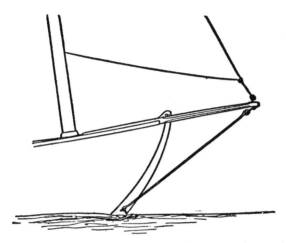

Figure 3. Removable bowsprit and bobstay used on early (1850) Narragansett Bay or Point boats.

about five hundred and fifty pounds, seemed to have beaten all other boats of her size in the bay. My father, Captain Nat, in describing this gear says:

The ballast box was amidships in light weather but was always used when there was wind enough to heel the boat to any appreciable amount. In a freshening wind and wishing to get the box to windward, it was not hauled there, but by luffing up into the wind suddenly and releasing the trigger or ratchet at the right time the box would roll to windward from the momentum of the boat's turning when the helm was suddenly put up to bring her back on her course. It certainly made "Julia" pleasanter to sail and also safer and faster. Although this ballast box and similar ones were used in four different boats I do not recall any accident by its getting adrift.

In describing the care that was taken of these sailboats of Bristol in the eighteen fifties and sixties my father has written as follows:

In those days there was a great rivalry between the owners of boats in Bristol in keeping them in fine order and spick and span in every way. Before going aboard my father's boat, "Julia" (and all his boats were named Julia after my mother) each shoe or boot had to be examined to see if any nails were protruding from the bottom; if they were they had to come off, and the same happened if they had boot blacking on them that might come off onto the paint work. The sail was kept clean and white and held from ever touching the deck by lazyjacks. Only washed hands were used in furling it.

Any boat coming along side must be held clear and not touch "Julia" for fear of leaving a mark. Both air and water were clean in those days, and so all these particulars were possible. It may be unnecessary to add that the painting was done with the greatest of care and only after thorough sand papering till the surface was faultlessly smooth.

At each full and new moon "Julia" was laid ashore and the bottom scrubbed so as to keep her in racing condition and ready for an afternoon scrap with four or five other Bristol boats that were kept in the same condition. These boats were owned by retired sea captains and characters to be remembered.

Our subject, then called little Natty, was eight years old when the family moved over to the town, and although his mother had been teaching him before, he now started to regularly attend the Bristol public schools. He and his brothers soon found the rendezvous of several sea captains past their active days but fond of spinning yarns. Natty was an intent listener who was much impressed by these old seagoing characters and often recalled those scenes in his later life.

Even before the family left the farm, Nat's older brothers had started boatbuilding and the oldest brother, James, had developed into quite a mechanical genius. Another brother, John, who was seven years older than Nat, started his first boat named "Meteor" in 1855 when only fourteen, and as it happens that many people ask the author when John Brown Herreshoff started at boatbuilding, I will say again it was in 1855. Surely this small boat built by a boy may not be considered much of a beginning, but John Brown, whom we will afterward refer to as J. B. was continually at boatbuilding from that time until his death. "Meteor" was designed by J. B. and started by him while the family was living at the Point Pleasant Farm on Popasquash. She was what was called a skip-jack in those days and now called a V-bottom boat. She was twelve feet long and five feet wide; her bottom planking was laid crosswise; she had an enormous sail plan and was later used as both cat, and jib and mainsail. When "Meteor" was about half completed, J. B. lost his eyesight and this brings up the subject of blindness in that generation of the Herreshoff family. Four of C. F.'s children—three sons and a daughter—were stricken with blindness in their youth. They suffered with glaucoma. It is not hereditary or contagious but a serious condition characterized by increased interocular pressure which I believe can be controlled today. It is interesting that the other brothers and one sister had rather remarkably good sight, and you can imagine Captain Nat as a designer had to have good eyes. Yes, I will say more, Captain Nat not only had the best eye for lines or shapes of anyone I have ever known but he had remarkably keen eyesight when at sea. When in middle life he was inspecting his various boat shops—sail loft, machine shop, foundry, or pattern shop he could see at once almost the length of the shop if some piece of work was being done wrong.

Well, let us get back to the "Meteor" and J. B. When he first lost his sight J. B. was very despondent for a few months but his energy to do things soon returned and he, with the help of his father, finished "Meteor" in 1857. In spite of his blindness she was sailed and raced by J. B. with his younger brother, Nat, aged nine acting as his eyes. "Meteor" was sailed by the boys for three years, capsizing twice, but each time their father in "Julia" picked them up and righted "Meteor."

Almost in front of the house where the Herreshoffs lived at Bristol, and right on the water, was a building called the Tannery which previously had been used for dressing leather. C. F. either acquired this building or the use of it, for from 1859 onward all Herreshoff boats or yachts were built in this locality and other adjoining land acquired later.

The next sailboat the Herreshoffs built was "Sprite," and I will give you some notes on her written by Captain Nat.

In fall of 1859 John decided to have a larger boat and "Sprite" was planned and modeled by my father & John, together, and I, at age of 11½ did all the drawing and figuring for the full size moulds. The boat was built by my father and John in the Old Tannery after being begun by Mr. Wm. Allen Manchester who died in fall of 1859.

Launched June 28, 1860. 20′ long, about 9′ beam. Centre-board, about ½ ton of inside ballast (old grate bars) and 5 or 6 cwt. of shifting weights, part lead. Centre-board 6′ 6″ long and forward end 8′ 10″ from outside of stem. The mast is stepped quite near the stem, and boom very long. Has a bulkhead supposed to be water tight about amidships—from that there is a cabin trunk or house. The ash coaming 4″ high begins at the house, and circles around 13″ from the stern.

"Sprite" was very fast, and easily the fastest sailer in the Bay. But she was a brute to steer, due principally to the very long boom, wide and weak rudder.

When only a few weeks old she made a cruise to New York in company of my father's "Julia" (3rd). The crew on "Sprite" was John B., Georg C. D'Marini & self. On "Julia," my father, (E. F. H.) James B. H., Lewis H. and Henry Slocum taken as pilot. The run was made in 27 hours in fog & light s. wind to Watch Hill, and brisk N.W. during night from New London to New York. The trip was specially made to see the steamship "Great Eastern." She was anchored in North River, but we could not get on board. We stayed over two nights at Hoboken. Our trip home was made in 26 hours in a brisk south wind.

The latter part of summer "Sprite" had her first race. It was from Jerry Angels' Clamhouse—an old stern-wheel steamer moored a little north of Fields Pt. and twice around a course down the river in moderate n.w. breeze. There were two 24′ boats of Ben. Appleton, the "Planet," 25 ft. of Davis & Childs, and "Sprite." Our crew was John, Lewis, Benjamin, Appleton, and myself as helmsman, (at 12 years). "Planet" 25′ beat us a little, but we won easily on time allowance.

"Sprite" was going much of the time in three long seasons. The longer cruises were to New Haven, Block Island, Vineyard Haven & Clinton, Conn.

By this time the Civil War had started and prices of food and other commodities were going up which must have been quite alarming to Charles Frederick Herreshoff living on a modest income with nine children, four of whom had lost their eyesight. But he succeeded in giving three of them a college education and helped to start almost all of them off on a career.

Charles Frederick was a large, strong, broad-shouldered man with a quiet, patient disposition. He had inherited strong characteristics from the Brown family for which he must have had a high regard, since four of his children had Brown as a middle name. He died in 1888 at the age of seventy-nine, and his wife, Julia Ann, although frail in the latter part of her life, lived to the age of ninety, dying in 1901.

I have not said much in this chapter about Captain Nat's brothers and sisters for this chapter is intended to describe his ancestors and his early life, but in the next chapter his brothers will be written about separately for most of them were somewhat famous in their particular lifework.

To sum up Captain Nat's inheritance—several of his ancestors had been ship captains or shipowners, and that would account for his nautical tendencies. His great-uncle, James Brown, seems to have been a very talented architect, so from the Browns he may have inherited his refined sense of proportion. I believe he received many other valuable traits from the Browns, not the least of which he liked to refer to as common sense. No doubt from the original Prussian Herreshoff he inherited stubborn determination, conceit, and self-sufficiency, and while these last characteristics do not seem desirable still they are absolutely necessary in designing. Conceit gives confidence, and self-sufficiency helps in making decisions, and designing or any other planning is mostly a matter of making decisions. Yes, endless decisions of shape, weight, strength, and methods of fabrication, and he that lacks either confidence or common sense should not attempt designing. Captain Nat was high strung, so to say—super-sensitive and easily irritated. Perhaps these traits are necessary for high accomplishment.

Naturally Captain Nat absorbed many of his mother's ideas and peculiarities for he was very fond of her. Julia Ann, among other things, was a strong prohibitionist or teetotaler but Nat even outdid her for he would not even take tea, coffee, or any stimulant whatsoever. The story is that the only time he took a drink was when the "Columbia" beat the "Shamrock" in the final race of 1899. It was on October 20 and a cold day, with a strong northerly wind, and "Columbia" had just beaten "Shamrock" six minutes in a magnificent fifteen-mile thrash to windward. The afterguard was celebrating the victory right after the finish, and Mrs. C. Oliver Iselin, who had sailed through the season on "Columbia," persuaded Captain Nat to have a drink.

Another thing this mother impressed upon the minds of her children was the value of truth, and none of her children were exaggerators in conversation. But truth is of even more value in engineering matters than in financial or personal affairs; perhaps truth is the most essential factor for logical thinking. It is probable that Julia Ann inherited her love of truth from the Winslow side of her family, for the Latin motto on the Winslow crest, "*Decoptus Floreo,*" may be translated to English as "Truth crushed to earth shall rise again."

CHAPTER THREE

The Herreshoffs

THIS CHAPTER will be used to describe Captain Nat's brothers and sisters for it will give the reader a clearer understanding of the ones who will be mentioned later, and because there is much confusion about just what some of them did or did not do. The chapter is called "The Herreshoffs" for in about 1890 there were no other Herreshoffs in the world that we know of except these brothers and sisters and their children.

The eldest child of Charles Frederick Herreshoff and Julia Lewis Herreshoff was named James Brown Herreshoff, born in 1834. In his youth James showed a strong inclination to experiment and invent, and one biographer, at least, has called him an inventor. While I have no intention of enumerating all of his inventions and experiments, a few of the most interesting or amusing will be mentioned. It is said that his first invention was a stool on runners to sit on while weeding the garden. In those days onions was the principal crop raised on the farms at Bristol, and the long rows were generally weeded by hand. Some people tied burlap bags around their knees and did the work kneeling—a very tiring work indeed. But Jimmie preferred to sit at ease on a seat on runners, and as he was only about fourteen years old, it was considered a good invention. He experimented with windmills quite a lot and developed a boat with a windmill connected to a propeller. When the size and pitch of both the windmill and the propeller are correct this type of craft will go to windward faster than a model yacht of its size, but it only performs well in strong winds, and for some reason or other a large one will not go materially faster than a small one.

Jimmie also developed what he called a "go-devil" which was simply a windmill or propeller on a stick, and when the propeller is carefully shaped this contrivance will fly to elevations of about fifty feet. It is run or flown by placing the stick under the propeller between the palms of the hands. Then by sliding the palms one by the other in the right direction the propeller will be so

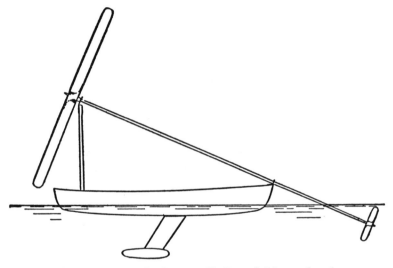

Figure 4. *Windmill propelled model boat developed by James Brown Herreshoff in his youth, about 1850.*

rapidly revolved that what with the momentum of the revolving blades it will screw its way up into the air. But it must be carefully shaped to fly well.

James attended the scientific department of Brown University. After being graduated in 1853, he became a manufacturing chemist connected with the Rumford Chemical Company near Providence, and between 1855 and 1862 developed what was then called cream of tartar powder, later called baking powder. Although quite a young man I believe he made enough through this baking powder development to live on most of his life. In

1862 he began the manufacture of fish oil and fertilizer derived from the large quantities of menhaden in the bay, and this industry, in other hands, became a large and successful business.

In 1873 he experimented with steam boilers and, in conjunction with Captain Nat, developed the so-called coil boiler of which we will speak later and will now only mention that it was the lightest steam generator of its time. He is also credited with inventing the fin keel for sailboats about this time, but I believe

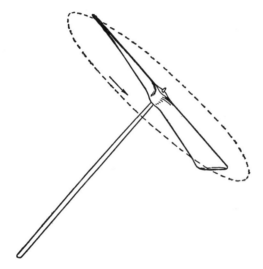

Figure 5. Another J. B. Herreshoff contrivance: a "Go Devil," or propellor on a stick, that would fly as high as 50 ft., designed about 1850.

he only used this invention on model yachts. While the first successful fin keeler, "Dilemma," was not built until 1891 (she will be spoken of later) there is no doubt that James experimented with model fin keelers both on windmill boats and sailboats, but Captain Nat told me that the fin keelers antedated both James and himself.

About 1875 he experimented with anti-fouling bottom paints and is credited with inventing mercurial anti-fouling paint, but I must mention that Charles Frederick, the father, as well as Charles Frederick, the brother, and Captain Nat all developed different anti-fouling paints of quite different formulae and color, two or three of which are now manufactured by various paint manufacturers.

In 1879 James invented, or experimented with, a steam engine run by super-heated steam which showed great promise of economy but, like many of his inventions, he dropped the idea before perfection was accomplished. It is probable that with the materials and lubricants then available the undertaking was most difficult. It is said that he invented the sliding seat for rowboats in 1860, and this apparatus is now used all over the world on racing shells. In 1864 he invented or worked out a process and apparatus for making nitric and muriatic acids which were used in the chemical industry.

In 1872 he built a power bicycle driven by a hot-air engine; it was a very ingenious affair in which the engine and fire box made up the frame. The whole thing was quite light as it was built up of iron and copper tubes brazed together. This was undoubtedly the first self-propelled vehicle to run on the roads of Rhode Island though, of course, there had been steam-driven coaches in use in England as far back as 1830, although English laws were soon passed that put them off the highways for many years to come. This motorcycle was built before the safety, or low-wheeled, bicycle came into use and I should think took some nerve to ride the first time, for it was quite a different proposition from the velocipede of that time. This early self-propelled bicycle had wheels about twenty-eight inches in diameter and was driven by a hot-air engine directly connected to the rear wheel. I must note that the hot-air engine was well thought of in those days because it was quite safe and simple, and at that time was much experimented with both in Europe and over here, but in its simplest form, where the air was heated and expanded in the working cylinder, which was right over the fire, it had lubrication trouble. Also most of the hot-air engines were not adapted or arranged to vary their power. Today, with heat resisting materials and the lubrication developed for internal combustion engines, a very interesting coal- or oil-burning hot-air engine might be built. James's motorcycle had no means of changing its speed and did not stop or run down until the charcoal fire burned out. Hence its few runs were made early in the morning when the roads were clear of traffic. On one of these runs, the last one so local legend says, James wrapped the cylinder with several layers of newspaper to hold in the heat. At the height of the run when quite a high speed was acquired the newspapers caught fire and James's legs were badly burned, so this early infernal machine was put one side.

James made many other inventions which included an ankle brace for skates in 1865, a thread tension regulator for sewing machines in 1866, an apparatus for measuring the specific heat of gases in 1872, and a sounding machine in 1874. Once James discovered that his inventions would work, however, he lost interest and made no effort to commercialize them. He did not marry until he was forty-one and spent many years after traveling in Europe where he studied engineering and other human endeavors. Of his five children one was born in Brooklyn, New York, one in London, one in Nice, France, another in England, and one in Bristol, Rhode Island, so we can see he was quite a traveler. He covered many of the rivers of Europe in a rowboat that he had arranged to be propelled when facing forward, and judging from his conversation he visited many places not usually seen by the tourist.

In his old age James was a most interesting conversationalist and could talk about the history of mechanical inventions in a very entertaining and scholarly way. He was remarkably spry at that time and many people expected him to live to a hundred, but he died in his ninety-sixth year of grippe and, I believe, had no organic trouble.

The second child of Charles Frederick, Captain Nat's oldest sister, was named Caroline. Born in 1837 she married Stanton Chesebrough in 1866. One child, Albert Stanton Chesebrough, became a yacht designer and designed several quite large and very good yachts, including the steam yachts, "Alcedo," "Elvina," "Cassandra"; the schooners "Hildegarde" and "Invader"; some steel torpedo boats for the U.S. Navy, and several smaller craft that were particularly able and good looking. It is interesting that one of Captain Nat's nephews also seemed to inherit a marked ability for naval architecture from some mutual ancestor.

The third child, born in 1839, was named after his father and grandfather, Charles Frederick Herreshoff. He was perhaps the most lovable and friendly of all the brothers; he was a farmer all his life but also quite a sportsman, passionately fond of shooting and fishing; he had several good and fast sailboats and sailed a great deal. A man of great size and strength; he weighed over two hundred and twenty pounds. Most all of the other Herreshoffs were teetotalers and could not stand the smell of tobacco, but Uncle Charlie told me that he started to smoke when he was sixteen and had never stopped. He was such a wholesome, good-natured man that he was a favorite with the ladies, and at times to tease him the ladies would say: "Mr. Charles, most of your brothers are famous for something, now what are you famous for?" And he'd answer: "About all I can claim fame for is being a rather good judge of whisky and tobacco."

The fourth child was John Brown, born in 1841, and the one we will speak of throughout this book as J. B. for he was for many years the senior partner of our subject in their yacht-building business. J. B., as a child, saw the necessity of money for any undertaking and made and saved money at a very young age so that by the time he was twelve or thirteen he was able to set up a rope walk with a rope-making machine he had partly constructed. One of the products he made was a very tightly laid cotton rope that was used for the hoops of the ladies' skirts then in style. He next fitted up a small machine shop with fairly good tools, including a good lathe which I think some of his Brown relations in Providence helped him with. At fourteen he was building the small boat, "Meteor," when he was stricken with blindness which was, of course, a serious handicap. But his great ambition and determination soon started him working again so that, with the help of his father, he finished "Meteor."

In the meantime, the family had moved from the farm at Popasquash to the town of Bristol, and in spite of J. B.'s blindness, he had fitted up a machine shop with four lathes. He soon took up building small boats to sell, and while at eighteen he was building boats for the trade he did not employ workmen in a real business until he was twenty-two, in 1863. At this time, besides boatbuilding, he had a sawmill in which most of the lumber he required was manufactured. In spite of his blindness, he modeled several of his early yachts, aided by his father. The designs for the sail plans and other drafting was either done by his father or his younger brother, Nat, but apparently entirely to or from J. B.'s descriptions and verbal specifications.

In 1864 he took a partner and the firm name was changed from John B. Herreshoff to Herreshoff and Stone. It is interesting to note the emphasis of building by steam power, but it must be remembered that before that time the work was nearly all done by hand. This partnership only lasted two years and then J. B. took over the business alone continuing this way without much expansion

HERRESHOFF & STONE,

YACHT AND BOAT BUILDERS,

BY STEAM POWER.

Yachts and Sailboats of all sizes, built to order at short notice, with special reference to SPEED, COMFORT and SAFETY, and warranted equal or superior to any others, as to style of model and construction. Also,

SURF BOATS, QUARTER BOATS, SCHOONER'S YAWLS, CLUB BOATS AND ROW BOATS,

OF ALL STYLES AND SIZES.

Boat Lumber on hand for sale. Logs sawed and Lumber Planed to order.

BRISTOL, R. I.

JOHN B. HERRESHOFF.   DEXTER S. STONE.

Figure 6. A boat builder's card of 1866.

until 1878 when he was joined by his younger brother, Nat, and the name of the concern was changed to the Herreshoff Manufacturing Company, the name it retains to the present time. While J. B.'s business had started in a small building on the water, a building that had previously been used as a tannery, he had enlarged that building and acquired the buildings of the Burnside Rifle Company, at one time called The Bristol Arms Company, which were close by. This small factory was run by General Burnside of Civil War fame and manufactured a very early model of repeating rifle.

After J. B. acquired this building he used it as a machine shop and, strange to say, started what I believe was the first attempt at quantity production of small boats, for he manufactured many skiffs, or flat bottom rowboats, for the South American trade. J. B. had a great capacity for business, and now that his brother, Nat, relieved him of the designing and construction work, he could devote all his energies to office work and business so that the company enlarged from the twenty or thirty employees when J. B. was alone to over four hundred workmen when they were building steam vessels, including the boilers and engines. As it was the intention of the company to make improvements when possible and keep the quality of their products at the height of perfection, Herreshoff yachts became noted. Therefore J. B. did not have to travel to get work—orders came in without going for them.

J. B. was a good business manager and kept up the enthusiasm of his employees, which I fear Nat sometimes rather dampened. He kept harmony through the works and, best of all, he was a most expert cost estimator, or perhaps I should say cost guesser. It is a well-known fact that the blind have wonderful memories, and perhaps J. B. could remember the cost of several hundred yachts. When an estimate of the cost of a new yacht was needed, and Captain Nat had explained her to J. B. in a very few words, J. B. would go home and think about it all night. The next morning when he came to the office he would say what the yacht would cost and, after she was built, his estimate was remarkably accurate. Many times he would answer cost questions over the telephone almost as quickly as the question was put to him, a feat that seems almost incredible today.

Strange to say J. B. was fond of fast horses and liked to go out driving in very smart rigs in which he took a great deal of interest, particularly the harnesses. One of the local myths about J. B. really not being blind sprang up from a harness maker's remark. It seems J. B. ordered a special harness from a local maker (each town had one in those days), and harnesses were priced or graded according to the number of stitches per inch in the sewing. Well, J. B. called on the harness maker one day to see how the work was getting along. Of course, being blind he had to feel of the work but he got his thumb in a certain position so the nail slid over the stitches and he could count them off.

Said he to the harness maker, "I thought you said there were to be ten stitches to the inch on this harness."

"So there are," replied the harness maker.

"Just put your rule on this seam where my thumb is," continued J. B., and when the harness maker put his rule there he found there were only about eight and a half stitches to the inch. After J. B. left the shop, the harness maker had to let off steam to the hangers-on in the place, so, after swearing some awful oaths, he brought his fist down on the saddle bench, ". . . he ain't blind at all, he only pretends to be."

Another time, J. B. was calling on a gentleman who thought himself a great connoisseur of antique furniture. The gentleman said, "I have just bought a very fine old chair and, although I had to pay considerable for it, it's the real thing," and he brought the chair over to where J. B. was sitting so that he could feel of it.

While the conversation was going on, J. B. had run his sensitive fingers over the chair and said, "I never knew before they had buzz planers in old times."

"What do you mean?" asked the gentleman.

"You turn this chair over," said J. B., "and you can see that the inside faces of the seat frame were gotten out on a buzz plane."

J. B. always carried a cane with him and with it he could measure almost anything, for he knew its exact diameter at several places, the length of the handle, the position of the ferrule, and several other points. He was a surprisingly rapid mathematician and could do quite involved problems in his head. Besides being in the yacht-building business, J. B. had owned many yachts, often three or four at a time, with a total of perhaps a hundred, large and small. Possibly he had owned more yachts than any other American. When business was slack in the boat shop, he would have a yacht built on speculation and very often he took yachts in trade when building new ones. He usually did well in these speculations and trades, for J. B. was a skillful trader.

In his younger life he had sailed and cruised a great deal in sailboats and entered his yachts in many races. He went on the Boston Yacht Club's first cruise in 1867 in his yacht "Clytie" and won several of the runs. In the Boston Yacht Club's first regatta on June 17, 1867 "Clytie" led from the start, making both the best actual and corrected time over the course. In this race the second was "Violet" and the third "Kelpie," all yachts built by J. B. "Violet," however, was modeled by N. G. and she raced with marked success for fifty years.

In his later years, J. B.'s sailing and cruising were confined to steam yachts of which he must have had about twenty in all at various times. He often stood for hours on the bridge or near the steering wheel and in some uncanny way could tell almost exactly where the yacht was. Perhaps knowing its speed and using his repeater watch, he could estimate where she should be, or perhaps he could make shrewd guesses from the conversation he heard from guests on board who undoubtedly did not know as well as J. B. where they were.

Soon after 1900, he took a great interest in automobiles and, from that time on, usually had three or four at a time. He was right on hand at the office everyday, bright and early, and went through the day's business with great speed and ability, but by four o'clock or so one of his automobiles usually called for him to take him for a ride in the country. The car was almost always driven by the engineer of his steam yacht, and somehow or other J. B. could tell pretty well where they were throughout the drive. He could literally recognize hundreds of people by their voices, and in fact I believe he could almost guess whether they were telling the truth or not by some hesitation or intonation in their speech. In asking a question he often grasped a person's hand or arm firmly and seemed to acquire their sentiments thus nearly as accurately as we do by watching the changes in facial expression. It is a strange thing that J. B. was such a good trader; if he got a good grip on a man's arm, that man was doomed and might have to trade in a good steam yacht at a low price and pay a stiff price for her successor. Yes, he was a man with a strong personality, strong will, and a great understanding of human nature. It is said of the elder J. P. Morgan that he could look right through a man and tell his exact character at a glance, and I believe if J. B. Herreshoff got a good hold on a man's hand or wrist he could tell almost as much.

I tell these things about J. B. mostly to discredit the almost international myth about "the blind designer." J. B. was certainly a remarkable man and deserves great credit for managing a complex industry successfully for fifty-seven years. Until his death he was always the president and principal owner of the Herreshoff Manufacturing Company, but to say that he was a designer is as ridiculous as to say that a blind man was a painter, engraver, or any other profession which is dependent on good eyesight. J. B. undoubtedly was very familiar with the shapes of boats between 1860 and 1870, but I doubt very much if he had any understanding at all of the shape of yachts built after 1890, although he did have a remarkable sense of their cost and a knowledge of the comparative cost of their parts.

When J. B. started boatbuilding about 1860, boats in Narragansett Bay were often built from models alone, apparently at times without any drawing at all, not even a sail plan, for the owners or builders would tell the sail maker the dimensions he wanted which were derived from previous boats of like size. Although J. B. could not have drawn any after he was blind (thus could not have been a designer in the accepted meaning of the word), he did, with the help of his father, model six or more yachts after he was blind, but as his father was a skillful modeler it is quite likely he did most of the cutting and J. B. simply described to him, as the shape developed, where he wanted it changed or cut away.

The yachts or boats modeled by J. B. are as follows:

"Sprite," 1860–62	20′ O.A., 9′ beam. Built by himself and his father and now preserved in the Ford Museum at Dearborn, Michigan.
"Kelpie," 1862.	26′ 9″ O.A. 10′ 6″ beam.
"Sadie," 1867.	50′ 6″ O.A. 16′ beam. Schooner modeled by J. B. with sail plan by N. G.
"Orion," 1869.	
"Ianthe," 1870.	
"Faustina," 1873.	
Other small boats between 1864 and 1870.	

He also built the following boats modeled or designed by his father or his brother, Nat.

Figure 7. Qui Vive II, typical of the yachts built by J. B. Herreshoff between 1860 and 1870.

"Qui Vive II,"   42′ O.A.
"Prudence,"   36′ O.A.
"Patience,"   36′ O.A.
"Hope,"   28′ O.A.
"Faith,"   28′ O.A.
"Henrietta,"   16′ O.A.
"Haidi,"   25′ O.A.
"Ariel."
"Violet."
"Psyche."
"Fannie."

So far as I can make out, these later yachts were designed or modeled by J. B., C. F. Herreshoff (the father), and Nat all working together, but C. F. and J. B. were depending on Nat more and more each year. After about 1870, when Captain Nat designed "Shadow," thirty-six feet O.A. sixteen feet three inches beam, all later Herreshoff yachts were designed by Captain Nat alone. So, while it can be said that J. B. Herreshoff modeled some successful yachts with the help of his father, he cannot under any stretch of the imagination be called a designer.

As time went on, after 1880, the construction of yachts became very complicated, and very exact construction plans were necessary. The designing of steam engines, boilers, and improved metal hardware required accurate, explicit drawings, and it is safe to say N. G. Herreshoff designed all yachts, their parts, and machinery *in toto* that were built at the Herreshoff Manufacturing Company between 1870 and 1915, and superintended almost all designing until about 1930.

I do not want to reduce J. B.'s reputation, but he was a remarkable enough man without being called, "the blind designer." J. B. was a large man with a full gray beard; he often wore a white vest and a conspicuous watch chain on which he rested his thumb. He died rather suddenly in 1915 in his seventy-fourth year and was active to the very end.

The fifth child was named Lewis, born in 1844. He became blind in his youth but, in spite of that handicap, sailed with his brothers in their yachts and sailboats. It is interesting to note that Captain Nat in some of his first races had two blind men for crew —John and Lewis. They were both big, strong men and apparently did quickly what their younger brother, Nattie, told them to do. I must say that in some of my racing experience I have wished at times some of the crew were blind if they could have done their work well. Perhaps then they would have done what they were told to do, instead of telling the skipper what to do.

In spite of his blindness, Lewis got about quite a lot and visited Europe where he made a cruise up and down the principal rivers with his brother in a small light sailboat which we will tell about in the next chapter on "Captain Nat's Education." Lewis was fond of rowing, with someone else steering, and of swimming; he was quite expert at playing the piano; he wrote correctly and neatly on the typewriter and the Braille writer, and carried on a large correspondence with people in several countries. He is best known to older yachtsmen by his writings in the yachting section of the Badminton Sports Library.

For some years Lewis tended the furnace in his mother's house, where he lived, and could tell which side of the fire needed coal by the direction the heat radiated when the furnace door was opened. He could keep the water at the right level by putting his sensitive fingers on the water gauge and feeling the difference in temperature above and below the water level. Altogether, Lewis was a good example of what a blind person can bring himself to do. He died at the age of eighty-two and perhaps would have lived longer if he had taken some exercise in his declining years.

The sixth child was Sally Brown Herreshoff, born in 1845. She, also, was blind from childhood but was a cheerful soul who played much on the piano, sang, and wrote both on the typewriter and the Braille writer, and carried on a correspondence with other blind people. She knitted hundreds of mittens and remembered the birthdays of all her young friends. She lived with her mother and her brother Lewis, dying at the age of seventy-two.

The next child, the seventh, was Captain Nat who was born in 1848 and died in 1938.

Captain Nat's next younger brother was John Brown Francis Herreshoff, born in 1850. He entered Brown University in 1867 and soon developed a marked aptitude for chemistry, so he concentrated his attention on that subject. In 1868 he was appointed assistant professor of chemistry at Brown University, but he preferred to enter the chemical industry. In 1876 he was superintendent of the Laurel Hill Chemical Works on Long Island, and was later employed by the Nichols Chemical Works. He was the most successful financially of any of the brothers. He invented, or developed, the present-day method of separating copper from copper ore by a chemical process. He invented the Herreshoff electric furnace for making steel castings. He received several medals and prizes for his contributions to the chemical industry and perhaps is nearly as well known in the chemical and metallurgical field as his brother Nat is among the yachting fraternity. John Brown Francis died in 1932.

The youngest child, Julian, born in 1854, was blind almost from his childhood, thus making a total of three brothers and one sister blind in this family. Julian was fond of music and could converse in several languages so, after studying in this country, he went abroad and continued his education at the University of Berlin. Later on, returning to this country, he ran a private school in music and languages besides dealing in real estate, setting a good example of a person afflicted with blindness earning his living. This perhaps was the reason this brother also was somewhat famous.

In a summary of this generation of Herreshoffs, it is interesting that out of nine children all lived to an advanced age, in fact their average longevity was about eighty-three years. Six of these brothers had either traveled or studied in Europe, and that includes three who were blind. Although none of them but James was fond of conversation, they all were well versed in some subject.

I want to apologize to the reader for taking so much space in describing Captain Nat's brothers and sisters, but to describe nine different people naturally takes some space, and I have preferred to put it all into one chapter instead of spreading it throughout the book.

CHAPTER FOUR

Captain Nat's Education

MANY PEOPLE today think of education as a standardized training of the mind where the student is instructed to memorize endless laws of physics, mathematics, art, and history, but where little is done to stimulate original thought or to become expert at observation, and critical in analysis.

Yes, I often hear it said with awe that A was educated at Harvard, and B went to Yale, but when you ask what they learned there you will find A learned to carry his liquor well and acquired an accent, while B's four years were used in making acquaintances somewhat below the standard of his former friends. Neither A nor B is what you can call a keen minded man although sometimes, I think, they might have been with a different education. As it is, they must depend entirely on memory for they can no longer see, hear, or think. While it is very doubtful if A and B would have become Lincolns if self-educated, still they would at least have open minds. Some psychologists class a person's intelligence by the number of years he can absorb knowledge, and class this one at eight years and that one at twelve, and so on, but it is very probable that the experiences and opportunities for observation that one has may create a type of intelligence that can go on absorbing knowledge for fifty or sixty years, or, as has been said of Michelangelo, for eighty years. While the primary function of the college is to give the student an opportunity for observation, it is much feared that the present-day college curriculum confuses rather than enlightens the student. While it no doubt trains the memory, it also seems to diminish the student's ability to think for himself. Perhaps too much theory without practice is partly responsible for this condition, but it is more likely that the college student lacks opportunities for actual experience. There is no doubt that experience is the greatest teacher, and so in this chapter I will tell more about Captain Nat's experiences than about his college life, and though having studied at the Massachusetts Institute of Technology may have helped him in acquiring his first position, I should say that his powers of observation and quick understanding, together with opportunities for experience, were the principal means of his education. But I will preface no longer.

Captain Nat's education was very much accelerated in his early youth because he was the constant attendant of his brother, J. B., who was blind. J. B. was a dynamo of energy and had an indomitable ambition which forced little Nat to do things for J. B. which are generally far beyond the capacity of children of his age. Little Nat was acting as helmsman for J. B. on his sailboat when he was only eight years old, and at twelve years steered J. B.'s boat "Sprite" in several races. J. B. was seven years older than Nat and had set up a small machine shop with three lathes just before becoming blind, and after his blindness, he continued doing machine work with little Nat guiding his hands at the lathe. J. B. had quite a temper and disciplined and dominated little Nat so that Nat never had the usual life of a child, nor played much, which left an unmistakable mark on his character. To quote from some writings of Captain Nat:

I thus got a rather early training in machine work and in boat building and sailing. Even when ten or eleven I became quite apt at tempering small tools, and when eleven had the job of taking the sections from a model and scaling them up to full size, what we call today laying down the lines.

He also started at a very early age to make all the drawings that were necessary for the spars and sails. By sixteen Nat had modeled the sloop "Violet," twenty-five feet long, which while owned by Eben Denton became a very noted winner around Boston, racing for nearly fifty years.

Nat had become a noted helmsman when very young—fifteen to eighteen—and between 1863 and 1866 acted as sailing master in many races in several boats which raced in most all the racing localities between the Hudson River and Boston. He kept up an interest in the steam engine and, when sixteen, originated, designed, and made a small rotary engine somewhat like the ones used to drive model aeroplanes seventy-five years later. Probably there were not many New England boys who had a workshop and tools at that time, or could devote all of their hours out of school to working on most interesting things, but this early start at the mechanical arts no doubt helped him more than any scholastic education.

Captain Nat attended the regular public grade schools in his native town of Bristol, and then went to the high school which at that time, 1861 to 1865, had few students, I suppose partly because of the Civil War. In the fall of 1866 he entered the Massachusetts Institute of Technology for a three-year course in mechanical engineering. His teachers were President William B. Rodgers, the founder of M. I. T., Professors Runkle and Osborn in mathematics, Professor Edward Pickering in physics, Professor Charles Eliot in chemistry, and Professor Watson in mechanics. One day in the class of analytical geometry he spoke to the professor of a curve he had used in constructing a rotary steam engine when he was sixteen. (I suppose the curve was for valve settings.) The professor became quite interested because curves were not used for that purpose at that time, and spoke to President Rodgers about it. The president requested Nat to exhibit the engine before the Society of Arts which held fortnightly meetings at that time in one of the M. I. T. buildings, so he had the little engine sent up from Bristol and connected up to run by steam for the next meeting of the society. He was asked to give a short lecture or explanation of the engine, and received very complimentary applause from both the audience and President Rodgers. I suspect Captain Nat's lifelong love of the steam engine was strengthened by that incident.

At the time he went to M. I. T., that region that is now called Back Bay was composed of swamps and brooklets with but few buildings on the higher and firmer ground, and he and the other students used to skate on the numerous ponds that were where Huntington Avenue now is. The Charles River was a tidal river and at times overran much of what is called Back Bay, a region that besides having been leveled off has had its level raised a few feet.

During Captain Nat's first year at M. I. T. he became affiliated with Boston gentlemen who were interested in sailing. At first, they had an informal club of those who liked to talk about sailing, but on November 21, 1866, he attended the first formal meeting of the Boston Yacht Club and was elected a committee of one to formulate measurement and time allowance rules for rating the various sized yachts then owned by the members. He was elected a member of the Boston Yacht Club in its second meeting on December 5, 1866. The club held its first meetings in the Parker House until a room was fitted up at the corner of Tremont Street and Pemberton Square. Although Captain Nat was not a charter member of the Boston Yacht Club he did attend its first meeting. He dropped out of the club in 1869, but on January 30, 1877, was elected an honorary member because of his services, I believe, in formulating their first measurement rule and for making up the tables of allowance in minutes and seconds per mile that a yacht of one rating allows one of a smaller rating. I will say something, in passing, about this table for it is still in use almost throughout the world with but few slight changes.

There had been earlier time allowance tables in England based on tonnage, but they were unsatisfactory for yachts that varied much in size, and they did not give direct readings without considerable mathematics. In other words, those early tables did not give the minutes and seconds per mile for lineal rating. But, in 1867, Captain Nat made up direct reading tables for time allowance on yachts ranging in racing lengths between twenty feet and eighty feet. The next year he extended the tables to range between fifteen feet and one hundred and ten feet, all of which entails considerable mathematics—which was pretty good for a first year M. I. T. student. I do not know what process of mathematics he used to determine the speed of various size yachts, but he must have had some quite accurate data to work from for these tables have only been changed or adjusted slightly for the larger classes of later years. The present-day tables of the New York Yacht Club range from fifteen feet to one hundred and fifty feet.

The tables have been the greatest boon to yacht racing of any one factor in the game, and they themselves have been the means of allowing boats of various ratings to compete satisfactorily. The Boston Yacht Club deserves considerable credit for publishing these tables in their first club book, and few members today realize what an important contribution their club made to yachting at its start.

While Captain Nat attended M. I. T. for three years, and I believe did well in all his studies, he is not listed as a graduate. It seems that as soon as he completed his special course he left and obtained a situation as a draftsman in the Corliss Steam Engine Company of Providence, Rhode Island, which at that time was the leading engine builder in this country, if not the world, and certainly manufactured one of the most economical steam engines of the time. Besides his work in the drafting room Captain Nat visited the engines when they were set up at their final destination to take what is called indicator diagrams of the engine while running, and make the final adjustment of the valves. This was a great opportunity for a young engineer, for the Corliss Company not only built large engines for driving factory machines, but also built the pumping machinery for several large cities.

In 1876, Captain Nat had charge of setting up and running the very large steam engine which furnished the power for the Centennial Exhibition at Philadelphia. This engine was afterward used to furnish power for the Pullman Car Works.

During the time Captain Nat worked for the Corliss Company he was designing the yachts and small steam engines his brother John was building at Bristol. This he did by working nights and Sundays, but by so doing his health suffered so that in 1874 he was obliged to take a vacation to regain it. At the time his next older brother, Lewis, and some cousins were living at Nice in the south of France, so Nat decided to go over and visit them. He sailed from New York February 10, 1874, and kept a complete log of this trip and a subsequent cruise across Europe in a small sailboat, both of which I have before me as I write this, and at times I will quote from these logs of nearly seventy-five years ago. I quote from them mostly to give an idea of Captain Nat's love of mathematical data, and his constant preoccupation with the work in which he was interested. He landed at Cherbourg on February 20, 1874, the ship having carried sail most of the time with strong westerly winds. Throughout the trip Captain Nat recorded courses, length of run, and revolutions of the propeller.

Feb. 10.

Steamer left dock at 2h. 40m. Passed the Castle Garden at 2-55. Engine 46 rev. Passed S.W. Spit at 4 h. 5 m. Engine 50 rev. Have a strong breeze from the N.W. but very pleasant, feels like March or April. Left pilot off Gedney Channel buoy at 4-35. He was taken by N. 7 a very handsome vessel. She was under double reef mainsail and foresail and fore staysail. We have on board 2 first class, 5 second class, and 30 steerage passengers. At 6 PM set foresail and fore topsail, course about true E. Wind N.W. a good breeze. Quite cold. Engine 52½ rev. Ship very steady. Had dinner at 3 o'clock of soup, roast beef, veal, stewed potatoes, all very nice. Supper at 6. Spent the evening in reading, writing and walking the deck. At 8 o'clock wind W.N.W. strong, sea beginning to make but ship quite steady. Engine 52 rev. Thermometer in state room 45°.

Feb. 13.

We are under closed reefed fore and main topsails, foresail and main staysail. The ship is very easy and I had no idea there was such a gale before I came on deck. We have been logging about 14½ miles. Engines are making 53 rev. per min. Wind moderates a little at 9 and we set jib and increased our fore and main topsails which have a patent reefing arrangement. The sails roll up on spars which are held at the ends to the topsail yard by pintles, and at two intermediate points by clasps with rolls which pass part of the way round the spar permitting the sail to roll up inside. Chains run from pulleys at the mast head to ones at the yard arms and then wind around the ends of the spars in opposite direction to that of the sail, so that by hoisting or lowering the yard it at the same time unwinds or winds the sail on the spar.

Captain Nat's description of the steamer he went over on is as follows:

The "Goethe" is a Clyde built vessel of 3600 tons burthen belonging to the Eagle Line steamer between Hamburg and New York. Is 375 feet long, 40 ft. beam, 32 ft. deep. Engines of 3000 effective horse power around 600 nominal. Compound engine, cylinders one of 60″ and one of 104″ diam. with 4 ft. stroke. Are inverted direct acting with cranks at right angles. Have reservoir between cylinders which the high pressure exhausts into. Plain slide valves worked by link motion with cut off valves to each. Air pumps and circulating pumps worked by beams off one side. The engineer drove me out of the engine room the first day and they pretend not to understand English, so I cannot get much information.

The vessel has a flush deck from end to end. Two smoke stacks fore and aft from each other, the aft one about midships. Two masts of iron about half way between smoke stacks and stem and stern. Topmast and top gallant mast in one stick. Has no topgallant yard aloft now. Stem nearly upright with no bow sprit or figure head. Quite round fore foot under water. Water wash board about one foot high above waterway. The rail about 3½ ft above deck is supported by iron stanchions. There are two iron rod stringers between washboard and rail, and up to the second one there is a network of rope.

The following sails are now bent on. Jib, fore staysail, fore and aft foresail and fore topsail. Square fore topsail. Main staysail, square main topsail, fore and aft main sail and top sail. Carries eight clinker built boats, three on a side forward of main rigging and one abaft it. They are set on cradles supported by cast iron columns about four feet above deck and directly under their davits swung inboard. The davits are held by heavy cast iron sockets four feet high bolted to the deck by large flanges.

I can occasionally hear a sea break against the weather side and wash across the deck as I sit here comfortably writing in the second cabin, and once in a while the lee side lights roll under water. My stateroom is the next one forward of the foremast and on the port side inboard, and is lighted in the daytime by a prismatic deck light about 10″ long and 2½″ wide. The ship's bell is nearly over my head and is quite a comfort to hear ring out its half-hour and hour of the watch while I lay awake in my berth. I believe it has never been so unkind yet as to wake me out of my sleep. I have much more to describe about the "Goethe" yet. The captain said today we were 50 miles farther on our course than on the last trip at noon of the second day, and then they reached Cherbourg Friday morning.

Among the notes of the fourteenth of February he continues:

The propeller is 19 f. diameter and 27 f. pitch, making 52 rev. per minute; without slip it would go ahead $27 \times 52 = 1404$ ft. per min. Taking her speed at 12.8 knots or 1281 ft. per minute the slip $1 - \dfrac{1281}{1404}$ = .088. The distance run today is 308 miles. Lat. 44° 6′ N. Long. 47° 29′ W.

This afternoon the weather is quite fine; the wind is directly aft but not enough to render any assistance by setting sails. The sun shows himself once in a while. There is quite a heavy swell from the N which makes the vessel roll considerable. I have a clear space of about 330 ft. on deck to walk. This afternoon I walked it 32 times. $\dfrac{330}{5280} = \frac{1}{16}$ $32 \times \frac{1}{16} = 2$ miles. The time of walking sixteen times was 19½ min. I make about 121 steps in the distance. In the evening the wind is a little fresher and nearly dead aft. Have set foresail and fore and main topsails.

After traveling across France and visiting Paris, Captain Nat arrived at Nice on the twenty-third of February, and shortly thereafter, around the middle of March, strangely enough Nice had a snowstorm. After resting and visiting places in the neighborhood he began to want to do something, and so, after putting his cousins' sailboat into shape for launching, he started to build a small double-ended sailboat, the "L'Onda" in which they sailed around Nice until he and his brother, Lewis, decided to make a larger sailboat which they named "Riviera." She was especially designed for sailing along the coast of the Mediterranean and for cruising in the rivers and canals of France, Belgium, and Holland. She was V bottomed, very lightly built. Her frames were made of mulberry, a native wood that is very sound and strong. She was built principally by Captain Nat with the help of his blind brother, Lewis, and a local carpenter. "Riviera" was about seventeen feet long and had a very large sloop rig for the light weather in the Mediterranean, but also arranged so the mast could be stepped farther forward when she was cat rigged.

After sailing and cruising about Nice for a while, they started on a trip up the Mediterranean coast of France, July 14. The first leg of the trip was along the coast to Marseilles. On the way they visited many quaint places and slept either on board or on the beach. They also visited a French navy yard. Then, from Marseille they went inland by river, canal, and railroad to Basle, then on to Strasbourg, Speyer, Mannheim, and Worms, from there continuing down the Rhine to Emerich and shortly after reaching the German outpost and registering the boat, entered Dutch customs in mid-afternoon of Saturday, the eighth of August. They went on by comfortable degrees to Rotterdam where they took a steamer to London and sailed and cruised on the Thames while sightseeing in London. After receiving funds from home, Captain Nat purchased Scott Russell's gigantic tomes on naval architecture, some English drawing instruments, and had made a special logarithmic slide rule.

This trip in "Riviera" through western Europe was an unusual opportunity for education where Captain Nat had the chance to visit navy yards, manufacturing companies, and to study the local types of shipping. He took full advantage of his opportunities by visiting the pumping stations of London as well as other European cities to gather data for his work at the Corliss Company.

The two brothers left Liverpool for America on the steamer "City of Brussels" of the Inman Line. On arriving at New York they lowered "Riviera" from the steamer and started at once for home, down Long Island Sound. On the third day of their trip near the east end of Long Island Sound, they were met by their brothers James and John in the first steam launch that J. B. had built, which had a coil boiler invented by James Brown Herreshoff and a steam engine designed by Captain Nat. This launch, "Vision," took "Riviera" in tow and they started for home. After they had gone a short distance, they met their father and a neighbor in the "Julia" who also had sailed down to meet the boys on their return from Europe.

This trip through Europe in a small sailboat was quite a feat for the time, 1874, but to accomplish it with one of the brothers totally blind seems amazing. However, Lewis, the blind brother, had sailed and rowed a great deal before this so was quite at home in a boat. He was a large, strong young man and an accomplished linguist both of which must have been helpful. "Riviera" was a light boat with an enormous sail plan, almost like the sandbaggers of the time, and of course easily capsized. She was

Figure 8. The Riviera, in which Captain Nat and his blind brother Lewis cruised the Mediterranean and the inland waterways to Rotterdam in 1874.

very fast and on one occasion, at least, sailed seventy miles in one day, and went through this remarkable cruise and the trip across the Atlantic on the deck of a steamer almost unscratched. She was later used by Captain Nat at Bristol for several years and finally used by his children under very much reduced sail plans. Later she was stored in a boat house on Captain Nat's property but was destroyed when this boat house was swept away in the hurricane of 1938, at the time when "Riviera" was sixty-four years old.

At the period when "Riviera" crossed western Europe many of the inland towns and villages were very provincial and not only did the "Riviera" cause astonishment but the dress of her crew at times seemed to the natives most novel. The brothers went ashore in tennis shoes that they had brought from America, and nearly the whole village followed them about for few of the inhabitants had ever seen any other shoes than wooden sabots and to see people walking noiselessly was quite a novelty.

I believe on the whole that the people of France, Germany, and Holland were quite friendly to the "Riviera" and her crew, and she did not have the serious holdups at the custom houses, or from extortionists, that some later cruisers in Europe were to experience. Perhaps the brothers traveled in such an unpretentious style that the natives thought they had no money. Perhaps they thought that people who slept and ate in an open sailboat were to be pitied.

Nothing could have been more educational than this cruise in Europe in a small sailboat, for the brothers could stop where they wanted to and move on when they wanted to. Of course, the voyager in a small boat sees things from quite a different point of view than the traveler who arrives at the Grand Depot, for the voyager sees the true nature and heart of the place rather than the rouged face prepared for the tourist. In those days, apparently, strangers could visit the navy yards, and watch the various manufactories unmolested, and Captain Nat learned much that was to be useful to him both in engineering and naval architecture.

After returning from Europe, Captain Nat continued his work at the Corliss Steam Engine Company, mostly working on the designs of pumping engines, but he was allowed many long holidays and given leave several times when he acted as sailing master in races on the yachts which J. B. had built at Bristol. By this time, J. B. was building steam launches and larger steamers, all designed by Captain Nat including boilers and engines.

In 1877 J. B. got the order for a larger steamboat that was later named "Estelle." Captain Nat's written description of her is as follows:

Estelle. Steamer building number 39. [The Herreshoffs had separate building numbers for sail boats and steam boats.] 120′ long, 16′ beam with coil boiler and compound engine. High pressure cylinder, 12″ bore; low pressure cylinder 24″. Stroke 21″. The vessel was contracted for by a New York lawyer who turned out to be an agent for Cuban Insurgents. She was to be built as soon as possible with a bonus for quick delivery. J. B. made contract for her about the last of May. I got leave from the Corliss Co. for the summer and went to Bristol; made the model and general drawings for laying down the lines, but as she was too large a vessel for J. B. to build, her hull was built by Job Terry who had a ship yard in Fall River. Then with the assistance of a draftsman I designed and made drawings for the engine which was built by the Rhode Island Locomotive Works very quickly and well. The hull, engine, and boiler (the latter built by J. B. Herreshoff) were ready in October and we had preliminary trials the last of November.

A few days after this the revenue cutter "Dexter" arrived at Bristol and anchored close to the Herreshoff boat shop with orders from Washington not to allow "Estelle" to leave the dock. After some time arrangements were made for the official trial trip, taking the "Dexter"'s officers and armed guard along. The trials were successfully completed, making a six-hour run at 16 m.p.h., and the craft was paid for. The U.S. officers immediately seized her and put her in charge of U.S. keepers. Some time later "Estelle" was sold and released; she became a successful tow boat at the mouth of the Mississippi, being able to tow two or three ships at a time from the Gulf up to New Orleans faster than any other tug. She was, after some years service, burned and lost in the Gulf of Mexico.

The "Estelle" was certainly an extremely fast steamer for her time, 1877, and it seems most remarkable that she could maintain a speed of sixteen miles per hour for six hours for she was partly designed to carry cargo in rough water. The most remarkable thing about "Estelle" was that she was designed and built, including a new model of boiler and engine, in about one hundred and eighty days, and while they talk today of assembling ships quickly you will find that from the commencement of the first drawing to the trial trip it takes much longer, except where the vessel is made up of parts previously designed, tried out, and made. "Estelle" must have had very sweet lines under water, and a perfect propeller to accomplish this speed for her engine was quite small. However, a new coil boiler is a remarkably good steam producer and no doubt "Estelle" ran with much higher pressure than was customary in those times, which was safe to do with a boiler that had no large drums or parts that could be stressed at high temperatures. No doubt, also, these coil boilers, when running just right, produced very hot steam which has several times the expansion of steam at the temperatures then customary. And this may be a good time to say something about the coil boiler.

The coil boiler was invented in 1873 by James Herreshoff, Captain Nat's oldest brother, and I believe the first one used in a launch was built by J. B. for his steam launch "Vision," built in about 1874. "Vision" was forty feet long with a four and one half feet beam, had a single cylinder engine with three and one half inches bore, seven inches stroke designed by Captain Nat. I do not know who modeled "Vision" for at that time four different Herreshoffs were working for J. B., off and on. They were his father, Charles Francis Herreshoff, James Herreshoff, who was working out the coil boiler, Charles Herreshoff of whom we have spoken before as a farmer but who about that time had charge of the woodworking part of the boat yard, and Captain Nat, himself, who apparently even then made all of the working drawings. At that period it would be difficult to tell just which of the Herreshoffs did certain things for they were all working together. However, James is credited with the idea of the coil boiler and did superintend making the first crude ones, but as the development of the coil boiler advanced Captain Nat made all the working drawings and, in fact, got out some patent papers for the machinery to manufacture them. I only mention this as there is some discussion as to who invented this boiler, but it is of little consequence for the coil boiler was later given up as impracticable.

As the name suggests, the coil boiler consists of coils of tubing over the fire box, and a type of boiler, nowadays called a "flash boiler," or one where the water turns to steam almost instantly. These boilers do not have a water level or carry little water in any but the first length of tubes where the water is injected. This boiler is arranged somewhat as follows:

At the top, where the flue gases escape somewhat cooled down, there is a coil of tubing which acts as a preheater and warms the incoming water. The tubes in this first coil are cool enough to absorb the latent heat in the waste gases so that they escape quite cool. This first coil is of small diameter tubing, but the next coil, and the one nearest to the fire, consists of quite a long length

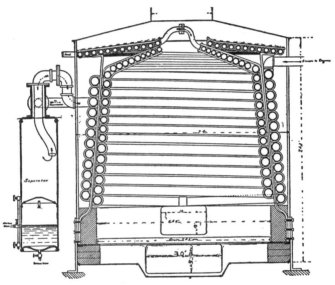

Figure 9. The Coil Boiler, invented in 1873 by James Herreshoff, Captain Nat's oldest brother.

of tapered tube, and here the steam is generated. The tubes are tapered because the volume of the steam is greatly increased in this section, and circulation in this section is downward so that the coolest end of the tubing is up toward the escaping gases, while the hottest end is down near the fire.

After the steam has passed through this section of the coils it enters a separator which separates the dry steam from any water that may have traveled this far, which, I believe, sometimes happens with a change in the amount of feed water, condition of fire, or amount of steam used. After passing the separator, the steam went through a length of parallel diameter tubing which acted as a superheater. This was the outside coil, apparently, so that it would be less apt to be burned. From here the steam went to the engine. These boilers were very light indeed compared to other boilers of the time, and quite safe, for where there are no tubes or drums of large diameter the bursting strains are small; in fact in the largest of these boilers, where the largest tubes got up to three inches inside diameter, the wall thickness was only one quarter inch, and they carried working pressures up to one hundred and thirty pounds.

The small end of the coils on the large boilers had a diameter of one and one half inches and a wall thickness of three sixteenths inch. The smaller boilers, of course, had tubes with diameters in proportion to their size. These boilers apparently weighed about seventy pounds per horsepower, and used 2.21 pounds of coal per horsepower hour. While these weights and fuel consumption seem large today, they were remarkably good for their time and allowed the Herreshoffs to build steamers which in two or three cases held world speed records for their time. These light boilers also made possible the first light steam launches that were practical to haul up on the davits of a larger vessel, and J. B. built many small launches of this class.

The principal disadvantages of the coil boiler were, first the difficulty of manufacture. The long tubes, of course, had to be made up in J. B.'s shops from strips of sheet iron which were first brazed together to make one long strip (several hundred feet), and then this strip was rolled up until it made a tube whose seam was also brazed. Although to a great extent this was what you may call handwork, it did have the advantage that a tapered tube could be made nearly as easily as a straight one. Then, bending the tubes to make the coils of proper size and shape to fit together was difficult. All this called for very skilful work. But perhaps the greatest difficulty with the coil boiler of those days was that it soon lost efficiency when the inner surface of the tube became scaled, or built up a deposit from the evaporated water. This, of course, happens to all boilers, but most boilers can have their separate short tubes cleaned, or they can be retubed at a nominal cost while with the coil boiler the whole thing had to be renewed. I will mention here that one or two of the first coil boilers used salt water, and the engine exhausted up a stack, as it does on a locomotive, creating a very strong draft. These outfits were very simple and consisted solely of the boiler, engine, and feed pump. However, these boilers only lasted a few months, as the salt water deposited scale very rapidly in the tubes.

For these reasons the coil boiler was given up about 1885. Then some so-called square boilers were built which had short lengths of tubes until 1890 when the Herreshoff Manufacturing Company started to make the somewhat conventional three-drum water tube boiler which had a water level halfway up the upper drum with all small tubes below this level.

But that takes us to a later date and we must now go back to 1876, the year Captain Nat brought out his first catamaran, "Amarylis." It seems that while sailing in Europe in the "Riviera" he worked out in his mind a double-hulled boat which he thought would be very fast. In 1875 he designed her and had her built by J. B. at Bristol. "Amarylis" had hulls twenty-five feet long that were rather deep and narrow so that no centerboards would be necessary. She had one central rudder instead of two like his later catamarans. Her original rig consisted of a single lateen sail with bipod masts the lower end of which terminated near the center of each hull, and was shaped like the sail on the flying proas of the Pacific, a rig similar to that used on many iceboats at one time. However, he found this rig both structurally weak and hard to steer, so that he soon changed her to a jib and main-sail rig with the mast stepped on the central backbone. It seems that on a catamaran of large sail area for her length it is advis-able to have a large jib to slack out when the weather hull rises. At that time the resistance of the depressed leeward hull tends to make her head off which is most alarming in a strong gust of wind when one wants to luff up into the wind.

Well, at any rate, the "Amarylis" finally got straightened out and Captain Nat entered her in the Open Centennial Regatta held at the head of Long Island Sound on June 23, 1876. She was in a class that contained an assortment of boats ranging from extreme sandbaggers to larger cabin yachts, most all of which, I believe, had larger sail area. At the beginning of the race the wind was quite light—a condition when a catamaran is slow on account of their rather large amount of wetted surface—so that the sandbaggers sailed by her. As they did they hailed the "Amarylis" with ridicule and abuse for the sandbaggers were notorious for their tough crews. Presently, however, a breeze sprang up and "Amarylis" sailed merrily through the whole fleet and won easily. I suppose in a good beam wind "Amarylis" could log thirteen or fourteen miles, but it is doubtful if the sandbaggers often made over nine miles. At any rate, the success of the "Amarylis" induced Captain Nat to build other catamarans, so that in the year 1877 he again got leave from the Corliss Company and went to Bristol where, working in J. B.'s shop with the help of workmen, he built the four catamarans, "John Gilpin," "Teaser," "Tarantula," and one whose name I do not know. They were all thirty-one feet long and I believe all quite similar. He also designed at least two other catamarans which were built by the Herreshoff Manufacturing Company after he had become a partner in the firm. They were "Goody-Two-Shoes" in 1879, rigged with a leg o' mutton mainsail, and "Lodola" in 1879. This latter craft Captain Nat used himself in the seasons of 1879, 1880, and 1881, and, as he said, was the best of the tribe. I do not know just how many catamarans Captain Nat designed or built, but of those before 1880 the number seems to be seven.

On January 1, 1878, Captain Nat went into partnership with his brother, John B. Herreshoff, which we will tell about later, and, while I think Captain Nat had a type of mind that kept absorbing knowledge for many years to come, I have chosen the years before 1878, when he was thirty years old, as the years of his education. We will make a slight review of those years.

In his extreme youth he was an expert helmsman and had become practiced at both wood- and metalwork. Next, he studied mechanical engineering at the Massachusetts Institute of Technology. Then he cruised across Europe and visited many museums and mechanical institutions. He worked in the designing department of the Corliss Steam Engine Company for about nine years, and no opportunity could have been better for training a young engineer. Then came his experience in designing steam- and sail-

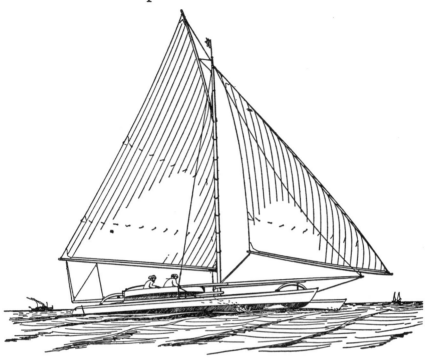

Figure 10. One of Captain Nat's Catamarans.

boats for J. B., and last, but not least, his experience in designing the catamaran, which certainly was an opportunity to exercise designing ingenuity.

All things considered, it seems doubtful if one could have had a better opportunity for education as a designer, particularly one who was to specialize in light steam engines and racing sailboats.

CHAPTER FIVE

The First Designs of
N. G. Herreshoff

I BELIEVE the first yacht of any consequence that Captain Nat designed was the sixteen-foot catboat, "Henrietta," whose name was later changed to "Popasquash." The same year he made a model from which the twenty-five-foot sloop "Haidee" (later named "Fanchon") was built. "Violet" was also built from this model as well as "Ariel." These boats were modeled in 1864 when Nat was only sixteen years old, although "Violet" was not built until 1866.

This brings up the story of a strange incident that Captain Nat told me in his old age. When the "Violet" was completed young Nat sailed her in a trial race against an older boat designed and sailed by his father, and "Violet" was beaten. Nat was so disappointed that as soon as he got home he took an ax and chopped up the model from which "Violet" had been built so that no other boats would be built from it. Strange to say, all the boats built from this model turned out very well later and were much liked by their owners. This incident, Captain Nat told me, made him more patient in later life and taught him to wait until a boat was thoroughly tried out before he condemned her.

The model from which "Violet" was built is the only one missing in his collection of models. "Violet" was built for Mr. Eben Denton, a charter member of the Boston Yacht Club, and an early secretary of the club. She raced successfully in the length-over-all classes for about fifty years and I believe was finally destroyed in the Chelsea fire although she had been in active use right up until that time.

In the winter of 1866, when Captain Nat was a student at Massachusetts Institute of Technology, he designed the sail plan and other drawings for the schooner "Sadie" which J. B. built for himself. "Sadie" was modeled by J. B. and his father and was fifty feet six inches O.A., forty-seven feet W.L., sixteen feet beam, five feet draft and of course, a centerboarder. "Sadie" was rerigged as a sloop in 1868 and had a large sail area— 3,876 square feet. She was sold in 1869 to R. Franklin Burgess, an older brother of Edward Burgess. The Burgess and Herreshoff families, who were distantly related, kept up a friendship from that time on, so I will say something about the Burgess family.

The family consisted of six brothers of about the same age as the Herreshoff brothers; their father had been a wealthy Bostonian engaged in shipping and owning sugar plantations in Cuba. Besides their home in Boston, they had a summer residence at Sandwich on Cape Cod where the boys started sailing from their youth and, as they grew up, they owned several Herreshoff-built boats. Edward Burgess, who was to become the leading yacht designer of his time, was born the same year as Captain Nat (1848) and, strange to say, there was a striking similarity in their appearance. They both attended college at the same time—Edward Burgess at Harvard and Captain Nat at M. I. T.

Edward Burgess had intended to devote his life to the study of natural history, and especially entomology, in which he was active the first ten or fifteen years after graduation from Harvard. On account of financial reverses, however, he was obliged to take up a more remunerative profession so that with his youthful love of sailing he decided to become a yacht designer. It is certainly most remarkable that in a few years he climbed to the head of the profession. This is principally outstanding because he could not have had time to study construction, although he had first gone to England to observe and study English yachts. The most remarkable thing about Edward Burgess was that he designed many large and fine yachts in the short span of about seven years

—about 137 vessels—and at this time, between 1884 and 1891, Burgess specialized in large sailboats while Captain Nat was concentrating his energies on small, fast steam craft.

These two were very friendly, and Mr. Burgess often visited Captain Nat at Bristol. Edward Burgess died in 1891 just before Captain Nat became famous for designing the larger sailing yachts. W. Starling Burgess, his son, continued the father's profession and each of the Burgess's designed three cup defenders so between the Burgess and Herreshoff families the cup has been defended twelve times. These defenders were as follows:

"Puritan"	1885	
"Mayflower"	1886	designed by Edward Burgess
"Volunteer"	1887	

"Vigilant"	1893	
"Defender"	1895	
"Columbia"	1899	designed by N. G. Herreshoff
"Columbia"	1901	
"Reliance"	1903	
"Resolute"	1920	

"Enterprise"	1930	
"Rainbow"	1934	designed by Starling Burgess
"Ranger"	1937	

So the Burgess and Herreshoff families designed all the cup defenders from 1885 to 1937. The cup was only defended five other years, and no other man designed more than one defender.

Now we must go back to Captain Nat's other early designs. In the year 1868 he modeled the steamer "Annie Morse," sixty feet long, the first steamer J. B. built. While speaking of "Sadie" we should find it interesting to note that Captain Nat and J. B. were on her during the famous gale of September 8, 1869. "Sadie" was anchored in East Greenwich Harbor; she dragged her anchors and fortunately just cleared the steamboat wharf when her crew succeeded in passing a line around a spile. She was the only boat in the harbor, and perhaps the neighborhood, that rode out the gale. Although they were just starting out on a cruise they returned to Bristol as soon as the wind went down to inform their parents of their safety. After this, they sailed to Newport, not seeing another vessel afloat but counting between forty and fifty vessels and boats that had been driven ashore.

In 1879 Captain Nat designed the steamer "Seven Brothers," sixty-five feet long; this was a steam fishing vessel, I believe the first one in America, and the first of a long line of Pogy steamers. She was built for some of the seven brothers of the Church family and, as Captain Nat and his brothers numbered seven, she was built by seven brothers for seven brothers. This was the first steamer for which J. B. built the engines and machinery, and Captain Nat designed the vessel, engines and all. The "Seven Brothers" was unusually successful and made money as a Pogy steamer for about thirty years.

The same year Captain Nat also designed the thirty-eight foot steam launch "Anemone," machinery and all. "Anemone" was built for J. B.'s own use and Captain Nat ran her quite a little during that summer and made one trip as far as New York to watch the yacht races in the Lower Bay there. All of these vessels and several others he designed while working at the Corliss Engine Works.

The most notable sailboat of his early design was the "Shadow" which he made the model for in the pattern shop of the Corliss Steam Engine Company in November 1870. Captain Nat's written description of "Shadow" is as follows:

"Shadow" was about 36' O.A., 33'6" W.L., 14'3" beam, and about 5' 6" deep, with hollow sections nearly full length, and bilge almost all above water line. The centerboard was 11' 6" long and 12' 6" from wood ends (bow); mast 9' from bow, 40' 6" above deck. Mast head 5', topmast 16' 9"; bowsprit from stem 16'. Mainsail 38' foot, 27' hoist, 21' head, 43' 6" leach = 740 sq. ft. Jib 25' foot, 38' luff, 29' leach = 361 sq. ft. Club topsail 27', 30' luff, 19' leach = 235 sq. ft. Total of three sails 1336 sq. ft.

I give all these dimensions for several people have made models of "Shadow" and tried to reconstruct her sail plan. The principal reason "Shadow" is famous is that she is considered the first of

the so-called "compromise yachts," the type that Edward Burgess perfected in "Puritan" and "Mayflower."

Around 1875 our American yachts were wide, shallow vessels
while the English, under their tonnage rules which measured

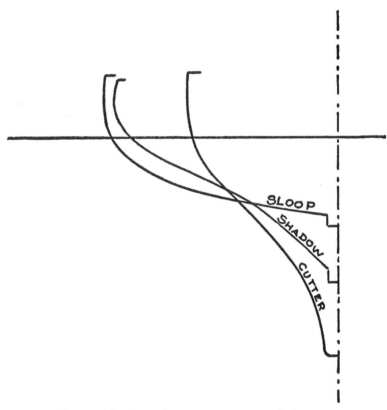

Figure 11. Typical sections of an English cutter,
American sloop, and Shadow, illustrating her
"compromise" between the two types.

beam twice, had developed the so-called "cutter model" which
was deep and narrow. Typical sections of a cutter, an American
sloop, and the "Shadow," shows that "Shadow" was someway
half between or what later was called a "compromise type." To
be sure, "Shadow" did not look very different above water from
other American sloops of her time, but she was surely a shadow

of coming events with her wine-glass sections below water. During the cutter-sloop controversy in the eighteen-eighties "Shadow" was the only American yacht that held the imported English cutters.

During "Shadow" 's first years, Captain Nat sailed her in several important races, some of which he liked to review in after life. He used to say one of the reasons for her success was that she had a nearly perfect suit of sails made by Jonathan Alger, an old time Bristol sail maker. He did not seem to think the low, full garboards of "Shadow" such a revolutionary feature, and when asked why he modeled her that way would say: "simply to get her ballast lower." (She had all inside ballast.) He would also sometimes say: "Shadow" is a direct descendant of the old Narragansett Bay boats which carried their ballast low and frequently beat the shallower boats of New York." However, I assume he thought a lot of the model of "Shadow" for this was one of only two of his models on a backboard, and it also had a frame around the backboard. After the first few years "Shadow" was owned by Dr. John Bryant and under his management was an almost unbeaten boat for fifteen years, accumulating, I believe, about one hundred and forty prizes altogether.

In 1871 Captain Nat modeled and designed the keel schooner "Latona" which was built by J. B. By this time J. B. was building good size sailboats and several steamers, all designed by Captain Nat; in fact N. G. Herreshoff made all designs from which Herreshoff yachts were built after the "Shadow," or the year 1870. Some of the steamers with the coil boilers were very fast for their day, and in 1875 the U.S. Navy ordered the torpedo boat "Lightning" which made the speed of twenty-two miles per hour. This was the first torpedo boat ordered to be built by the Navy although before this they had had steam launches which had been converted to torpedo boats. "Lightning" was a long, narrow, double-ended launch only partly decked, fifty-eight feet long, and carried what is called "spar torpedoes," that is, bombs on the end of a long spar which were intended to be rammed against the side of a vessel below her armor plate.

I believe the first launch built as a torpedo boat was built by Thornycroft in England for the Norwegian Navy in 1873. Her

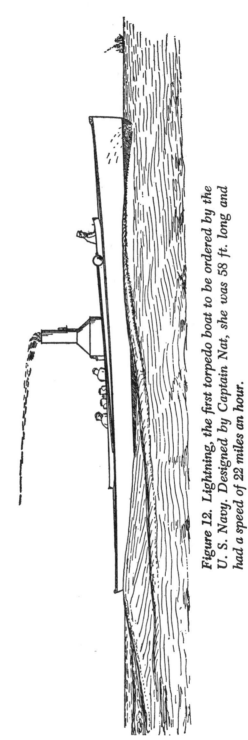

Figure 12. Lightning, the first torpedo boat to be ordered by the U. S. Navy. Designed by Captain Nat, she was 58 ft. long and had a speed of 22 miles an hour.

name was the "Rasp," fifty-eight feet long, speed about seventeen and one-half miles per hour. All the principal navies soon began to have torpedo boats built so by 1896 they numbered about as follows: England, 262; France, 254; Russia, 224; Italy, 181; Germany, 168; Japan, 116; Spain, 56; U.S.A., 22. So you can see the light steam engine was developing rapidly.

In 1876 Captain Nat designed the racing catboat "Gleam," and worked out a rather new construction for her for she was the first boat built upside down and fastened with screw fastenings, a construction that the Herreshoffs used on all later small craft: in fact they later built steamers upside down up to ninety feet long. While Captain Nat did not originate the use of screw fastenings for the planking he did introduce it in this country. Screws for planking fastenings had been used in France before this.

Captain Nat was now concentrating his attention almost entirely on light steam plants and working out improved construction for the hulls to reduce the weight without sacrificing strength. Almost all of this development was done in connection with the light steam launches they were building, and although these early improvements in methods of construction were at the time severely criticized by the nautical public, it is a fact that the modern small boat throughout the world is now built approximately as he worked out the construction seventy years ago. Personally, I believe N. G. Herreshoff's greatest contributions were in the line of construction, and believe he was the world's greatest authority in that matter, the principal proof of which is that his yachts and boats lasted longer than any others although they were much lighter.

One of the important products of J. B. Herreshoff at this time, 1876, seems to have been small steam launches, many of which were built to be hoisted up on the davits of ships so that extreme lightness in both power plant and hull was paramount. Strange to say, these light launches stood up better in service than heavier ones by other builders, the reason for it being two-fold. When a launch comes alongside in a seaway she is bound at times to come against the ship heavily, and in hoisting and lowering there are unavoidable strains. The weight of the heavy launch in itself makes these concussions more severe than with the light launch, but the light launch with steam-bent frames and properly constructed gunwales will spring or give, cushioning the shock that would have smashed a stiff unyielding construction like the usual boat of that time with sawn frames.

Some of these early launches were built for the U.S. Navy, some for the Ordnance Department, the U.S. Coast Survey, and the U.S. Fish Commission. One of these early models was twenty-two feet long, five feet three inches beam. This model, which was built between 1876 and 1878, is very interesting as it represents, I believe, the first attempt at the modern powerboat model. The greatest draft was a little aft of the forefoot, and greatest beam near the stern which was flat, the underwater shape being a gradual twist from bow to stern. These launches were said to be quite satisfactory and drove very easily into a moderate head sea. But as Captain Nat abandoned the model after 1878, it is probable that the sharp-bowed launches with the wide flat sterns were not good sea boats under all conditions, a bit of knowledge most designers at the present time have not yet learned.

The power plant of the small launches between 1876 and 1880 showed a small coil boiler over a circular fire box and ash pit, the whole enclosed in a cylindrical casing not so dissimilar in shape from that of a donkey boiler but certainly much lighter, and a boiler capable of making steam in a few minutes. The engine was a single cylinder one, I think, three and one half inches bore and seven inches stroke, and developed about five horsepower but a different size of horse from that used in the gasoline era. The whole business was neat, simple, and light, and, of course, reliable and quite economical.

One pattern of propeller used in the early Herreshoff launches and steamers was twenty-four inches in diameter and thirty-six inches in pitch, but Captain Nat designed a series of similar propellers in the early eighteen-seventies, varying greatly in size but not much in shape. However, the small launches generally used a two-bladed wheel. These propellers were a true screw, or had the same pitch throughout the blade, and blades slightly concave on the pressure side both ways. When Captain Nat first designed steam craft there were no commercial propellers made, and he

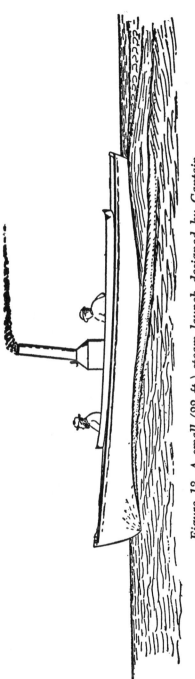

Figure 13. A small (22 ft.) steam launch designed by Captain Nat. Several were built between 1876 and 1878. This was probably the first attempt at the modern power boat model with flat stern.

continued to design his own wheels as long as the Herreshoff Manufacturing Company built steamers. The later wheels were all cast in the company's own foundry, and were generally considered the most efficient propellers in the world. His later screws, however, had the profile of the blade narrower at the outer ends, and the leading edge rounded off, and therefore were less apt to foul ropes and weeds. While a propeller in itself may not interest the average reader still it is likely that the shape of a propeller is of as great importance as the model of the vessel it propels, and there is no doubt that the refinement of these early Herreshoff propellers had an important effect on the performance of Herreshoff yachts. Captain Nat designed a great many propellers during a span of nearly sixty years.

In the preceding chapter I have spoken about the one-hundred-and-twenty-foot steamer "Estelle" and the several catamarans he designed about this time, 1877, but it must be remembered that Captain Nat was still working at the Corliss Steam Engine Company most of the time and apparently doing original and valuable work for he got out some patents on steam engines, I believe, in connection with the variable valve gear and the so-called dash pot which allowed very quick closing valves. These patents he turned over to the Corliss Company and they, in return, were very patient with Captain Nat, giving him time off apparently whenever he requested it. During this time, he acted as helmsman or sailing master on several of the yachts J. B. built, and won a great many races on Long Island Sound, Narragansett Bay, Buzzards Bay, and in Massachusetts Bay, altogether acquiring quite a reputation as a helmsman, and maybe that is the principal reason he was called Captain Nat.

But I must tell of a rather amusing incident in one of these races for I fear the gentle reader has become somewhat wearied with this listing of boats and dates. This particular race was way back in 1864 off Bridgeport, Connecticut, and Captain Nat was sailing the sloop "Magic" owned by J. B. "Magic" won handsomely.

The next boat was the "Go Softly," a fine boat from the west end of the Sound, but the third boat was owned by General Tom Thumb, the famous midget of that time who made quite a fortune

by appearing with the P. T. Barnum interests, and took up yachting as a hobby. To quote from some of Captain Nat's notes,
"When we returned to the yacht club landing, Tom Thumb, who
was half seas over, gave us a most unusual and profane tongue
lashing from his about thirty-three-inch stature, and very much to
the delight of all his friends." A later entry about "Magic" shows
things rather reversed. "I sailed 'Magic' against some of Brooklyn's best boats and one of them named 'Laura,' Commodore
Whiting, handsomely beat us and indicated that for racing
'Magic' was not equal to the best Penny Bridge boats. We then
sailed home."

I must note that the Penny Bridge boats were early sandbaggers kept in a shallow water region at the mouth of Gowanus
Creek, Brooklyn where there was a toll bridge from which the
boats derived their name.

Captain Nat did not act as sailing master in races after about
1880 with the exception of sailing "Gloriana" in 1891 for Mr. E. D.
Morgan and steering the "Vigilant" for Mr. Oliver Iselin in the
cup races of '93.

In the eighteen-seventies there sprang up many builders of
small steam craft throughout the world, and the young men of
that time were as much interested in them as a later generation
were to be in the airplane. Many of the early builders were in
England, and among the successful ones there who specialized
in small, fast steamers were Thornycroft and Yarrow. Thornycroft
built some of the world's first fast launches, and Yarrow, who was
born in 1842, six years before Captain Nat, specialized in high
speed steamers and light craft.

Yarrow was a remarkable man—he started life with little capital or education but at a very early age developed into a genius at
designing steam engines. When only nineteen years old he and
his partner designed steam traction engines for agricultural purposes and a successful steam road carriage in 1861, but as these
undertakings did not prove profitable, he started building steam
launches in the late eighteen-sixties. Between 1868 and 1875 Yarrow built three hundred and fifty steam launches. They were of
beautiful model and superb workmanship; in many cases the
model was like an enlarged rowboat. By about 1870 he was build-

ing some of these small craft of iron, and soon began building iron, steel, and aluminum alloy torpedo boats in large quantities for various navies. However, these early English torpedo boats all had heavy fire tube boilers and rather heavy hulls so that, in most cases, they were not as fast as the torpedo boats and launches Captain Nat was designing at the same time.

But the contributions to marine engineering that were given by Thornycroft and Yarrow in England, Normand in France, and N. G. Herreshoff in the United States are of much greater importance than is generally known. To quote a few sentences from the fine book, *Alfred Yarrow, His Life and Work.*

We do not wish to imply that those firms who have devoted themselves to the construction of small vessels have more ability than those who build large ones, but the record of progress from the very commencement of steam navigation shows that advances have first been made with vessels of small size, the reason clearly being that experimental research can be carried out with small vessels at an expense which is within the means of many firms, whilst corresponding experiments on a larger scale would involve too much financial risk.

Yarrow specialized on torpedo boats and destroyers while after 1890 Captain Nat devoted much of his skill to racing sailboats. Yarrow had tact enough to get along with the naval authorities, and built up a large organization which employed three thousand men, and his contributions to the English Navy in World War I were of such value that he was eventually knighted for his services.

Yarrow has this to say about tact: "If you need money, you can work for it; if you want grace, you may pray for it; but if you are without tact, there is no hope for you."

It must be conceded that both J. B. and N. G. Herreshoff were a little lacking in tact, but Yarrow's dealings with the Admiralty were with such fine gentlemen as Lord Fisher, Admiral Jellicoe, and Mr. Churchill when he became First Lord of the Admiralty, while the Herreshoffs had to deal with most difficult political appointees, so that after building the torpedo boats for the Spanish-American War they preferred to deal with civilians, as will be told later.

It is interesting to note that "Shamrock I," although designed by William Fife, Jr., was built by Thornycroft and Company. Though some of the Shamrocks were equal to the defenders in model and sail plan, they never equaled them in workmanship or structural design. This writer, at least, believes that if the Herreshoff Manufacturing Company had continued building torpedo boats and destroyers they, too, would have proved superior to all others.

But we must go back again to the eighteen-sixties, -seventies, and -eighties for it was during this time that the steam yacht came into popularity. The growth in numbers can be somewhat gauged by the steam yachts listed in England. These are as follows: 1863– thirty; 1873–one hundred and forty; 1883–four hundred and sixty-six. Of course we in this country had many less, but these figures show the proportionate growth of the steam yacht quite well, and it is not surprising that Captain Nat concentrated almost all of his attention on the steam launch and steam yacht between 1870 and 1890.

CHAPTER SIX

Captain Nat Forms a Partnership
with His Brother John

THE YEAR 1878 was an important one in the life of N. G. Herreshoff, for in that year he went into partnership with his brother, J. B. Herreshoff, in the boatbuilding business that J. B. was running at Bristol. It was an important step for Captain Nat as apparently he had good prospects in the steam engine industry which was then flourishing. But perhaps he realized that J. B.'s business was dependent on good designs and careful superintendence, and if Captain Nat did not give his full time to the works it could not expand or even become financially successful. So far as I know the agreement between the brother partners was very simple—in fact Captain Nat told me it consisted principally in his agreeing to join the partnership if J. B. would keep all bills paid promptly and not borrow money for expansion or construction, and never undertake work that would require more capital than they had on hand. Before this time, I believe, J. B. had been somewhat reckless in his business affairs but it may have been necessary for by this time, 1878, the works had expanded quite a little and had quite a lot of machinery for engine and boiler building. After this time the brothers must have been quite successful financially for I believe they financed the building of many yachts without borrowing money, and, in the case of tor-

pedo boats for the various governments, the payments were undoubtedly slow.

With yachts J. B. had made an early rule that the yacht must be
fully paid for before she was delivered to the owner. This rule
caused criticism and hard feelings in some owners, but as one of
the well-known clients said, "If a man can really afford a yacht he
can pay for her today as well as tomorrow." This policy of being
paid promptly and paying promptly gave the Herreshoff Manufacturing Company an enviable name among the suppliers of
materials, and no doubt made it possible for them to get the best
materials promptly at a reduced rate. I only speak of their
financial policies because at the present time it is quite usual for
a builder to take on large contracts with little more capital than a
shoestring, but the Herreshoffs always made a dollar before they
used it, and this, no doubt, very much simplified the management
of the company. In other words, having no creditors they could
make decisions quickly.

After the partnership was formed, the company was incor-
porated under the name of the Herreshoff Manufacturing Company with the two brothers the sole owners. They had intended
to manufacture other things as well as yachts, and in fact did
build steam engines and boilers for stationary work. For many
years they made steam engines to drive rotary water pumps,
dynamos, and for other stationary use. Their stationary engines
were all horizontal and quite small. The Herreshoff engines acquired a very good name both for economy and reliability and
one of their later types, which had an enclosed crankcase and
splash lubrication and was used in New York in the chemical
industry, ran continuously night and day for one year, a feat that
probably few engines before or since have accomplished.

The first sizable order after the partnership was formed was
from the Spanish government for a gunboat to be used at Cuba
to chase or capture vessels the insurgents might use to import
arms. Apparently the "Estelle," of which we have spoken before
and which could maintain a speed of sixteen miles per hour, had
greatly impressed the Spanish government. This gunboat, which
was named "Clara," was somewhat similar to "Estelle" but was
one hundred and forty feet long.

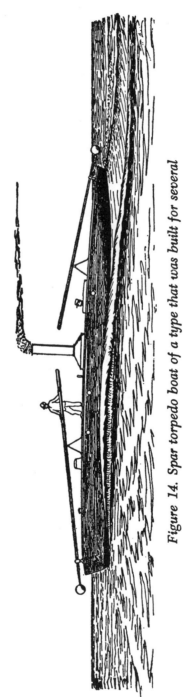

Figure 14. Spar torpedo boat of a type that was built for several governments.

After this, they began building so-called "spar torpedo" boats for several governments. They were about fifty-six feet long and only six feet six inches beam. They were nearly perfect double-enders and intended to run either end first just as well and at about the same speed. Previous spar torpedo boats had only carried one spar with its bomb in place over the bow, but these double-enders were, you might say, repeaters. For those who are not familiar with the spar torpedo, I will say this weapon was developed just at the close of the Civil War when many of the fighting ships had armor plate which extended only a little below the water line. These early torpedo boats were intended to sneak up quietly to a ship at anchor and thrust the spar with the bomb on its end against the wooden underbody of the ship below the armor plate, when the resulting explosion right against the ship's side, and backed up by the incompressible surrounding water, caused a terrific local concussion.

These little torpedo boats were painted gray and could run very smoothly and quietly up to around twenty-one miles per hour. One of the most remarkable things about them was that they could slow down or stop quickly; this was because the boats were very light and because they had relatively large propellers connected to engines which could be instantly reversed with the throttle wide open, and, of course, the engine developed the same power running either way. The propellers, being quite near the middle of the boats, did not cavitate. It is said that these craft could stop within a few lengths when running at full speed, and a few seconds later would be going some twenty miles per hour astern which, of course, was a most valuable accomplishment in the life and death feat of launching a spar torpedo.

Another unusual feature of these craft was that the propeller shaft was run on a slight curve so that the engine, which was forward of the boiler, was on quite an angle, while the shaft at the propeller was more horizontal. The shaft, which was of steel or iron, ran in a snug-fitting brass tube its full length, and as the tube was well lubricated, you might say the shaft ran in a continuous bearing. This shaft ran very smoothly and with little friction. The long strut which supported this curved propeller shaft was made up of brass or bronze plates which acted as a streamlined keel condenser. These little vessels were light enough to hoist aboard a man-of-war. They were very reliable when kept in good condition, and good sea boats when slowed down. Incidentally, with these coil or flash boilers they could get up steam from a cold boiler in about three minutes with a specially built fire of split hard pine saturated with oil, and I believe in about five minutes had a full head of steam. I will note for those not familiar with boilers that with most boilers of that time, and even now, it is injurious to the boiler to get up steam rapidly for some parts expand more rapidly than others which causes internal strains and often starts seams, but rapid steaming did not injure these Herreshoff coil boilers.

One of these spar torpedo boats was left on the Herreshoff Manufacturing Company's hands when the war between Peru and Chile ended. She was stored for many years on the Herreshoff Farm at Popasquash where, at times, I used to play in her hull, but then she was manned principally by a crew of wasps who had built several nests in her ends so that we boys generally kept away from her. Even if the wasps did not have torpedoes they had stingers in one end at least. This particular torpedo boat had been built between 1879 and 1880, and although she was uncovered she remained in remarkably good condition up until about 1910. I speak of this principally to show the fine workmanship and scientific construction that went into their hulls—a type of construction lighter, stronger, and of better materials and workmanship than any I know of being made today.

One of the last of the spar torpedo boats built by the Herreshoff Manufacturing Company was hull No. 64, built in 1880 for the Russian Navy, fifty-nine feet long, six feet six inches beam. She made a record speed for those days of twenty-three miles per hour on her trial trip. The model of this steamer is now at the Massachusetts Institute of Technology. She was higher at the ends than the previous spar torpedo boats built by the Herreshoffs. This was accomplished by having depressions or launching ways on her four quarters so that she could carry four spar torpedoes. Although this craft had several hatches she was run and steered mostly from below deck with the helmsman's head only above deck. Altogether, she was more streamlined than any

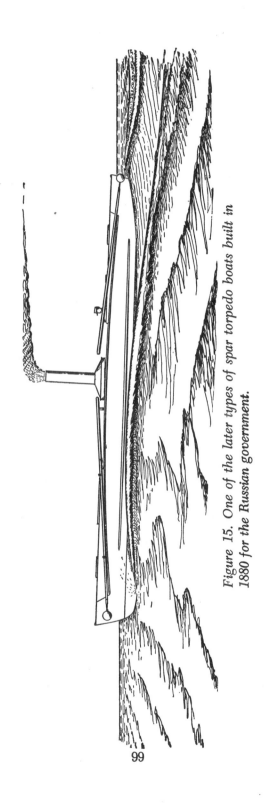

Figure 15. One of the later types of spar torpedo boats built in
1880 for the Russian government.

modern craft. The engines in these craft and in some of the steam yachts built by the Herreshoffs about 1880 were made in several sizes. They had cast iron columns or frames which contained the so-called guide rods all in one casting. They were beautifully simple, easy to make, and performed remarkably well. Some of these engines made for stationary work were used nearly forty years. Because they had very light moving parts they were quite free from vibration.

In 1878 the Herreshoffs had built a torpedo boat for the British government. She was fifty-nine feet six inches long and seven feet six inches beam, and I believe the first vessel they built that used much steel or iron in the hull. Below the sheer line, she had wood planking over steel frames, but the upper sides and deck were of one sixteenth inch sheet steel. Her engine was compound with bores of six inches and ten and one half inches; stroke ten inches. The coil boiler was four feet in diameter, and had three inch diameter tubes about three hundred feet long, using a working pressure of one hundred and sixty pounds. J. B. and N. G. Herreshoff took this torpedo boat to England on the deck of a steamer along with a small double-ended launch, No. 47, twenty-nine feet long, five feet beam, named "Ibis," which they had built for G. R. Dunell of London. They took over with them a crew and ran the trials of the torpedo boat on the Thames before the First Lord of the Admiralty, Chief Constructor Barnaby, and other naval officers. The weight of this little ship was only six tons, but the crew of four, fuel and torpedoes brought her weight to seven and one half tons. She ran the same speed astern as ahead and turned in a circle of about three times her length. It is said she got up steam from the lighting of the fire to the blowing of the safety valve in five minutes. I believe she made only about eighteen miles per hour on the Thames, but her runs were slightly hampered by floating ice. Her deck was enclosed and clear, except for the smoke stack and a small turret aft for steering.

During the next few years the Herreshoff Manufacturing Company built several so-called "Vedette" boats for the French and English governments. These were high speed launches, forty or fifty feet long, and I believe some of these were the first boats the Herreshoffs built with steel plating. The works at this time, 1880,

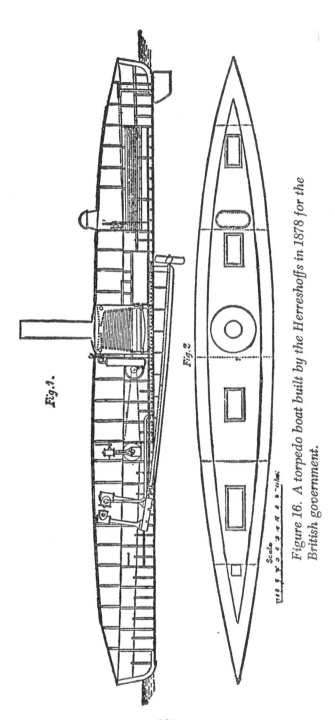

Fig.1.

Fig.2.

Scale

Figure 16. A torpedo boat built by the Herreshoffs in 1878 for the British government.

were greatly enlarged, and the number of employees was in the neighborhood of three hundred.

Some of the steam yachts they built in the 1880's were:

	L.O.A.
"Gleam"	120'
"Edith"	60'
"Sport"	45'
"Lucy"	42'
"Leila"	100'
"Siesta"	98'
"Permelia"	95'
"Orienta"	125'
"Nereid"	76'
"Permelia II"	100'
"Magnolia"	99' -twin screw.

Sailboats were almost entirely dropped between 1880 and 1890 with the exception of some racing catboats and other undecked craft.

By 1885, the brothers were quite prosperous so they decided to build for themselves a high-speed steam yacht, the "Stiletto," ninety-four feet long, eleven feet six inches beam.

"Stiletto" had a very unusual engine, designed particularly for her, with unique valves that let a large flow of steam in and out of the cylinders at the top and bottom of the stroke. It was a compound engine with bores of twelve inches and twenty-one inches and stroke of twelve inches. Her boiler was seven feet square and consisted of tubes alongside the firebox and many tubes above, some running fore and aft and some athwartship. This boiler was a step between the coil boiler and the three-drum water tube boiler later adopted, but it must have been a good steamer for apparently "Stiletto" could easily maintain a speed of twenty miles per hour and is said to have made one long run of eight hours at twenty-six and one half miles per hour. However, "Stiletto" is considered by many to be the first high-speed steam yacht and, in her type, as outstanding as the "Gloriana" was among racing sailboats.

"Stiletto" was made famous because of her race with the

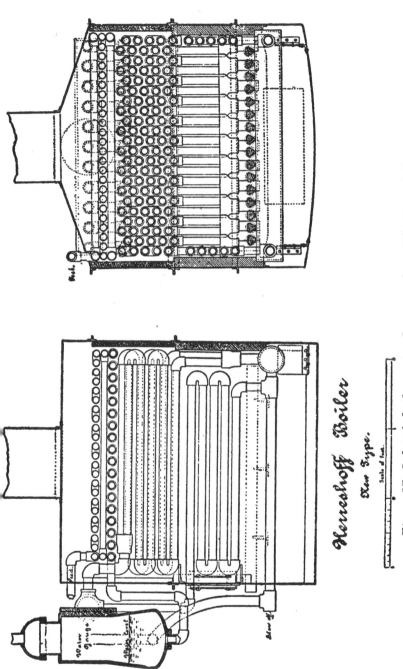

Herreshoff Boiler

New Type.

Scale of feet.

Figure 17. Stiletto's boiler; a step between the coil boiler and the three-drum water tube boiler later adopted.

Hudson River steamboat, "Mary Powell." The "Mary Powell" was the fastest American steamboat, and perhaps the fastest vessel in the world, for a few years around 1880. Her speed was around twenty-five miles per hour and, although there had been other steamers that were said to have been as fast, the "Mary" had beaten them when they were alongside. On the tenth of June, in 1885, "Stiletto" had her famous race with "Mary Powell." At first she ran alongside of her for a few miles but when Captain Nat gave the jingle, the bell signal for full speed, "Stiletto" ran ahead, crossed "Mary's" bow, slowed down, let "Mary" pass her, crossed "Mary's" stern, went ahead again and, after a run of thirty miles, was five minutes ahead of "Mary." This race was headline material for the papers of the time.

I must say a few words about the "Mary Powell" for she was one of the most famous steamboats ever built in America. She had originally been built in 1861, three hundred feet long, and, although rebuilt and, I believe, lengthened forward around 1880, she was considered the Queen of the Hudson and was called "The Peerless Mary." At one time, at least, she was owned and managed by one family, but the most remarkable thing about her was that she ran on the Hudson for about fifty summers. She was also a very handsome vessel of her type.

After about two years, or in 1887, "Stiletto" was sold to the U.S. Navy for a torpedo boat and as such ran in naval service for over twenty years. She was the second torpedo boat our Navy had; the first one, "Lightning," has already been spoken of. "Stiletto" had a torpedo tube built into her after the Navy took her over and was the first U.S. Navy torpedo boat to fire an automobile torpedo.

The Herreshoff Manufacturing Company was very busy during these years and had to erect new buildings to accommodate the work. The north construction shop was built in about 1884, the machine shop much enlarged, and the south construction shop built in 1887. Both of the construction shops were approximately one hundred and sixty-five feet long by forty feet wide, had launching ways down their middle, and two overhead traveling cranes in each shop so that weights could be picked up in any position in the shop. The shops were also heated, which was un-

usual at that time or even now, in large yacht construction buildings. The two brothers were working together as a good team,
J. B. attending to the financial business while Captain Nat did the
designing and superintending.

In the meantime, Captain Nat, when he had a chance, experimented with towing models which he did somewhat as follows.
He had a gangway or platform temporarily built on the side of a
steam yacht about eighteen inches above the water where one or
two people could stand. The models were always towed in pairs
from a balanced yoke so that if one had the least bit more resistance she would lag backward. The models towed against each
other always weighed exactly the same. The speed of the steam
yacht was determined by having tachometers or revolution counters on the engines, and the yacht had previously been run several
times over the measured mile until the scale speed of the models
had been determined. Then, by noting the reading of the revolution counters, the engineer could hold the yacht to the desired
speed. I believe Captain Nat learned a great deal from these towing tests and much about wave action which somewhat influenced his later designs. But it must not be thought for a minute
that he was blind to the full size action of his yachts, which he
always ran on their trial trips, for he certainly had unusual
powers of observation. Where the average person was somewhat
bewildered on a trial trip, he seemed to have taken in everything
and, best of all, remembered it, so that he could later make a
complete mental analysis of the results. And this is the only way
in which a designer can make improvement.

In 1887 the Herreshoff Manufacturing Company got the contract to build a steel torpedo boat for the U.S. Navy. She was
classed in the Navy as "Seagoing Torpedo Boat No. 1," and
when completed was christened "Cushing." She was one hundred
and forty feet long and, I believe, she was the first vessel built in
the south shop. She was lightly built but most of her steel parts
were electrogalvanized. Captain Nat designed a new model of
engine for the "Cushing," and these engines were so unusual that
I will describe them briefly. They were five cylinder, quadruple
expansion engines with two low pressure cylinders. If the valve
gear had been between the cylinders, like the usual engines, the

engine would have been abnormally long, so he had adopted the scheme of having the valves at the side of the cylinders, and the valves were driven by a separate crankshaft as nearly all internal combustion engines today have their camshaft at one side. This separate valve crankshaft also much simplified the reversing mechanism for the valves could be put in position for going ahead or reverse by changing the timing of the valve crankshaft in relation to the main crankshaft. This was accomplished by having the driving gear on the valve crankshaft mounted on a spiral cut in the valve crankshaft, and by shifting a sliding nut on the valve shaft the desired valve position was accomplished.

I believe these were the first large engines mounted on diagonally braced forged steel columns, an arrangement that saves much weight. In fact there were no parts between the engine bed and cylinders that were not forged steel with the exception of the crossheads. There were many features about these engines that Captain Nat used on several later models and much that was copied by the light steam engine designers of the world. I believe there were five of these engines built—two for the "Cushing," one each for the "Ballymena," "Say When" and "Vamoose." Although these engines were a designing triumph, as far as the mechanical parts were concerned, they did have too many cylinders so that they often gave trouble from the steam condensing and causing water knocks in the low pressure cylinders. In fact some of them cracked their low pressure cylinder heads so that Captain Nat never designed more than a triple expansion engine after this model. I also believe these engines did not develop as much power as was expected, or as their general size might indicate, so that the "Cushing" only exceeded her contract speed by about half a knot. However, her trials were run in February which may have somewhat slowed her down, but it is rather surprising that she did not go materially faster than "Stiletto," or somewhere around twenty-six miles per hour. But the most surprising thing about the "Cushing" was that she only cost $82,750, while it is likely a similar vessel today would cost the best part of a million.

The next vessel set up in the south shop was the steel steam yacht, "Ballymena," one hundred and forty-eight feet long, but in the meantime two very interesting steamers were built. They

were the "Now Then" and "Say When." The "Now Then," eighty-
five feet long, was quite a departure in model from previous
power vessels and had a wide flat stern with a very straight run
aft. Her stern, as you can see by her photograph, had a pro-
nounced tumble home and terminated in a sharp point at the
water line, and although this model was copied by literally hundreds of later power vessels, Captain Nat did not like it at all. He
said the sharp point at the water line was an abomination but,
worst of all, one day when "Now Then" was backing out of the
slip at the Herreshoff works she struck a couple of waves which
this stern brought right up on deck and soaked a couple of ladies
(one of whom was the author's mother), sitting in chairs on the
after deck. So he never used this type of stern again.

Nevertheless, "Now Then" was a remarkable yacht and if she
had been built without the clipper bow, masts, etc., certainly
would have looked very modern. On her first run after delivery
she traveled from Newport, Rhode Island, to Twenty-fourth
Street, New York City, a distance of one hundred and seventy
miles, in seven hours and four minutes, or at a rate of over twenty-
four miles per hour, a speed between Newport and New York not
often beaten since by privately owned yachts. When one considers that this record was made in 1887, it seems amazing. I know
there will be many of my younger readers who will say, "Oh,
there are plenty of launches nowadays that go more than twice as
fast as that," but I wonder if many of them have made the run
much faster from Newport to New York through the sea off Point
Judith and the tide rips of the Sound. At the time of "Now Then,"
a fast steam yacht was the fastest privately owned conveyance
that a person could own. Of course, the horse could go faster for
a few miles, and a few people could ride a bicycle faster for a
mile or two, but nothing but the steam locomotive could travel
faster for long distances, and the locomotive or steam train could
only run in the direction the tracks were laid. So, in its day, the
high-speed steam yacht was quite a thing, and for several years
Captain Nat designed the fastest of them. In fact, the owner of
"Now Then," Mr. Norman L. Munro, offered to race "Now Then"
against any American steam yacht without time allowance, but
received no acceptance to his challenge. I must mention that the

design of a yacht like "Now Then," including her boiler and engine, required much more brain work than the design of a yacht like "Gloriana," and in my opinion the practice and training Captain Nat got in designing high-speed steamers put him head and shoulders above other designers of the time, particularly in regard to construction and most particularly in the design of metal parts.

But perhaps Captain Nat was going a little too fast at this time, for he was to receive somewhat of a setback on his next fast yacht. While some people may criticize me for bringing up this incident, I feel that it had some effect on his career and may have turned him partly toward the sailboat again. This happened with the steamer "Say When" also built for Mr. Munro. "Say When" was

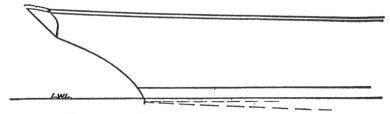

Figure 18. The overhung stern of Say When.

very much the same model under water as "Now Then," but her stern above water was carried out in an overhang, somewhat like other yachts of the time. She was one hundred and thirty-eight feet long, planked of mahogany, and had an engine like the ones in "Cushing." These engines had a stroke of fifteen inches and bores of eleven inches, sixteen inches, twenty-two and one half inches, twenty-two and one half inches, twenty-two and one half inches and developed in the neighborhood of eight hundred and seventy-five horsepower. On her trial trips "Say When" rather disappointed her designer and because the safety valve blew just before she got up to the speed anticipated, Captain Nat himself screwed down the safety valve adjustment. I suppose he did not increase the boiler pressure materially, but in running a trial it is most annoying to have the safety valve pop and at times lower the whole boiler pressure five pounds or so before the valve closes again. At any rate it was Captain Nat's hard luck that in getting up steam before the next trial run a boiler tube burst when the fire door was open, and the steam and fire that was thrown into the boiler room fatally asphyxiated a fireman. At the inquest of the accident the steamboat inspectors not only severely reprimanded Captain Nat but also, I believe, took away his steam engine license forever.

In an attempt to justify Captain Nat, I will say the boiler tubes of that day varied in strength considerably, particularly at different temperatures and this particular boiler, which was of the Thornycroft type, had some tubes above the water level. Also if the fire door had not happened to be open for the fireman to stoke the fire probably no harm would have been done. Also I have heard, and this happened before I was born, that the boiler was only getting up steam and did not have a high pressure when the tube let go, so Captain Nat had bad luck. For those not familiar with water tube boilers I will say that generally a tube that gives out opens only with a small crack and allows a small escape of steam, in fact so small that you would not know anything had happened excepting for the loss of steam pressure and, at times, the use of more water than comes from the condenser. Almost always you can complete the day's run without difficulty, so the severity of this accident with a water tube boiler was hard luck.

I do not know the speed of "Say When," but believe it was about twenty-five miles per hour. Mr. Norman L. Munro, who was a wealthy publisher in New York, also had built the high speed Herreshoff launches, "Henrietta," forty-eight feet; "Lotus Seeker," forty-eight feet; "Jersey Lily," forty-eight feet; "Our Mary," sixty-four feet—six notable Herreshoff steamers in all.

I do not mean to give the reader the impression that the Herreshoff Manufacturing Company specialized in high-speed steamers, for by far the greater number of their yachts were comfortable cruisers of ten or twelve miles an hour. Also much of their work was building small open launches. They in no way had a monopoly of small steam yacht building, but through the excellence of Captain Nat's designs and the high quality of the work, they enjoyed a generous share of this business at the time.

Before closing this chapter, I feel that a description of the

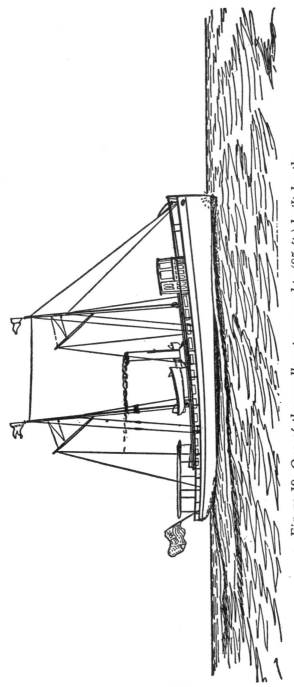

Figure 19. One of the smaller steam yachts (85 ft.) built by the Herreshoff Manufacturing Company in the 1880's. They used about one ton of coal each 150 miles at 10 to 15 miles an hour speeds.

small steam yacht of the eighteen-eighties would be in place. Several of these built by the Herreshoff Manufacturing Company were around eighty-five feet long, and sensible, economical, and reliable craft. The crew generally consisted of a captain, a deck hand, a steward, and an engineer, all of whom slept in a forecastle forward. Next aft of the forecastle was a galley, then the space for boiler and engine room (and the Herreshoffs built very compact boilers and engines. Aft of the engine room was usually a sort of main saloon with table in the middle and folding berths at the side, and here meals were sometimes served at night and in rainy weather. Aft of this usually there was a toilet room and a single stateroom or two. These little vessels were fine sea boats and very economical, only using about one ton of coal in one hundred and fifty miles at speeds of between ten and fifteen miles an hour, a cost of fuel much below the usual modern craft of the same displacement and speed.

Quite a number of these small steam yachts were built and owned or used all along the coast from Lake Ponchatrain at New Orleans to the coast of Maine, besides some on the fresh water lakes. These little steamers were pleasanter to cruise in than most modern craft; they were noiseless, safe, reliable, and comfortable. They had a very pleasant smell about them and one never worried about fire or explosion. To be sure, some of them were notorious rollers, but you could get used to that. Some of these little steamers lasted a long time, and about their only disadvantage was that they required a comparatively large crew which today would bring their running expense to more than the saving of their low cost of fuel. All of my early experiences in cruising were in small steam yachts and I will say without hesitation that it was a pleasanter life than any that I know of today on the water.

Most all of these little steamers built by the Herreshoff Manufacturing Company were quite different in size, model, and type, and it is perfectly amazing that Captain Nat could have designed them all in such a short time, for he did almost all of the designing himself and only employed draftsmen to ink in the drawings he had made in pencil. Some people who know something about the matter say that Captain Nat designed more models and sizes of steam engines than anyone in the world, and I think this statement is quite likely, and probably the various models, sizes, and types combined might number thirty or more. Among other things, he designed at least two very small side-wheeled steamers, about forty feet long, for some of the shallow water regions of the south, and I am sorry I cannot find a photo of them for they were pretty little craft.

CHAPTER SEVEN

Captain Nat's Home Life

CAPTAIN NAT's home life was closely connected with his work. In fact nearly all of his designing was done in a drafting room in his home. At a very early age he had accustomed or trained himself to work nights and Sundays on the designs of steamers that J. B. was building, and to have accomplished this while he was a student at Tech and later a designer at the Corliss Engine Company seems most remarkable. But this early concentration at designing in the hours when most people were having their recreation or rest seemed to harden him so that through a very long life he worked approximately twelve hours a day, and sometimes even more. I would like to emphasize this for no doubt this ability to work long hours was the principal reason for his great accomplishments. Not only was the quality of his work the best in the world but the quantity is most amazing. It is generally conceded that he designed more boats or vessels of various kinds than anyone who has left a record. Some steam engineers also say he designed more models of steam engines than anyone else, and I think this very likely.

Strange to say, when he had passed middle life he often designed or modeled yachts which had not been ordered; in other words these extra designs were simply for the amusement of a mind that was capable of doing even more work. "Work" is the wrong word for I believe it was more pleasure than work for him. No doubt it was extra practice, and it is my opinion that great accomplishment is always dependent on much practice. For in-

113

stance it is stated that the great piano player Paderewski practiced many more hours than anyone else.

For many years Captain Nat's day was divided up and used
about as follows, although he had no fixed schedule. He arose at
6:00 A.M.—even earlier in the summer—worked in his drafting
room or model-making room until 8:00 A.M., and used to say the
early morning was the best time for him to work, then had break-
fast at eight, and sat quietly thereafter for a half hour or so reading the paper or some engineering magazine. At nine or before he
went to the boat shop, usually at first visiting the drafting room at
the shop where there were three or four draftsmen who inked in
his drawings or made working drawings of various parts taken
from his original pencil plans. In this first call at the drafting
room he often brought in a drawing that he had made the night
before. Next he talked over the day's business with his brother
J. B., who by that time had had the morning's mail read. Perhaps
then by 10:00 A.M. he started on a walk over the whole boat
plant to inspect every piece of work that was being made. This
was quite an undertaking to do rapidly; not only did he have to
answer many questions, but the distance traveled would often be
the better part of a mile with many stairs to climb. Captain Nat
could usually tell at a glance if everything was going as it should,
and many people believe the high quality of the work that was
done by the Herreshoff Manufacturing Company was to a great
extent the result of Captain Nat's careful inspection and superintendency.

Often by eleven-thirty he would return home, about a two-
minute walk from the works, where he set to work at his
designing or model making again until one o'clock, when he had
his noonday meal. Then perhaps from one-thirty to two he sat
quietly reading before he went back to the works to spend perhaps an hour or so in the office and drafting room before making
another complete inspection of the works. This inspection lasted
until 6:00 P.M. in the old days, but after the works were closed
down for the day at 5:00 A.M., he returned home and set to work
again at his designing until six-thirty when he had supper. From
seven to about seven-thirty he read again and then went to his
drafting room where he did either designing or model making
until ten o'clock when he retired. He apparently kept up a sched-

ule somewhat like this, or worked an equal number of hours a day, for a term of nearly sixty years. If he designed "Violet" in 1864 and "Belisarius" in 1935 that would add up to seventy-one years that he had worked altogether at his profession. The last fifteen years of his life he took a great deal of time off for sailing and cruising, spending his winters in Florida.

I have said before that he worked Sundays and holidays also, but in the summer he usually went sailing on Sundays, and as a matter of fact on nice Sundays in the winter he often took a few hours' sail in one of the several small boats he kept for that purpose. These were light open boats, which could be launched or hauled up quickly and easily, and it may be well to list some of these small sailboats in which he took his recreation during the time he was designing steam vessels, and while making this list possibly list as well all the larger yachts he owned.

At first, or in the years between 1874 and 1889, he used the "Riviera" of which we have spoken before, but her original sloop rig was taken out to use on an iceboat he built in 1875. In 1880 he had "Riviera" replanked, and in 1882 put a catyawl rig in her which was especially designed to stow inside the boat but still could be quickly rigged and unrigged for winter sailing. With this rig "Riviera" had three mast holes which were used as follows: In light weather the mainmast was stepped in the mast hole near the stem, and the mizzen in a hole well aft. In stronger breezes the mainmast was stepped in a mast hole about one-third her length from the bow, with no mizzen set; and in strong winds the mizzen was used here in place of the mainsail.

His next small boat was named "Sabrina," a sixteen-foot cat-boat, narrow on the water line but with wide flaring sides above. She was built in 1878 and sold in 1879 going to the Gulf of Finland where she became famous for her sailing.

Between 1876 and 1881 he used catamarans mostly for his pleasure sailing, and often spoke of the great enjoyment he got from these fast craft.

Captain Nat became a married man in 1883 and required a more comfortable sort of craft so he had the catyawl "Consuelo" built. She was a roomy, able little ship with sections somewhat like a cutter, and the first sailboat built by the Herreshoff Manufacturing Company that had all outside ballast. She was thirty-two feet O.A., twenty-nine feet W.L., eight feet eight inches beam, and five feet two inches draft. She was heavily ballasted with six and one-half tons of lead, all outside. He used the "Consuelo" between 1883 and 1886 when she was sold to Pierre Lorillard.

His next boat was the "Clara," a catyawl thirty-five feet O.A., twenty-nine and one half feet L.W.L., nine feet eight inches beam, and five feet draft, which was used in the seasons of 1887 to 1890. Her model was somewhat like the English cutters which at that time were popular in this country, but her sail plan was similar to the sailing canoes of that era with full length battens and a batwing sail. "Clara" must have been carefully built for she was used on the east coast for some fifty years and is now in use as a yacht on the west coast at the advanced age of sixty-two years, and no doubt is one of the oldest American yachts now in use.

But Captain Nat's love of sailing open, unballasted boats was so great that in 1889 he had "Coquina" built. She was a very light boat designed to be hoisted up in tackles as the boats of a yacht are, but "Coquina" had a boathouse which extended out over the water and entirely enclosed her when hoisted. However, she could be quickly lowered away and rigged for a sail in any of the four seasons. She was sixteen feet six inches long, five feet beam, and decked in along the sides for a width of about seven inches. The stern was also decked in for a length of about two feet making a compartment where clothes or food could be carried and kept dry. Her weights were as follows:

	Lbs.
Stripped hull	275
Removable bronze centerboard	37
Rudder, etc.	10
Oars and rowlocks	11
Mainsail and spars	30
Mizzen and spars	13
Captain Nat	170
Sandbags	140
Total displacement while sailing	687

"Coquina" had two rigs, both catyawl; the large rig had one hundred and eighty-three square feet area, and the small rig one hundred and thirty-one square feet. Although "Coquina" was lightly built, planking five sixteenths inch cedar, she was a nearly perfect piece of workmanship. Captain Nat used her off and on for about fourteen years, when she was turned over to his oldest son who also took good care of her so that she was almost without a blemish at forty-nine years of age when she was in a boathouse that was swept away in the hurricane of 1938. "Coquina" was the first boat the author remembers being in under sail, and he may have been five years old at the time.

Although youthful impressions may be exaggerated, I believe "Coquina" was as fast for her sail area as any useful boats in existence today.

Captain Nat's next sailboat was the famous finkeeler "Dilemma" built in 1891. She was the first so-called fin and bulb keel boat, but as I am to describe her in a following chapter I will only say now that he used her but one season.

His next boat or yacht was the first of his yachts to be named "Alerion." She was built in 1894 and had for her keel the fin and bulb that had originally been made for Mr. E. D. Morgan's "Drusilla," building No. 417, but was found to be too light for the sail area of No. 417. This "Alerion" was thirty-three feet W.L. and had two headsails—what Captain Nat called a full sloop rig— but he found her too large for his use as he sometimes liked to go singlehanded, so he sold her during her first season and her name was changed to "Memory."

In the fall of 1894 he had built "Alerion II," thirty feet W.L. fin keel, jib and mainsail. This "Alerion" had the second suit of crosscut sails that had ever been made. The crosscut sail had been invented by Captain Nat about 1893 and, I believe, the first one used was on one of the Larchmont one-design fin keelers built by the Herreshoffs for Mr. W. B. Duncan. Captain Nat liked this "Alerion" very much and used her between 1894 and 1897 when he was so busy designing steam torpedo boats for the Spanish-American War that he was unable to take time off even for sailing, so she was stored in his boathouse until 1899 when she was sold to Mr. A. H. Alker and went to Long Island Sound. This "Alerion."

by the way, was the prototype of the Newport thirty foot one-design class only differing very slightly from it.

By this time Captain Nat was very much troubled with rheumatism and it was thought then that this condition was partly aggravated by his often being wet to the skin in sailing small sailboats in all seasons of the year. He had also acquired a large family—six children—and perhaps now that he was designing more sailboats than steamers it was a pleasant change to use steam launches or steam yachts for his sailing and cruising, so for the next several years he used steamers principally. These steamers were much the best for following the races and studying the action of the larger sailing yachts that he was now designing. However, in the fall, winter, and spring he took occasional sails in the "Coquina" which he seemed to relish very much although by this time he was nearing fifty years of age. In the season of 1896 he used the steam cabin launch "Loon," sixty-two feet long, which had been built for Mr. R. M. Riddle and had taken a winter cruise in the West Indies about 1895. "Loon"'s speed was approximately twelve miles per hour and she could cruise comfortably at over ten.

His next steamer was named "Item," built in 1896, building No. 183. She was forty-eight feet long and had a darling little triple expansion engine with bores of four and one half inches, seven inches and eleven and one-fourth inches, and stroke of seven inches. This launch had a good size cockpit aft and was the first steamer the author remembers sailing in. She ran at about fourteen miles an hour.

In the year 1898 Captain Nat took over a steam launch sixty-five feet long which had been started as a torpedo launch in 1886. He drew up plans to convert her into a pleasure launch, and named her "Squib." She had a triple expansion engine with bores of five and one fourth inches, nine inches and fourteen inches, with nine inches stroke. She was used mostly for day sailing between 1898 and 1901 and followed many of the races off Newport, but as she was a little small for his growing family of six children he had her stern lengthened to make her seventy-six feet O.A. When speeded up she ran with her forefoot at water level, and the stern wave came up to a level a little below the after deck. When opened up, I think she went about eighteen miles per hour. She had a light airy engine room and was a pleasure to sail in for she was nearly noiseless and vibrationless.

About this time, perhaps 1898, Captain Nat chartered for a few months the one-hundred-and-nine-foot steam yacht "Neckan" that he had designed for Mr. H. C. Baxter and took his whole family for a cruise down the Maine coast. While I remember going on this cruise, I do not remember the exact year. On this cruise Captain Nat's family all had such a good time that he decided to build a roomy yacht for himself, so "Roamer," building No. 215 was built. She was ninety-three feet ten inches O.A., seventeen feet beam, and four feet ten inches draft. She was an extremely roomy craft principally because her machinery was very compact. Her boiler was only four feet three inches fore and aft, five feet ten inches wide though it had 394 square feet of heating surface, and grate area of seventeen and one half square feet. She had a triple expansion engine with bores of five and five eighths inches, eight inches, and twelve and one half inches, and seven inches stroke. The engine was of a type he was designing at that time and called a triple expansion steeple engine, having the low pressure cylinder above the high and intermediate cylinders so the engine was very short fore and aft, also remarkably free from vibration. The crankcase was enclosed, and the moving parts lubricated by the splash system as later internal combustion engines were to be. This engine turned a propeller of forty inches diameter and forty inches pitch and enabled the "Roamer" to cruise at ten miles an hour very quietly and economically. Captain Nat cruised many thousand miles in "Roamer" and at one time or another she visited most every harbor from Bar Harbor to Sandy Hook; that is most every harbor that had over a fathom of water. He owned "Roamer" between 1902 and 1911 and often took twelve guests (mostly his family), himself, and a crew of four, totaling seventeen. They all had a separate berth and were well fed and made perfectly comfortable in all weather, barring some seasickness.

In 1904 the Herreshoff Manufacturing Company built the fast steam launch "Swiftsure," and Captain Nat used her a season or two. She was fifty-two feet three inches, O.A. and only six feet

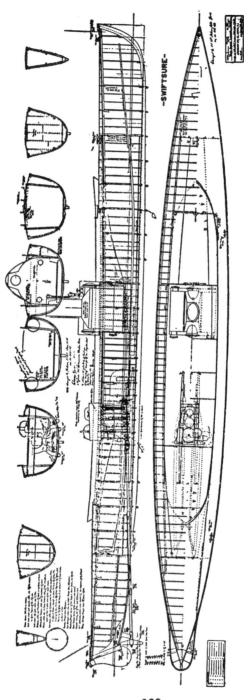

Figure 20. Swiftsure, the last fast steam launch that Captain Nat designed in 1904. Her race with Vingt-Et-Un was almost the last race between steam and gasoline launches to be made in open salt water.

one inch beam. She had a light, double-ended hull of light construction and must have been a model easy to drive through the water for her steam power plant was similar to ones used in two launches he had designed that went twenty-one miles per hour, but "Swiftsure" under a good head of steam could get up to some twenty-six miles per hour. However, she could not hold that speed for long runs or on courses that had some turns, but she made good time, nevertheless, in two races she ran in 1904. The first was on July 30 off the Atlantic Yacht Club when she raced the big sixty foot powerboat "Standard" that had a two hundred horsepower engine. In this race, including the turns, "Standard" made an average speed of 24.29 miles per hour while "Swiftsure" averaged 23.16 miles per hour. On August 18, at Newport "Swiftsure" and "Vingt-et-un" ran over a course of sixteen nautical miles which was in two laps, "Swiftsure" keeping ahead the first round but "Vingt-et-un" passing her just before the finish with both launches averaging 25.64 statute miles per hour, which was very good going considering the strong wind and choppy sea and the turns of the course, for it is well known that the turns of a race course much reduce the speed. This I think was about the last race between steam and gasoline launches in open salt water.

Captain Nat did not use "Swiftsure" much but I remember one run I had in her between Newport and Bristol in a fresh northerly breeze. She may have been going twenty-four or twenty-five miles an hour and running almost noiselessly; it certainly was a run to be remembered. I believe if "Swiftsure" had had an oil-fired boiler so she could hold her steam better, had carried slightly higher boiler pressure, and had not had a rather clumsy tube condenser under her bottom she would have been several miles per hour faster. At any rate she ran remarkably well for her horsepower and weight, and went very smoothly in a choppy sea, and I cannot help thinking a model like "Swiftsure" would carry her weight at twenty-five miles per hour with less power than any launch afloat today, for most launches of her weight and speed today have nearly double her horsepower. "Swiftsure" was the last small, high speed steam launch Captain Nat designed, and although he designed larger and slower steamers for a few years longer the internal combustion engine was surely taking the place of steam.

The next boat he had was the small keel sailboat "Delight" built in 1908—twenty-eight feet six inches O.A., nineteen and one half feet W.L. and six feet three inches beam, designed to fit the Universal Rule—and a remarkably pretty little craft.

In 1911 he designed a sailboat to take to Bermuda for sailing there in the winter. She was named "Oleander" and was twenty-three feet six inches O.A., twenty feet six inches W.L., was quite shallow, but had a centerboard passing through her outside lead keel. He found her too small and not seaworthy enough for the choppy waters and strong breezes of Bermuda winter weather, so sold her.

In 1912 he built "Alerion III," building No. 718. She was a fine, able little boat, twenty-six feet O.A., twenty-one feet nine inches W.L., seven feet seven inches beam, and twenty-eight inches draft with centerboard and outside lead keel. He used "Alerion" at Bermuda in the winters of 1913, '14, and '15. After the war she was shipped back to Bristol where he used her between 1920 and 1929.

In 1912 he had the powerboat "Helianthus" built. She was sixty-four feet long and thirteen and one half feet beam, had a deck house which was a combination pilot house and dining saloon. This was his first gasoline yacht for his personal use and he was rather disappointed with her economy of fuel compared to the steamers to which he was accustomed. Although "Helianthus" was built in 1912, she had a reduction gear of his own design and a system of distant controls so the engine could be managed entirely from the pilot house. She ran at about ten knots, and he cruised quite a little along the New England coast in her between 1912 and 1916, and sold her to the U.S. Navy for a patrol boat in 1917.

In 1918 Captain Nat had the powerboat "Helianthus II," sixty-five feet long and seventeen feet beam. She was twin screw, had quite a long deck house, and was really a houseboat. He took her to Florida but was never satisfied with her gasoline engines on account of their noise, vibration, and cost of fuel, so in 1919 he took out the gasoline engines and replaced them with a small

Herreshoff triple-expansion steam engine and a special boiler of his design, fired with burners, and automatic controls as used in the Stanley steam automobile, using kerosene for fuel. He took this "Helianthus" to Florida the following winter and said he liked the power plant very well, but he sold her in 1920 and designed and had built a smaller yacht, "Helianthus III," which was sixty-two and one half feet long and twelve feet nine inches beam. This power yacht had a single gasoline engine. He spent the winters of 1921, '22, '23, and '24 on this yacht in Florida. One or two winters at least he towed the fifteen foot open sailboat "Lantana" to Florida where he sailed her in the waters around Coconut Grove. "Helianthus III" was sold in 1924 to a Mr. Peters of Boston as Captain Nat was then seventy-six years old and thought himself too old for long distance cruising.

However, he still loved sailing, and even short distance cruising, so designed and had built "Pleasure," a yacht thirty feet O.A., twenty-four feet six inches W.L., eight feet four inches beam, and thirty-one inches draft, which he shipped to Florida and used there in the winters of 1925 to 1928, when, being eighty years old, he thought he was too old for even sailing so he sold "Pleasure."

Soon after he had the urge to sail again so he sent to Florida the small half-decked sailboat "Water Lily" which he used at Coconut Grove in the winters of 1928 and 1929. This was his last boat.

Altogether he had owned twenty-eight very interesting boats and yachts, and if we take into consideration others like "Stiletto," which he owned together with his brother John, it makes quite an array of small vessels.

I want to apologize to the reader for listing all these boats but I am sure several of Captain Nat's friends and their children would enjoy a list of them together with some of their dimensions.

However, this chapter was intended more to describe his home life so we must go back to the year 1883 when on December 26 he married Clara Diman DeWolf, the eldest daughter of a family intimate with Captain Nat's parents, who lived only about a mile away in an attractive farm house or country estate. She was descended from a family that had even more of a nautical association than Captain Nat's for the DeWolfs had been successful captains and owners of slave ships, privateers, whaling ships, and merchant ships. She was a grand-daughter of a governor of the state, and great-grand-daughter of Episcopal Bishop Griswold whose see was all of New England excepting Connecticut. She not only sailed and cruised with Captain Nat in many yachts but was an expert manager of his home and bore him six children in about nine years.

Just before Captain Nat was married he designed and had built a small house only about an eighth of a mile from his parents' home, and as the Hereshoff Manufacturing Company had been built almost around his parents' home he was close to the shop. To be sure it was a strange-looking house as we think of house architecture nowadays, but in the eighteen-eighties very strange-looking houses were built. The house was built on a small point of land protruding slightly into Bristol Harbor, and on a site which many years before had been occupied by a windmill of the type common in Rhode Island in Colonial times. At the extremity of this point, jutting right into the harbor, was a rocky ledge that for generations had been known as the Love Rocks, so the house was quite automatically named Love Rocks, a name that it still retains. But I must mention that this southern end of the old town must have been in the past looked on with approval by Venus for within a mile of the Love Rocks was a shady lane, known as Lovers' Lane, and a small pastureland beside a wood lot, known as Cupid's Garden, which even in my time was a well-known retreat for amorous couples.

The original house at the Love Rocks was painted dark red and was capped by a weather vane which had Captain Nat's private signal on it. It had a piazza most all the way around it, with some very good places for children to play. The property had two boathouses and a good size stable for Mrs. Herreshoff had a coachman and pair of horses until the advent of the automobile. As the children grew up the house had to be added onto from time to time, and as the young trees which were planted in front of it originally grew up the house had quite a different appearance.

For many years Captain Nat's family moved each summer to what had been his wife's home, an estate of about one hundred and fifty acres which had been called "The Farm" throughout the town for many years. It was a pleasant location with one side of The Farm bordering on Mount Hope Bay and the other side in sight of Bristol Harbor. Near the middle of The Farm was a fine old farmhouse built by Mrs. Herreshoff's great-great-grandfather.

However, Captain Nat never spent much time at The Farm; in fact he was too busy to rest or relax, but generally rode over on a bicycle for his meals. He did not like riding in a carriage unless it was raining; in fact he seemed to have a dislike for things that were of the land, and often went back to the Love Rocks to sleep or even slept on one of his yachts where he was closer to his element and the work he loved.

But I must say he was very kind to his children and saw that they all had many things to play with. He made model yachts for the older ones, and had a workshop for them with all sorts of good tools, and as they grew up each child had his boat and bicycle, later to be replaced by motorcycles and automobiles. For Mrs. Herreshoff he payed the expenses of The Farm which for many years must have been quite a burden as it was run more as a country estate than a farm. But he was altogether too busy a man to give his family much time; to produce the designs that he did seems today most miraculous. For instance in the winter of 1891–92 he designed the three large sloops "Navahoe," "Colonia," and "Vigilant"—all metal vessels and nearly ninety feet on the water line—besides several steam yachts and smaller boats; and again in 1897 he produced the designs of five steel torpedo boats —engines, boilers, and all.

Many people at this time thought him a short-spoken, unsociable man, but perhaps they themselves would have been much shorter spoken if they were accomplishing as much work or taking as much responsibility. Captain Nat was on call night and day for as early as the eighteen-nineties there was a private telephone to his home from the works. If anything went wrong at the works or with the vessels at the dock then he was called on the telephone for he seemed to take the responsibility for the whole works and never seemed to turn the responsibility over to the several superintendents. But Mrs. Herreshoff took such good care of him that he was able to stand this overwork.

She also nursed him through two sicknesses. The first I think was pneumonia in 1888 and came about as follows. In February of that year there was a heavy southerly storm that broke up the ice in Bristol Harbor and when the tide was high, much higher than normal, the piled-up ice broke in the large doors over the launching ways of the south construction shop. The seas and ice then ran up into the shop underneath the 145-foot steel steamer "Ballymena," which was then in frame, and threatened to throw her out of line. The night watchmen summoned Captain Nat at about 2:00 A.M. He put on his rubber boots and heavy clothes and went to the south shop, but in superintending the securing of things, with only lantern light, he walked along the main floor that was partly under water and covered with cakes of ice. This floor had some removable sections in it that had floated away. When Captain Nat came to one of these holes in the darkness he fell through and a receding sea pulled him under the floor below water. Fortunately the next sea, as it rushed in, carried him under the hatchway again and, although he had been under the icy water some time, he was able to climb with difficulty between the ice cakes in the darkness and with hip boots full of water. But he was only about forty at that time and must have had a strong heart. He then had to walk home in the winter storm with clothes freezing to him and boots full of water. In a few days he came down with pneumonia which I believe was quite severe.

His next sickness was typhoid fever in 1895 when the cup boat "Defender" was being built. The severity of this sickness was probably partly the result of overwork which had put him in a run-down condition but in after years he regretted this sickness most because at the time he could not inspect the "Defender" as she was being built, and some of the work under her mast step was not carried out properly, gave trouble, and had to be rebuilt.

Almost all of his life Captain Nat was troubled with rheumatism and this was a particular aggravation to him when he had to sit still for hours which apparently made him stiff and caused him much pain. Fortunately his home life was ideal for undisturbed work, and he had most excellent food. By the way, he was rather a big eater although his weight remained at about one hundred and seventy pounds for most of his life. He almost never went out of the house in the evening, and unless on a cruise worked in his model room or drafting room every night, so altogether his home life was arranged so that he could work entirely undisturbed, which undoubtedly was one of the principal reasons for his great accomplishments.

The next chapter will describe some of his methods of designing, and a later chapter will describe some of his later life.

CHAPTER EIGHT

Captain Nat's Methods
of Designing

C APTAIN NAT's method of designing will seem to many a queer combination of old-fashion techniques together with most modern and scientific methods, but to me at least it seems that he had selected the most efficient methods of both the old and the new school, with methods of his own. So, altogether we must admit he was a most versatile man who was well acquainted with the whole gamut of the art of design.

It is well known that many of the great artists of the past were nearly as skillful at painting in water colors as in oil, and many of them also produced etchings, lithographs, woodcuts and other prints, and, while no doubt the mastering of each new craft greatly increased their general ability, it is strange that but few like Michelangelo took up sculpture in a serious way. Thus in art as in design the schools of planographic art and sculpture have usually been in separate hands. In speaking of design this way I, of course, refer to the schools of developing shapes with line drawings as planographic art, and of model making as sculpture, and in my opinion sculpture is not only the most exacting of all arts but it is by far the most expressive.

While Captain Nat used models only in developing the shapes of his yachts, I do not for a minute want to give the reader the idea that he was deficient at making drawings or designs on

128

Nathanael Greene Herreshoff

1848-1938

Left: The John Brown
House on Power Street,
Providence, R. I. (p. 28)

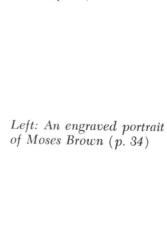

Above: James Brown Her-
reshoff as a small boy in
1840 (p. 47)

Left: An engraved portrait
of Moses Brown (p. 34)

CAPTAIN NAT'S FAMILY

Below: The parents of Captain Nat: Charles Frederick and Julia Ann (Lewis) Herreshoff (p. 37)

Bottom: The Herreshoff's in about 1890. Capt. Nat at left, standing.

FIRST DESIGNS

Below left: The steamboat Estelle, designed by Captain Nat in 1877, including hull, boiler, and engine (p. 73)

Below right: Edward Burgess, an outstanding yacht designer of his time and a lifelong friend of Captain Nat (p. 81)

Bottom: A light portable sawmill, boiler and engine, designed and manufactured by the Herreshoff's in 1881

Left: An early Herreshoff launch (p. 76)

Left: Shadow sailing. She was considered the first of the so-called "compromise" yachts (p. 83)

Right: A small, horizontal Herreshoff steam engine, now in the Ford Museum of Steam Engines, Dearborn, Michigan (p. 87)

PARTNERSHIP WITH BROTHER JOHN

Right above: The boatshop of J. B. Herreshoff in 1866 (p. 94)

Below: Ballymena (p. 106) and Now Then (p. 107)

Below: in descending order

1) *Stiletto, considered by many to be the first high-speed steam yacht. She made an 8 hour run at 26½ miles an hour (p. 102)*

2) *One of the Cushing's five cylinder, quadruple expansion engines (p. 105)*

CAPTAIN NAT'S HOME LIFE

Left: Clara, with a reef in her mainsail (p. 116)

Right: Coquina and Clara (p. 116)

Right: Neckan (p. 119)

Top: Roamer, 93 ft. 10 in. over all and with a 17 ft. beam, was a roomy yacht on which Captain Nat and his family cruised for nine years. She accommodated 17 persons comfortably (p. 119)

Bottom: Captain Nat sailing Pleasure in Florida waters in his late seventies (p. 317)

Above: Captain Nat's home at Love Rocks, Bristol Harbor in the 1880's (p. 124)

Below: Three views of the workroom where Captain Nat cut his models

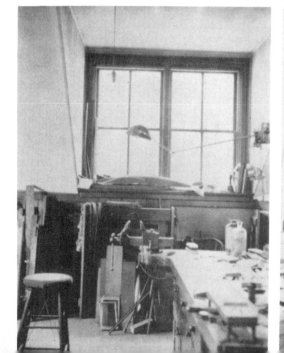

Above: Captain Nat and Mrs. Herreshoff with five of their children in about 1892. The author is in the baby carriage (p. 125)

ONE OF CAPTAIN NAT'S DESIGNS OF THE 1890's. *Gloriana sailing* (*p. 162*)

Left: El Chico (p. 166)

Left: Reaper (p. 166)

Above: Alpha (p. 166)

Below: Navahoe, in England (p. 169)

Right: Vigilant and Britannia, racing (p. 170)

Left: Colonia (p. 178)

Left: Corona (ex Colonia)
rigged as a schooner (p.
178)

Left: Vigilant with yawl rig

Right: Dacotah, sailing (p. 179)

Right: Isolde, sister ship to Niagara (p. 180)

Left: Niagara at the end of the 1895 racing season (p. 181)

Left: Japonica (ex Niagara) about 1897 (p. 181)

*Right above: Defender,
stuck on the ways (p. 185)*

*Right below: Morris, firing
a torpedo at broadside (p.
193)*

Above: Vaquero II, racing in England (p. 197)

Below: Start of Newport Thirties race in 1896 (p. 197)

Right top: Steam engine of the 1896 period (p. 203)

Right center: Racing cat-boat, Wander (p. 204)

Below: The twenty-one footer, Cock Robin (p. 203)

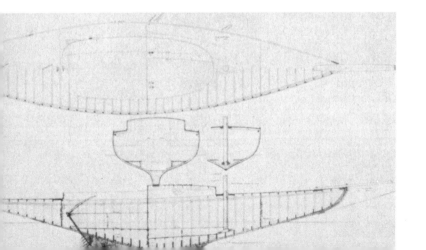

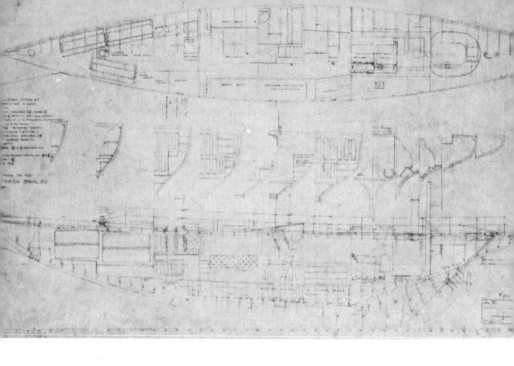

Above: Construction plan of Spalpeen (p. 204)

Below: Plans of the yawl Petrel (p. 205)

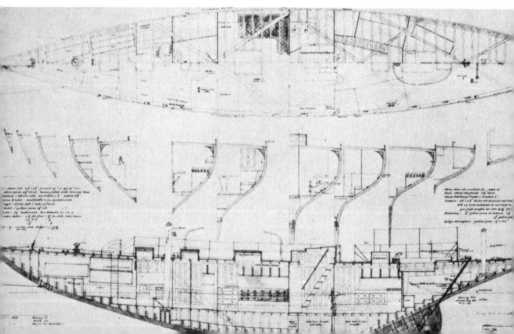

Above: Columbia in drydock (p. 205)

Above: The afterguard of Columbia in 1899 (p. 206)

Left: The sloop Athene, seventy foot waterline (p. 214)

Below: Columbia, winning the final race of 1899 (p. 206)

Right: Columbia and Shamrock rounding leeward mark in the cup race of 1899

Right: One of the seventy footers off Newport, R. I. (p. 215)

Left: One of the Seventies in later years.

Right: Altair, sister ship to Shark.

*Left: Humma, built in 1901
(p. 220)*

*Right: Columbia, the Gem
of the Ocean (p. 221)*

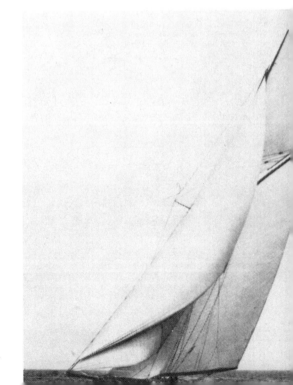

Left: Steam yachts racing back to New York after the finish of the last race of 1901

Left: Reliance sailing (p. 231)

Left: Reliance emerging from the building shed (p. 231)

Left: Reliance, after floating off cradle (p. 231)

Right: The big three: Columbia, Reliance and Constitution.

Left: Reposo (p. 241)

Right: Helvetia (p. 242)

Left: Wana (p. 248)

Right: Vasanta (p. 250)

Left: Sunbeam (p. 244)

Left: The Burgess designed sloop, Outlook

Below: XPDNC (p. 250)

Right: Doris, the first yacht designed by Captain Nat under the Universal Rule (p. 254)

Above: One of the Bar Harbor Thirties (p. 272)

Below: Two views of the mechanism of Captain Nat's recording anemometer (p. 264)

Right: Queen sailing off Newport, R. I. (p. 267)

Right below: Irolita (ex Queen) off Marblehead

Above: Polaris (ex-Irolita) with yawl rig (p. 269)

Below: N.Y.Y.C. fifty-seven foot Istalena sailing on Long Island Sound (p. 270)

Above: Irolita II, rigged as a schooner (p. 269)

Below: The seventy-four-foot Avenger (p. 270)

Right: Chewink IV (p. 274)

Below: Adventuress (p. 271)

Designs between 1910-1920

Above: Westward in the 1935 Royal Yacht Squadron Regatta (p. 276)

Below: The seventy-one foot schooner, Queen Mab (p. 279)

Above: The schooner Elena (p. 280)

Below: The sloop Joyant (p. 281)

Above: Vagrant (p. 282)

*Right: Flying Cloud in 1950
(p. 282)*

Above: Katoura, 162 foot steel schooner, the largest yacht built by the Herreshoff company (p. 284)

Below left: Pleione, a N.Y.Y.C. Fifty, under schooner rig (p. 283)

Below right: Start of N.Y.Y.C. Fifties race

Above: Resolute, in 1915, off Oyster Bay (p. 287)

Right: Resolute and Vanitie racing (p. 288)

Below: Ohonkara, a steel schooner similar to Vagrant (p. 282)

Below: One of the Forties, owned by Henry L. Maxwell (p. 302)

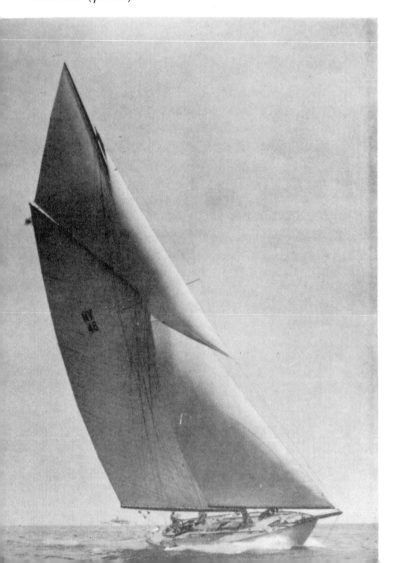

Right: The first S Boat (p. 305)

Right: A Fisher's Island thirty-one footer, rerigged (p. 306)

Right: Ventura, a sixty foot cruising sloop, designed for George F. Baker, Jr. (p. 306)

LATER DESIGNS

Left: Grayling, a Q boat, built for J. P. Morgan, Jr. in 1923 (p. 307)

Left: Grayling, an R boat, built for Junius Morgan in 1926 (p. 309)

Above: Wildfire, rigged as a staysail schooner (p. 308)

Below: Wildfire, in 1923, under original schooner rig (p. 308)

LATER LIFE AND FRIENDS

*Above: Thistle, the 102 foot bronze yawl designed
and built for Robert E. Tod (p. 310)*

*Below: Captain Nat's cottage at Coconut Grove,
Florida (p. 315)*

Above: Aida, a shadow draft center board boat (p. 317), owned by Henry C. White

Left: Captain Nat sailing Water Lily, his last boat (p. 318)

Left: Commodore Ralph M. Monroe and Captain Nat trying out a model (p. 316)

Center: Model yacht with steering vane on mizzen-head (p. 317)

Right: Captain Nat building a model yacht at Coconut Grove (p. 317)

paper, and the reader can well imagine that the drawings necessary in designing steam engines, boilers, and particularly construction plans, call for the highest type of drafting. But with good reason he chose to develop his shapes with models only. There are no lines drawings of the yachts and boats he designed. He was perfectly familiar with looking at lines drawings, and I believe nearly as capable at judging them as judging a model, but in the last analysis perhaps it is safe to say no one living can judge a set of lines as accurately as he can a model. This writer has designed boats both ways and can say from actual experience that the model method is the quickest and most natural way to develop a shape. And, having worked with both Captain Nat and Starling Burgess (who only made lines drawings), I can say that Captain Nat usually made a model in from one-half to one-quarter the time that Starling needed to develop a set of lines.

The model-making method, however, requires more training and practice, and it may be that very, very few individuals combine the manual skill with a sufficient sense of proportion to make the model-making method the best for them. In my case, and I have designed more yachts with lines than with models, it perhaps would take me two-thirds the time to make the model as the lines. While I am not trying to persuade anyone to adopt the model method I will say that I believe it is by far the most advanced and scientific way. However, it is out of the question with the average yacht designer for he must usually mail sets of lines back and forth between owner, builder, etc. Models also are difficult to store, and to make the model-making method practical it takes special equipment for taking off the sections for the construction plan and making the table of offsets.

Later in this chapter I will describe how Captain Nat did this, but now I will try to describe how he made his models. First, he made a small sketch of the yacht for which he was to fashion the model. This sketch was often quite small and almost always made on a pad of paper ten and one half inches by eight inches. This sketch sometimes included some construction if points of construction were to affect the model, and the dimensions worked out on this sketch were the length overall, length on water line, draft, beam, and freeboard at three points. The principal thing on the sketch would be a carefully drawn midship section at the same scale the model was to be.

With these general dimensions he could glue up some blocks of soft pine to the size necessary for the model, and sometimes with the larger models he had this block made at the pattern shop of the Herreshoff Manufacturing Company. His first operation on the model was to fair the back side, or center line, to a perfectly flat plane; then he drew the profile and sheer line in with pencil on this plane using French curves, battens, and

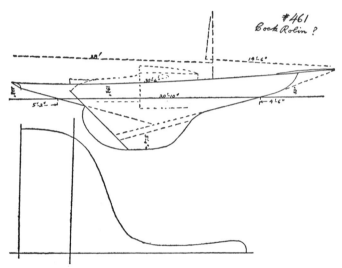

Figure 21. A preliminary sketch for making a model. (Cock Robin, 20 ft. raceabout.)

straight edges. Next he cut down the sheer line, and after making the sheer a fair sweep fore and aft and at right angles to the center plane, he was ready to lay off the deck line which he did on the model block without any preliminary sketches or dimensions excepting to make the beam at the deck correspond with the midship section he had drawn. The deck line was drawn in pencil along a batten held in place with several small brads, and I would say that many of his deck lines were very much as the batten would spring if held at the center line forward and held at the width of the transom aft, and sprung out to the midship beam. This was no fixed rule for, of course, some of the flat-bowed boats built under the length-on-water-line rules had straighter lines along the side, while some of the yachts built under the Universal Rule around 1908 actually had some hollow in the deck line way forward. But it might be said that he sprung the battens over these three points and then moved it in or out to suit the type of vessel he had in his mind, so the deck line was

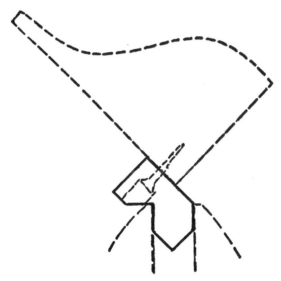

Figure 22. Block for holding model in vise.

a combination of the way the battens sprang when influenced by certain functional requirements.

After the deck line was laid out the model had a hard wood block screwed to its back side, so that in all later work of shaping the model, it could be held in three different positions in, or over, the vise.

After the model had been cut down to the deck line, as seen from above, and cut down to the profile as seen from the side, he would be ready to shape the sections. I might say the work so far had proceeded very rapidly for not only had Captain Nat been practicing these operations from childhood but also, as the reader may know, a combination of manual and mental work often proceeds faster than either one or the other practiced separately.

To get his midship section like the sketch he had drawn he took a thin strip of soft pine and laid it under the sketch. Then, with a sharp prick, he pricked through the paper to the wood beneath so that by joining these points with a pencil line he had an exact guide to cut to in shaping the template which he usually did with a sharp jack knife, then finishing off with sandpaper. At first he only tried the template in place to see where the first rough cuts were to be made, but as the section got down to approximate shape, he rubbed chalk on the template so that each time it was tried it automatically marked the high spots with chalk. Almost all of this roughing out was done with inside sharpened paring gouges, and these tools, when properly sharpened, can be controlled to take off either a very large shaving or thin sliver, so that with his skill the model would be cut down to approximate size in perhaps one hour's work with the paring gouge.

The next operation was smoothing up with several small metal planes. He had made up a set of these planes by reshaping the Stanley No. 101 plane. Some of the planes were concave crossways, and some convex crossways, and some curved both ways fore and aft. There were about ten planes in the set and some one of these would fit most any part of a model, and, of course, a plane with a proper curve to the sole helps materially in fairing. But his principal means of fairing was by rubbing small battens over the surface of the model and these battens, having first been rubbed with blue chalk, registered the high spots. While this fairing process takes quite a while if the model is not roughed out nearly to shape, still Captain Nat, with his trained eye, usually brought the model almost to its final shape with the paring gouge, so that in his case the final fairing took but a few hours. I would like to note that this method of fairing up with the battens is equal to laying off a thousand or more diagonals all at slightly different fore and aft angles.

After the model was perfectly fair he substituted sandpaper for the small curved planes, and the sandpaper was cut and folded quite small. This he held a certain way with the tips of his four fingers on top, and the thumb holding the partly turned up edge. As the sandpaper traveled back and forth his sensitive fingers could detect the slightest irregularity which he worked over until the whole surface was entirely fair. The stem, rudder,

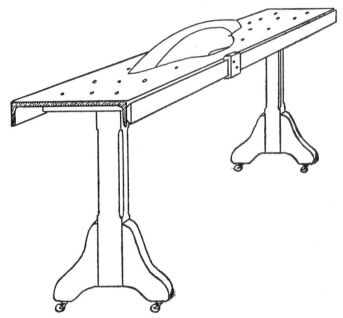

Figure 23. Machine for taking off sections and offsets.

and parts of the transom were all worked down to their scale size, and this necessitated the rudder blade to be very thin as, of course, it was but half thickness. After several coats of shellac the model was ready to mount on his machine for taking off what sections were needed for the construction plan, and for taking off the offsets.

I have described Captain Nat's model making at some length because I believe his ability to develop new shapes, which perhaps he did more than anyone else, came principally from his use of models. I must say that this procedure was quite different from most yacht designers who first of all set up a displacement curve with the center exactly at some predetermined point, and waste much time over various wave-line theories. But Captain Nat's methods of developing shape were pure art even if he did use science and mathematics lavishly on his construction plans, engines, boilers, rigging, and particularly in strength calculations. No doubt the shape of a yacht or vessel is influenced by so many factors that the necessary compromises and combinations may be

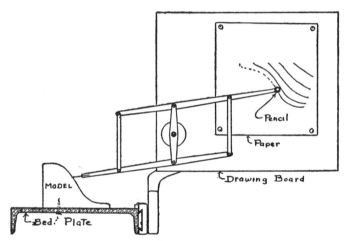

Figure 24. Pantograph for taking sections off the model (diagrammatic drawing).

best dealt with by art. I am sure Captain Nat enjoyed model making and seemed as fascinated by the shape as it developed to his ideas as any sculptor could be as the vision in his mind was taking form.

I am sorry I do not know how Captain Nat took the measurements for his offsets in the early days, but from the time of my childhood on he used a machine which he designed for that purpose which consisted of a cast-iron bed plate, planed up perfectly flat, upon which the model was laid, as shown, and firmly held down with wood screws. The bed plate had dove-tailed ways along its front side with a small carriage so that he could mount up a pantograph to take off sections as required. The spacing of the sections was determined by various wooden scales depending on the scale of the model and the frame spacing of the yacht. After the required sections were taken off he used them first to determine the displacement of the yacht and center of flotation, which he did in the usual methods with a planimeter. He transferred the shape of the sections from the small sheet of paper on

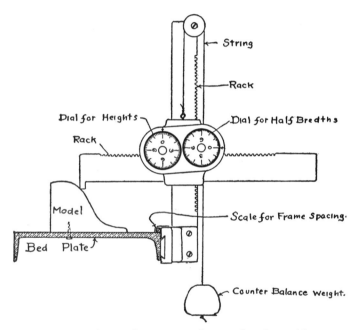

Figure 25. Machine for taking off offsets (diagrammatic drawing).

the pantograph to the construction plan by simply laying a sheet of carbon paper between the two and then drawing over the line on the upper paper again with a hard pencil. While this made only a faint mark on the lower sheet it was enough to follow with a pen or pencil.

For taking off the offsets he mounted a machine on the carriage of the slide where the pantograph had been, and this measuring machine had dials that were easily read so that in taking off the offsets there was little strain on the eyes. In fact it was such a simple matter that some of Captain Nat's children used to do this work when they were about eighteen years old. One of the dials denoted heights and the other widths, and, of course, there were different dials for models of different scale. The table of offsets was always written in a small, brown, covered notebook which measured about six inches by four inches, on the cover of which was simply the building number of the yacht while on the first page were such notes as the frame spacing, thickness of planking, half-widths of the stem, etc., and the following pages gave the offsets with each station on a separate page; all of which is a very convenient method for the mold loftman.

Captain Nat had made part of these instruments himself, for he was a skillful machinist. Part of his workshop had a Rivett Precision Lathe which could be set up for most any light machining operation including milling, gears cutting, and rack cutting. The bed of the machine was made by the Brown and Sharpe Company from Captain Nat's design.

To get the profile of the yacht on the construction plan he simply laid the model on the paper and drew around it with a pencil. Now that he had some sections on the plan and the profile his next move was to establish the line of the top of the lead, and here, instead of making weight calculations of a construction not yet drawn, he simply referred to his data book which, among other things, gave the percentage of lead of many previous yachts. He could make such a shrewd guess that for many years his yachts had all of their lead on the outside and floated exactly as designed.

Of course his calculations of displacement and volume of lead were made from the sections taken of the model with the pantograph, but with his early designs of steamers and inside ballasted boats, before he had a planimeter, perhaps before 1885, he used the then common method called the spill-of-water method, which consisted of carefully placing the model in a tank of water that had been filled up to the spill hole. This caused an amount of water to spill into a container which exactly equaled the displacement of the half model. He had made a very accurate weighing machine especially for weighing the water that had spilled into

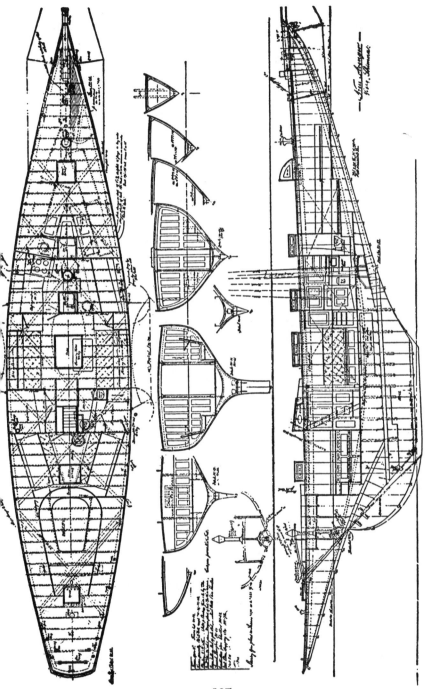

Figure 26. Typical construction plan made after 1900. The sloop Avenger.

137

the container, for any inaccuracy in this small weight would become large in the full size vessel.

Captain Nat drew his construction plans in pencil and could make them very quickly because he had developed several formulas for determining the size of the various parts. There was no hesitancy in working out the general scantlings. But in all his work one of the greatest helps was his data book where he had noted down the principal sizes, weights, and characteristics of each yacht for quick reference.

He had a particular knack of keeping his drawings simple and of only showing the information required by the workman. Many of his patterns of hardware were very ingenious in the way they could be adapted to yachts of different design. The Herreshoff Manufacturing Company had two testing machines for testing parts under tension and compression, and Captain Nat had his own small testing machine in his model room so that he had very complete data on the strength of all the hardware they manufactured which, as a matter of fact, included a more varied line of hardware than was manufactured by any other builder or marine hardware manufacturer.

This is but a slight description of how he developed the design of a sailboat, and for fear that further description of his methods in regard to steam engines, fittings, spars, and rigging would become boring to the average reader of this type of book I will note that the difficulties of describing involved processes to any but the professional designer makes it almost impossible. So I will only make a few observations.

Captain Nat is generally considered the designer who used mathematics most, and while he did certainly depend on mathematics in the design of steam engines and in strength calculations, it is my personal impression, after my having watched him work several years, that some natural instinct and superfine sense of proportion enabled him in most cases to proportion things so perfectly that he drew the taper and sizes of things out quite spontaneously, which I for one call pure art. I will give an example of this.

One day he was in the drafting room at the Herreshoff Manufacturing Company when the chief draftsman said, "How about the size and taper of the connecting rods we are to draw up full size for this new model of steam engine." So Captain Nat took from his pocket one of the very short pencils he was in the habit of carrying and without any hesitancy drew out the profile of the connecting rod freehand and said, "That ought to do."

Now the calculations for the size of a connecting rod are extremely involved for the motion of the upper end is reciprocating and the lower end revolving, but the chief draftsman who was highly educated went through the complete mathematical analysis of the strains and at the completion of his labor found that the connecting rod as drawn out by Captain Nat freehand was perfect in shape and size for the strains indicated. No doubt this ability to choose sizes of parts was the result of much past mathematical work and actual experience with the failure of parts as shown on the testing machine, for certainly by his middle age he had developed a sense of proportion and eye for shape so perfect that he could no doubt design the whole of a yacht or steam engine entirely by eye. While of course he never did this still his ability to draw spontaneously many of the parts without mathematics enabled him to accomplish his work very rapidly.

Some of the other factors of great help to him were that his yachts were all built in his own yard entirely under his own supervision. Any designer who has tried to use methods of construction that were improvements but were different from the traditional technique of some particular yard will readily understand Captain Nat's advantage in this matter. Another great help to him was the orderly arrangement of drawings at the Herreshoff Manufacturing Company, and their file system of cataloguing patterns, so that together with a personnel in the office and yard that he had trained (in later years many of the employees had worked under him from twenty to forty years), he had a unique organization. I must say that the very high standard of the employees at the Herreshoff Manufacturing Company contributed much to his success. Too, it was not only his ability to design but also his being able to have special parts made as he wanted them that put him at the head of his profession. And lastly, the experience both he and his organization had in building steam engines and boilers left them head and shoulders above other builders of the time who lacked both the equipment and experience to design and fabricate light parts from all sorts of materials.

CHAPTER NINE

The Works of the Herreshoff
Manufacturing Company

NATURALLY the first boat shop of what was to be the Herreshoff Manufacturing Company was very small; apparently my grandfather, Charles Frederick Herreshoff, thought that the boatbuilding was little other than the amusement of his blind son J. B., so at first they simply hired a vacant building almost across the street from my grandfather's house. This building had been a tannery but was right on the shore, in fact some of it was out on a small stone wharf or seawall. J. B., with his great energy, soon got orders for several sailboats as has all been previously told, so that the tannery was purchased and changed over to a boat shop with a suitable wharf, launching ways, etc.

Soon after J. B. began building steamers and their machinery he purchased the Burnside Rifle Factory which was on a street running inland from the tannery building about two hundred yards. This little factory had been run by General Burnside, the Civil War general, and here he made two or three models of early repeating rifles some of which had some rather complicated parts, so the factory must have been capable of somewhat intricate machine work. However, nearby in Connecticut several other manufacturers of repeating rifles were established so that the Burnside factory closed down. This also may have been partly because of General Burnside's death in about 1870.

After J. B. acquired the Burnside Rifle Factory he used the

lower part for building boilers and engines, and on the top floor he tried the experiment of manufacturing flat bottom rowboats (skiffs) in quantity production which were sold in South America. Some people say this was one of the first attempts to make small boats in quantity production. Although I have heard that this experiment was a success financially it is probable it was not interesting enough to long hold the minds of men like J. B. and N. G.

One of J. B.'s early activities was running a sawmill and selling lumber so that before long the tannery building was changed into a mill for working lumber, and all through the life of the Herreshoff Manufacturing Company the mill or most of the woodworking machinery remained in this place. This part of the works was on the water at about 1880 when they built their large vessels outside but sometimes under a framework that could be covered over with canvas. At this time the street which led up to the Burnside Rifle Company, and which was called Burnside Street, was often piled with lumber and unsawn logs.

Of course most of the work in those days was done by hand, and soon after 1880 the company had three hundred employees, or nearly twice as many workmen as they averaged in after years. However, J. B.'s love of mechanical things induced him to use as much steam-driven machinery in the works as was practical. While in the old days the Herreshoff Manufacturing Company used more power tools than other yacht builders did it is interesting to note that Captain Nat in his old age, with some seventy years of experience, said, "If I could get together some old-fashioned mechanics of the kind we had when we started business I could build yachts cheaper and better without many power tools than with a whole shop full of modern machinery." This statement may at first seem surprising, but it does show what a high regard he had for his early workmen. When we consider that yachts seem to cost about twenty times as much today while food, shoes, and real estate in the country are only about four times as much, and the workmen's wages about ten times as much, it does show that hand labor under good management can operate more efficiently in a simple shop with its little overhead cost. My own experiences also have shown the same to be true in later years for I had built from my designs about a dozen boats and yachts by Britt Brothers of Lynn, Massachusetts and, while they were of a quality comparable with those then built by the Herreshoff Company and the George Lawley Corporation, they were about 25 per cent less in cost. At that time the Britt brothers had little machinery but some men who could and were willing to do some handwork. I suppose their overhead, or fixed costs, such as taxes, plant depreciation, insurance, power, heat, etc., were 25 per cent less than the Herreshoff and Lawley companies. At any rate the great variety of work the Herreshoff Company did eventually necessitated building the works up so the overhead cost was over 30 per cent. In other words, the labor on a yacht may have cost 40 per cent, material 30 per cent, and the rest of the cost went into overhead. These are, of course, very rough figures, for different types of yachts at different times varied quite a lot. However, the profits of the Herreshoff Company, like many others, were greater when the plant was smaller, and my impression would be that the plant was not particularly profitable after 1910.

I speak of these matters now only to show the responsibility that falls on the shoulders of plant managers who have got together too much machinery in too many fine buildings. In other words, when a plant's overhead costs rise to more than 30 per cent then plant management must be very scientific or the plant will no longer be able to compete with the small builder with less overhead. While Captain Nat at least was conscious of this, J. B. had bigger ideas so the plant kept growing. But now, instead of telling when and why the various additions were made to the plant, I will describe from memory what the plant was like in about 1910 when the work perhaps was at its highest standard.

At this time the plant was conspicuous for its absence of signs or advertisements, and as I recall it about the only sign was a small black painted board which had on it in gold letters the word "Office." The office was about halfway up Burnside Street and consisted of three rooms on the ground floor. The front room, which was used for general office work, was presided over by Mr. Young who I believe acted as office manager for some fifty years. Next, back of this was the room used by the purchasing agent and where the company's letters were typewritten, while the room in

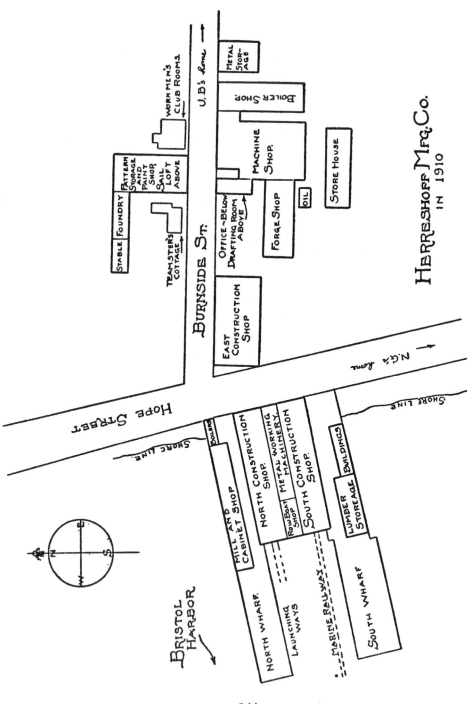

HERRESHOFF MFG. CO.
IN 1910

144

the rear was J. B.'s private office. Here the prospective yacht owners usually came to terms, and other important business was transacted without interference for one had to pass through the two outer offices to get there.

Near the street entrance to the offices was a flight of stairs which led up to the drafting room which was a good size room over the offices. Besides drafting tables for four draftsmen this room contained the large files for drawings which are now at the Massachusetts Institute of Technology. For many years Mr. Olson was the chief draftsman, and he had worked out a simple but good filing system which listed all the patterns for making castings, and here were issued the orders to the different departments which gave them a comprehensive list of the parts they were to make.

Above the drafting room was the blueprinting department and, of course, at that time the blueprints were made by daylight. From the drafting room there was a door that led most conveniently into the pattern shop, which was on the same level, for the drafting room and pattern shop must keep in close contact with each other. The head pattern maker for many years was Mr. Sandford; he had worked with Captain Nat at the Corliss Steam Engine Company. The pattern shop had three benches for pattern makers, and two wood-turning lathes, and a metal spinning lathe besides its band saw, circular saw, and buzz planer. They produced here the best patterns I have ever seen, many of which were for the steam engines, and therefore, intricate. Some of the patterns for small fittings were in multiple so that several pieces alike could be molded in one parting of the flask.

The pattern shop, the tool room, and the department for finishing off small fittings (blocks, etc.) were on a gallery which extended around the machine shop. Also on this gallery was the small testing machine, now owned by Merriman Brothers, which tested the strength of small fittings.

On the main floor of this building was the machine shop with a floor measuring about one hundred and thirteen feet by seventy feet. This shop had two overhead traveling cranes and very good light throughout. The center portion was used for assembling steam engines, and around this space were ranged two planing machines, two radial drills, a vertical boring mill, a horizontal boring mill, two milling machines, three shapers, and twenty lathes, the lathes varying in size from speed lathes and turret screw machines to engine lathes large enough to bore the torpedo boat cylinders or turn the crank shafts. The largest lathe swung sixty inches, and the longest one, which was used for propeller shafts, had a bed thirty-six feet long. There were also several upright drills and other small machinery, all driven by a Herreshoff steam engine right on the main floor.

It might interest some of my readers to know that part of the roof over the machine shop, the part where the cupola was and where the shop bell was hung, had been part of the Burnside Rifle Factory. This roof and one story had been jacked up in the air in about 1880, and the present front part of the machine shop built under it. Speaking of the shop bell, this was a familiar sound in the south end of Bristol for about half a century as it announced to the workers the time to commence and stop work, and the bell's pleasant but businesslike tone could be heard at the Cove half a mile away, at the yacht storage, and on any yacht moored in the harbor.

On the east side of the machine shop was a door leading into the boiler shop which was one hundred and ten feet by thirty-six feet and had suitable tools for boiler making. Among them were upright drills, power shears, punches, and boiler tube bending devices. The foreman of this shop for many years was Mr. Wood, and before 1910 it was a busy place building the boilers for steam yachts. In later years it was used mostly by the coppersmith who made the exhaust pipes, condensers, ventilators, and tanks. Some of this was very nice work. The plumbing or piping department also used this shop. It might interest the sailboat men to know that the smaller sail slides for sail track were made here, as of course the Herreshoffs were the only manufacturers of this article for the first thirty years or so after Captain Nat invented the modern sail track and slide. East of the boiler shop was a storehouse which usually carried a large stock of sheet metal, tubing, etc., which was used in the boiler shop.

Now we must retrace our steps through the machine shop to a door on its west side which led into the blacksmith shop, or forge shop. This building was about eighty-five feet by thirty-five feet and had two steam hammers and seven or eight forges, an annealing furnace, an oil-burning furnace about twenty-eight feet long for heating metal frames, and a bending slab for bending and beveling frames. Mr. Guisler was chief blacksmith at this time, and this shop certainly turned out nice forgings for the steam engines, special forgings for the cup defenders, and a large quantity of hand-forged Herreshoff anchors.

South of the machine shop was a high studded three-story storage building about one hundred feet by thirty-one feet. This building, besides storing a variety of large parts, including steam engines, contained the boiler, engines, and dynamos which generated the electricity for the plant. The upholstery department was also in this building, as well as the large testing machine which was a horizontal one with bed thirty-two feet long and a capacity of sixty thousand pounds. Here some of the rigging and many of the fittings of the cup defenders were tested or proved. So all these shops and departments were ranged around the office and drafting room, which was most convenient.

Right across Burnside Street from the office was a building ninety-six feet by forty-seven feet, the upper floor of which was used for the sail loft where for several years Mr. Hathaway was the superintendent, and here perhaps were made more sails for cup defenders, winners of Astor and King's cups than in any other one sail loft. It is not difficult to understand why the best sails of their time were made in this loft when one considers that Captain Nat invented the crosscut sail.

Below the sail loft the building was used for the paint shop and pattern storage. Patterns were methodically stored so that they were readily found even if they had not been used for years. On the west side of the pattern storage shop was a door that led directly into the foundry where bronze castings were made every day and iron poured about once a week. West of this were the stables and wagon storage.

Most of the shops we have listed until now were used for metal working, with the exception of the sail loft, but as we go down Burnside Street, we come to what was called the east construction shop, a three-story building one hundred and nine feet by fifty-six feet. Part of the lower floor was used for building medium-sized wooden yachts, and here the N.Y.Y.C. thirty-footers and many other yachts of that size were built. The north side of the building had metalworking machinery for fabricating parts of the metal yachts. Above this north side of the building was the mold loft where metal yachts were laid down, while on the top floor was the spar loft where hollow spars were built.

This brings us down to Hope Street, the street that runs along the water front in southern Bristol, and on the water side of this street were the two main construction shops known as the north and south construction shops, each of which was approximately one hundred and sixty-five feet by thirty-six feet. Each shop had launching ways down its center, and about thirty-eight feet of clear height for building, and each construction shop had two overhead traveling cranes which could pick up weights in any position in the shop.

Between the construction shops was a roofed-in space with overhead skylights, and here at one end was the metalworking machinery for hull construction (shears, punches, rolls, etc.). At the other end of this space was the rowboat shop with its band saw and molding machine. Tenders were built here as well as keel sailboats up to some twenty-five feet O.A. Although there was no advantage in this location for the rowboat shop it was quite advantageous to have the metalworking machines between the two construction shops for steel hulls at times were built in each shop. However, the south shop was generally used for steelwork, and the north shop for wood hulls. Perhaps three fourths of the steel vessels were built in the south shop, and this included most of the torpedo boats, all of the cup boats but "Vigilant" and "Resolute," and many other yachts and the steel schooners "Queen," "Westward," "Elena," and "Katoura."

The south shop, and in fact all construction work of steel, was under the superintendency of Mr. Brechin, while the north shop and all wood construction came under Mr. Murray's department. Above the south construction shop was the rigging loft under the martial law of Mr. Chase who had served as chief rigger for many years. The reader may wonder why I have spoken so often of the length of time some of the men had served, but that was one of the outstanding features of the company: several of the men had been employed steadily for forty years and, I believe, one at least worked there for a span of some sixty years.

Over the north construction shop was the mold loft where yachts constructed of wood were laid down. As there were several men who could lay down lines this shop was run by different men at different times.

Just north of the north construction shop was a building one hundred and fifty-six feet by twenty-five feet, in the lower part of which was the sawmill with, if anything, too much woodworking machinery driven by a Herreshoff steam engine. On the upper floor of this building was the cabinet shop where most of the interiors of the yachts were fabricated before being put in place on the yacht, and this at times included whole bulkheads and partitions of some size. This shop was also liberally supplied with power tools too numerous for me to list here. At the east end of the building was the boiler room located almost where the tannery had been. The boilers were of quite good size for, besides heating all these buildings, they at times drove four or five steam engines, but there was another boiler in the upper shops which made the steam for generating electricity. Altogether there were several miles of steam pipes to and in these several buildings which in themselves caused some expense in upkeep.

Many people, particularly those who arrived by water, thought of the Herreshoff Manufacturing Company as being only in those buildings on the water, but the group of buildings near the water contained less than half of the floor space of the company. While all of these buildings were quite necessary in the steam yacht era, it is my opinion that later they added much to the overhead cost of running the plant. On the other hand the Herreshoff Company made almost everything that was used on their yachts right on the premises, and that included the power plants, sails, blocks, all hardware, upholstery, and even the paint; this may have saved some cost and certainly much delay and purchasing complication. On the whole the buildings were quite conveniently arranged and, if I remember right, had seven overhead traveling cranes in all. Of course, if the complete layout had been built at once it would no doubt have been more compact and arranged so that there was less movement of parts during construction, but even the smartest man is confused by the layout of a yacht yard which may undertake quite different work from year to year. One year the work may be mostly large metal vessels, while the next few years may be devoted to small one-design classes; but if one knew beforehand what a yacht yard was to build in the future, he could quite easily make a layout that would greatly increase the efficiency. To make a layout that is truly versatile and capable of a variety of work is most difficult.

In my opinion the personnel of a yacht yard is of far more importance than the machinery or plant layout. Good men can turn out good work with few tools, but poor workmen can only make a botched up job even with the best of equipment. So I will say something about the men who worked for the Herreshoff Company as they were the best thing about the organization. At one time, around 1880, the Herreshoffs paid about the highest wages in the state, and this had induced good men to come there. But by far most of the workmen had come because they liked to work on high-grade objects, both wood and metal, and because each job was different the work was never tiring.

I remember talking to one of the machinists who had been there forty years or more, and said to him, "How did you happen to come here in the first place?"

He told me, "As a young man I saw one of the Herreshoff steam launches and I just had to come here to work, and have stayed ever since."

The whole crew around 1910 was the finest lot of men I have ever seen in any manufacturing business: they were mostly Americans—and Yankees at that—although there were a few French Canadians, who are always natural woodworkers, a few Nova Scotians who had come from the shipbuilding provinces, and, of course, in the machine shop a few British-born machinists. While some other nations were represented by one or two men a more harmonious group of men would have been hard to find. Many of them belonged to the Odd Fellows or the Masons, or both, and this seemed to create a brotherly feeling among them. In fact it was more like a big fraternity than a workshop, where each member tried to help the other and always called one another by his first name.

At one time I remember there were several of the men named Charlie, and to distinguish them certain prefixes were added to their names so that in several cases I never knew their right names. Among the Charlies were Pretty Charlie, Dark Charlie, Light Charlie, as well as Charlie Copper (the coppersmith), Charlie Black (the blacksmith), Charlie Tool (the toolmaker), and Charlie Grease, (the rigger). The men took their work seriously and did not play many practical jokes on one another. While this may not seem important, still in many other yards it has been the means of starting serious quarrels and grudges, which in the end are costly, for sometimes a workman will not forget a grudge for years.

One of the customs of the yard that helped the works as much as anything was that the workmen did not steal one another's tools. In some yards if you laid down a center punch to take a rule out of your pocket while your other hand gripped your hammer firmly, when you reached again for the center punch it would be gone; a man could not have any more tools than he could hold in his pockets and hands, or if he had he would have to keep his eyes on them so intently that he would neglect his work. This stealing habit, or joke, got to its height in World War II when many of the yards were flooded with the scum and riffraff of the race tracks, the saloons, and the city, who were lured there by the easy money they could make under the protection of the unions, and yachts will not again be built at a reasonable cost until this tool-stealing habit is broken. But in the old days at Bristol all the men left their tools scattered around the job and did not even collect them together or lock their tool chests at night or over Sunday. Yes, several thousand dollars' worth of the workmen's tools would be scattered over the works together with their overalls with the plug of tobacco in the hip pocket, so that on Monday morning they could start work at once with all their necessities right where they had left them. Occasionally one of the new men would turn out to be light fingered, but the other men soon spotted him and one of them would walk around and say to watch so-and-so, and the light-fingered man either corrected his ways or the men made it so disagreeable for him that he left the plant.

The superintendents were particularly co-operative with one another which was far from so in some other yards where they often were not on speaking terms. This spirit of co-operation seemed to permeate the whole works so that the men vied with one another in turning out the most and best work. It was not an uncommon thing for the men to pick out teams to compete in such things as planking up two sides of a yacht or in building some of the hulls in the one-design classes, etc. Although, of course, this much accelerated the work the quality of the work never suffered for the workmen not only tried to beat the others in speed but also in workmanship. Besides, they knew Captain Nat's eagle eye would detect any defect. In fact the men seemed to enjoy these competitions very much which seems strange to us today when most workmen vie with one another to see who can do the least and poorest work. The New York Yacht Club fifty-footers stand as an example of what was produced under this competitive work, and nine of them were built one winter with a comparatively small crew. They were seventy-two feet O.A. and I think cost but $17,000, still it is doubtful if any better constructed hulls have been built since.

So Captain Nat had a great advantage over other designers in being able to have his yachts properly built for it is one thing to make a good design and another thing to have it well built. I will say more—it is quite likely that some of Captain Nat's designs would not have turned out well if they had been built by other builders, so, although the personnel of the yard at Bristol and the plant itself had their definite effect in acquiring perfection, still Captain Nat had designed all the buildings and had practically trained the men with his constant and careful inspection. But there is another important requisite for a successful yacht yard, and that is, to have the men want to please their general superintendent. This may be hard to explain to the layman, but when the spirit is there men can accomplish more with poor tools and buildings than when there is the best equipment without the good spirit. Just how Captain Nat inspired the men to do their best is very hard to tell, for he had very little to say to them; in fact he was usually short and gruff in his conversations with them and only dealt with the superintendents. Apparently in a boat yard the workmen get a great kick out of working for a superman, one in whom they have confidence and who they know can answer all questions, as they would say, "one who knew his stuff." And Captain Nat certainly knew construction from a to z. The men got a great kick out of seeing each yacht, as she was launched, float exactly as she should with all outside ballast; they marveled at how the parts made in the different departments all fitted together perfectly. They had perfect confidence in his designs and went ahead with strange new things knowing that all would be well at the final assembly. And I must say that with new types of steam engines they would be built and put in the yacht without trial and functioned perfectly while other engine builders generally had to first give the engines a block test and then make several alterations in valve settings, counter balance, etc. So the men thought they were working for a genius and a wizard, would put up with any idiosyncrasies he might have, and were always most patient and respectful to him. I cannot say that they loved him, or that he would have wanted any affection from anyone, but, nevertheless, in about 1900 the workmen presented him with a very nice loving cup with a suitable inscription in raised letters, and the names of the most notable yachts he had designed and they had built.

This book is supposed to be about Captain Nat and not a history of the Herreshoff Manufacturing Company, but as I have taken you through the rise of the company I will try in a few words to describe its decline, although to me it is not a pleasant subject. Somewhere around 1913 Captain Nat's health began to fail; he had chronic and painful rheumatism and, although his teeth did not appear to be bad, it was decided to have them all out so he went to a hospital in New York and had his teeth removed, and other treatment. And by the way he lived twenty-five years after that and not only became free of rheumatism but was more congenial and affable than he had been around 1913. However, he spent several winters in Bermuda about this time when his oldest son, A. Sidney DeW. Herreshoff, carried on the engineering and designing work of the company, with J. B. of course as usual running the business end of the works.

In about 1915 the Russian government wanted the company to build several motor torpedo boats, and the preliminary plans and business arrangements had been made. I believe money had even been deposited in the bank at Bristol when Captain Nat came back from Bermuda and put a stop to the whole business. Just what his motives were no one ever knew, but this just about broke J. B.'s heart, so to say, and he went home and died. J. B. was seventy-four, and after a long life of struggling with small contracts that were not always very remunerative, this opportunity to do a good stroke of business was the height of his ambition. When his plans were frustrated it was too much for his nature. Some people say that if the company had gone ahead with this order very likely the French submarine chasers would have been built there also, as well as some of the U.S. Navy subchasers. This, of course, would have necessitated enlargement of the plant, and that in itself may have been what Captain Nat disliked, for he was always rightly concerned with the increasing overhead cost of running the plant. At any rate the company lost something when J. B. died that never was regained, and the whole place seemed different after his death. After all, J. B. was human even if N. G. was too busy to be, and a mechanical genius is not expected to be human. J. B. was the one who heard the workmen's grievances, and he was very good about keeping the men employed when the company was short of work. Sometimes he would have a yacht built on his own speculation, or he would put them to work repairing or painting the buildings. The men usually soldiered on these jobs, and J. B. knew it, but he also knew they would make up for it when work came in. J. B. knew the value of keeping a good crew together, and stimulated good feeling through the plant. I believe the superintendents were really fond of him. He could tell a good story, and appreciate a good joke; he was also a skillful purchaser of materials even if he were an old horse trader when dealing with some of the yachtsmen. Yes, I think the decline of the company can be dated from J. B.'s death on July 20, 1915.

At any rate within a year or so the trustees of J. B.'s estate wanted to liquidate their holdings in the Herreshoff Manufacturing Company. By this time the war had been going on in Europe two or so years, and it looked as if this country would become involved. This made some of the yachtsmen who had had Herreshoff yachts willing to buy into the company as they anticipated profits from war work in a company already tooled up to build torpedo boats, etc. Thus the stock in the company sold like hot cakes, and Captain Nat, seeing this, very wisely sold most of his stock also. The company was now owned by several wealthy yachtsmen of Boston and New York, and had a board of directors who unfortunately knew little about running a yacht yard, although their names were among the first in the social register of these two cities. They acquired a highly paid general superintendent and a sales executive and were all set to do big business, but for some reason or other failed to get paying work during World War I, although they did do much troublesome work for the government which included repair work, building the hulls for seaplanes, building steel pontoons or floats that were planned to carry seaplanes about as they were towed behind destroyers at high speed (in those days the flying radius of the seaplanes was small). Although they built three or four steamers for the government they failed to get the order for some of the two hundred foot Eagle boats so that at the close of the war the stockholders were quite disappointed. Then directly after the war followed a few years with little yachting activity when for some reason or other some of the directors seemed to think the trouble was that the men in the company were not working well, while the real trouble was that the executives had not secured work for them to do. So one of the directors got up at a board meeting and said, "I know how to make the men work; we will reduce the salary of the superintendents." Perhaps this man did not know what their salaries were, but if I remember right it was only about twenty-five dollars a week so that when notified of this cut some of the best superintendents resigned, and this included Mr. Murray who was soon to build up the Nevins Company at City Island.

The company then struggled along till 1924 when one of the directors at a meeting said words to this effect: Boys, we want to get out from under this calamity as soon as possible so I vote we auction the company off and liquidate without taking further loss. And the vote was passed. This was a very foolish move for during the next few years more yachts were built than at any other time, and almost every boat yard made money until the democratic dynasty started.

One of the reasons it was foolish to auction off the company suddenly was that they had a large stock of building materials on hand. The company in the old days used to keep a full supply of building material simply to do away with delay in purchasing, and in the case of lumber not only can it be bought cheaper in large quantities, but after you have stored it yourself for six or eight years you may be sure it is well seasoned. At the time of the auction the company had on hand some of almost all sizes of brass, bronze, sheets, tubes, etc., as well as much steel of different kinds, together with almost all varieties of yacht-building lumber, some in large quantities and very old. One item was about one hundred thousand feet of hard pine suitable for planking, etc. They certainly had on hand the components for several fine yachts, and some poeple have said that the whole company auctioned off for less than the stock on hand was worth.

Somewhere near the end of the sale a man named Mr. Haffenreffer, who had a country residence back of the town, came to the auction and, seeing some of the buildings selling at ridiculously low prices, bid and acquired a few; then he contacted some interested yachtsmen who wanted to see part of the company continue, and they got together and purchased other buildings and some of the machinery from other successful bidders, and at once formed a new organization to carry on some of the works. They had the construction buildings which were on the water, and some of the others on Burnside Street—in all perhaps one half of the floor area of the plant together with perhaps one third of its machinery and special tools. However, they had some buildings large enough to mount large signs, stating that this was the Herreshoff Manufacturing Company, for the benefit of those who believe in signs, but much of the personnel was gone, and the spirit was gone. To be sure some of the old buildings and some of the old tools were there, and an old company with a good reputation has a certain momentum that carries it along in spite of its weaknesses. This new organization with R. F. Haffenreffer as president built several sizable yachts including three "J" boats and three or four other metal yachts such as the "Manxman" and "Thistle," which are among our largest sailing yachts at the present time.

During these years Mr. T. P. Brightman, who had worked in the office since his youth, did almost all of the spade work and kept the remains of the old company on an even keel; without his guiding hand it is doubtful if they ever would have gotten under way successfully again.

No doubt the company made good profits some years but they also made expensive alterations in the wharves and marine railways which mostly increased the overhead cost of the yard. In World War II this new organization had to enlarge its buildings for constructing motor torpedo boats and other small naval craft that were built in some quantity. When peace came with little prospect of yacht building in the near future, or until the present political situation is changed, the yard was closed down, and to save taxation some of the main buildings have been either sold or torn down. The George Lawley Corporation and the Jacobs Yacht Yard both met similar fates, and time only will tell if the Herreshoff Manufacturing Company ever builds yachts again.

One thing is certain—good yachts will not be built again at a reasonable price until an organization is put together that has a personnel equal to the Herreshoff Company before World War I, and with a spirit of co-operation among the workers similar to that which the old company enjoyed. And last, but not least, they will have to have a leader whom everyone respects and has confidence in.

Perhaps Sweden or perhaps Germany may be the next builders of high-grade yachts, but at any rate it will have to be a country where the clear income of the yachtsman is considerably more than that of the mechanic who builds the yacht.

While this description of the last days of the Herreshoff Manufacturing Company has taken us up to the present time, in the next chapter we will go back to 1890 and tell of some of the yachts Captain Nat designed at that time.

CHAPTER TEN

Captain Nat's Designs of the Eighteen-Nineties

IT WAS during the eighteen-nineties that Captain Nat became famous for his designs of the larger sailing yachts. For ten years before this the Herreshoff Company had built steamers almost exclusively, and this sudden change in the type of yachts they built seemed surprising to some people, but Captain Nat, of course, had designed sailboats before 1880, and always had a sailboat for his own use. However, this shift from steam to sail was partly as a result of Captain Nat's acquaintance and friendship with Mr. Edwin D. Morgan. This Mr. Morgan, whom we will call E. D., is often confused with Mr. J. Pierpont Morgan because they were both wealthy men who were commodores of the New York Yacht Club within a few years: E. D. was rear-commodore 1887-8, vice-commodore 1891-2, commodore 1923-4, while J. P. Morgan was commodore in 1897-9. If J. P. were one of our leading bankers, E. D. was our leading yachtsman of the times, and perhaps for all time. He owned many fine yachts, large and small, sail and steam. E. D. had arranged his affairs so that he could devote most of each summer to yachting, and particularly racing, while J. P. kept his nose on the grindstone most of the time and used his different "Corsair"s for transportation and entertainment. But we will speak of him later in connection with the cup defender, "Columbia."

In my childhood I must say I heard E. D. and J. P. spoken of a great deal, and had formed a childish opinion that J. P. arranged the finances of yachting and E. D. sailed the yachts, just as at Bristol J. B. arranged the finances of building and N. G. saw to the building. At any rate just before 1890 E. D. Morgan became very much interested in the fast steam launches being built at Bristol, and eventually owned the three high-speed launches "Javelin," "Daisy," and "Vanish." His residence in the summer was at Newport where about this time, 1890, he had built a fine house on a large crag called Beacon Rock at the head of Newport Harbor. This house, or villa, was designed by Stanford White and was copied after a villa of one of the Knights of Malta. E. D. Morgan and N. G. Herreshoff both had the Maltese Cross on their private signals, and the reason for it was that that was the insignia that the Knights of Malta had adopted some three hundred years before when they made an effort to suppress piracy in the Mediterranean. The Maltese flag stands for exactly the opposite of the skull and cross bones: the Knights of Malta were always the sailor's friends, and had banded together to protect shipping and to succor those in distress.

There was fairly deep water almost to Mr. Morgan's residence on two sides, and Brenton's Cove right in front of the house was where the cup defenders and many others of the large yachts anchored at Newport. Here at that time Mr. Morgan kept the fine schooner "Constellation," which he had had built in 1889 from a design by Edward Burgess. He also kept in Brenton's Cove the forty foot racing sloop "Moccasin" as well as the Herreshoff forty-eight foot cabin steam launch "Henrietta." Mr. Morgan often owned five or six yachts at a time ranging in size from English steel steam yachts to Newport catboats, and in those days he often sailed or steamed up to the boat shops at Bristol. Not only was he interested in the steam craft building there but he took much interest in Captain Nat's own catyawl "Clara" which Mr. Morgan had both sailed in and tried out alongside the "Moccasin." So Mr. Morgan ordered from Captain Nat two catyawls—he did not believe in doing things in halves—which were to be improvements on "Clara." They were both built on the same molds and the first one, completed and launched on November 11, 1890, was named "Pelican." She was twenty-six feet six inches long on the water while the other one named "Gannet" was twenty-nine feet six inches long. "Pelican" is still in existence while "Gannet" made her home port Newport for nearly forty years, becoming almost a landmark in the inner harbor there.

Perhaps Mr. Morgan and Captain Nat were interested in the effect a change of length would make on yachts built on the same molds, but as Captain Nat always spoke of this model as the "Pelican," I will continue to do so now, and may do so at some length as she was really the model, or development boat, from which the "Gloriana" was evolved, and has been overlooked by other writers who would suggest that Captain Nat jumped in one leap from steam to sail, or the "Gloriana." This is, of course, ridiculous for, besides the "Pelican," he had designed many famous racers before 1880, and in the meantime always had a sailboat or two of his own.

At that time the beautiful little Scottish cutter "Minerva" was the fastest of the popular forty foot class, but "Minerva" had rather a pot belly below water with such long and fine ends that she not only had unnecessary wetted surface but was apt to hobby-horse or pitch too deeply. So in the model of "Pelican" he straightened the diagonals by using a slightly smaller mid-section and increasing the sections at the water-line endings. This in turn slightly increased the overhangs. He also cut off the deep forefoot always found on English cutters of that time and a feature making them steer badly at times and always requiring the sail plan to be well forward. "Pelican" may have been one of the first sailboats to be scientifically engineered in her construction so that she had approximately 60 per cent of her ballast all in an outside cast lead. Both her profile and mid-sections suggest the commencement of the bulb keel which in a few years was to come out in "Wasp."

Mr. Morgan liked "Pelican" very much but the next winter, 1890–91, he had Captain Nat design and build the high-speed steam launch "Javelin" which was a remarkable open launch ninety-eight feet long, double ended, planked with mahogany. I think she went around twenty-six miles per hour and was one of the fastest open launches of her time. She, too, like the "Stiletto," made a circle around the Hudson River steamer "Mary Powell." Right beside the "Javelin" in the north construction shop that winter

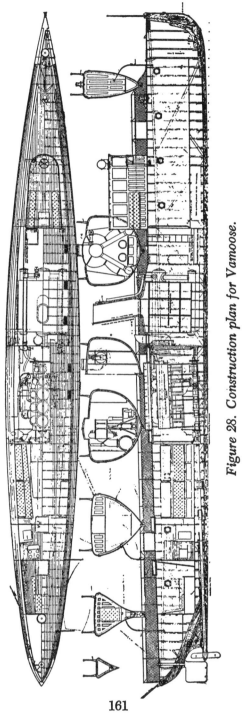

Figure 28. Construction plan for Vamoose.

161

the "Vamoose" was built for William Randolph Hearst. There is no doubt that she was fast, and perhaps the fastest yacht in America in 1891, although there were a few launches that were said to be faster, particularly the "Yankee Doodle" and "Norwood" which were claimed to go almost ten miles faster but never ran in public competition. However, on September of 1891 the American Yacht Club, which particularly sponsored steam yachts, gave a much publicized race with a five hundred dollar prize—the course a straightaway of ninety miles from Race Rock at the east end of the Sound to the club station. Perhaps the other flyers did not want to race ninety miles of the Sound; at any rate "Vamoose" was the only yacht that showed up at the start so we can assume the owners of other steamers considered her too fast for them. The speed of "Vamoose" was a little over twenty-seven miles per hour.

But to get back to the sailboats. In 1890 and 1891 the famous class of forty-six-footers was started, and I believe there were about a dozen built with more than half of them designed by Edward Burgess. Mr. E. D. Morgan had an acquaintance, Mr. Royal Phelps Carroll, who was to build in this class and he recommended that Carroll go to the Herreshoffs for his forty-six-footer, which he did. Soon after the design was completed, however, Mr. Carroll wrote and requested that the contract be canceled as he was to be married, and the Herreshoff Manufacturing Company agreed to do this. About the first of February Mr. Morgan called at Bristol to see his steamer "Javelin," then under construction, and looked at the model and design of the forty-six-footer which had been started for Mr. Carroll. Mr. Morgan liked the design so much that he decided to take it over, so the forty-six-footer was built in the south shop and when launched early in June was christened "Gloriana." So "Gloriana" was built for Mr. E. D. Morgan even if she had not been designed for him, and it is very possible that if Mr. Morgan had not managed her she might not have made a clean sweep the first year.

While the "Gloriana" model was certainly radical, or different from preceding yachts, it is my opinion that scientific construction, which allowed a large amount of ballast, together with very special fittings aloft and alow, had more effect than the model in her success. Perhaps "Gloriana" was the first sizable racing sailboat that was built in a plant that could make all of her special parts (and I must note that the stock marine hardware of those days was as crude and bad as it is today). Other designers had to depend on stock fittings which in most cases had originally been designed for a different type and size of craft. The sharp and deep forefoot of the prevailing model is entirely cut away which much shortened the water line. Under a rule that combined LWL and SA she was allowed more SA than others in her class, but on account of her full ends she not only had longer diagonals (better sailing lines), but the full ends with their buoyancy contributed much to stability when the yacht was heeled. When the cutter and compromise cutter heeled, the center of flotation did not move to leeward or as far from the center of weight as on the "Gloriana." Most of the others in "Gloriana"'s class were models similar to "Minerva," a model that is notorious for pitching. As a sailor man would say, some of them would even start to pitch if they saw a sea coming, but the "Gloriana"'s bow seemed to lift over a sea instead of bunting at it a couple of times and finally going through it. So the "Gloriana"'s bow was copied throughout the world and in the next ten years it was to be seen on everything from catboats to three-masted schooners.

As for construction, it is quite unlikely that the independent yacht designers such as Edward Burgess, Cary Smith or Gardner, even if they had been engineers, could have brought out so many innovations in one year. Although any of them might have taught a builder to use steam-bent frames one year, double planking another year, and diagonal strapping the next, etc., Captain Nat had a great advantage with his own yard and a crew whom he had trained in all these constructions on steam craft. "Gloriana" was built almost exactly as all high-grade yachts of her size are today, that is, steel angle frames, double planking, and strap diagonal framing which was quite a contrast to some others in her class which had single planking over sawed frames fastened with nails.

Above the water line everything on "Gloriana" was pared down in size and weight—even the hatches, companionways, and skylights—and every ounce of this saving in weight was put into the outside lead. Although her upper works were light they were strong because they were constructed scientifically, and the proof of this is "Gloriana"'s long life free from structural defects. But above deck is where "Gloriana" excelled mostly, for her fittings and rig in general were what might be expected from an engineer who had his own forge shop and machine shop—sail tracks, special winches, properly proportioned turnbuckles, together with special goosenecks, gaff jaws, topmast cap irons, etc. A photo shows "Gloriana" sailing and gives a general idea of the neatness of her rig, but the construction of "Gloriana," her special fittings, rig, etc., were overlooked by the writers of the time who were so fascinated with her bow that they either did not see or could not understand her other advanced features.

"Gloriana" entered eight races in the forty-six foot class the first year and won them all. In the first race E. D. Morgan was helmsman, and in the following seven Captain Nat steered her. Mr. Morgan then very sportingly withdrew "Gloriana" from the class to let the other ten or eleven yachts fight it out among themselves.

On July 12, 1891, Edward Burgess died from typhoid fever. It is said he had become run down as the result of designing so many yachts in the last few years of his life, and I should think he might have for he designed, I think, more than anyone else did in those years. However, this friend of Captain Nat was spared the knowledge that his several forty-six foot yachts were out-classed. Edward Burgess was only forty-three when he died and, I believe, he might have designed the world's handsomest yachts if he had lived to an age of greater maturity for in my opinion he was a great artist. The death of Mr. Burgess and the victories of the "Gloriana" automatically put Captain Nat at once at the head of American designers. Of course there were Cary Smith and Gardner at New York, but Smith was really a marine painter while Gardner had had most of his training in England, so for the rest of their lives they did very little in the sailing yacht field but copy Captain Nat, and, strange to say, they sometimes beat him with their copies. Cary Smith, however, designed some wonderfully good Sound steamers, and Gardner some nice-looking steam yachts that certainly were not copies of Captain Nat.

While Captain Nat was sailing "Gloriana" his active mind

worked out the structural problems which made the fin keeler possible. He used to say he did not invent the fin keel, that it had been invented before his time, but there is no doubt N. G. Herreshoff designed the first sizable boat that was to use a fin keel. Of course there had been many model yachts previously with a plate and bulb keel: there had been experiments with heavily weighted centerboards, and there had been some ill-shaped cast-iron keels tried which with a stretch of imagination

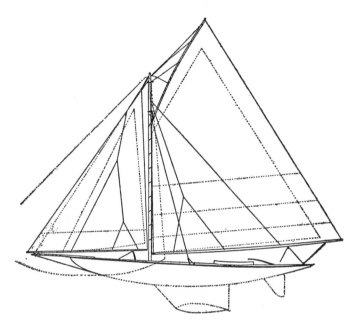

Figure 29. Sail plan of Dilemma.

might be called fin keels. But Captain Nat's "Dilemma" was the first successful fin keeler. "Dilemma" was built for himself and came out in the fall of 1891, the same year as "Gloriana." Her sail plan may look old-fashioned nowadays, the sails are of about the proportions then in vogue with the smaller yachts descended from the Sandbaggers. "Dilemma" was a decided success and was followed by many other fin keelers. The Herreshoff Company built about one hundred of them in all, and in the few years before they were barred from racing they quite took the place of all other types. It was with the fin keelers that the full spoon bow was developed, and among the first sizable fin keelers was the thirty-five foot water line "Drusilla," built for E. D. Morgan, rigged with long battens in the sails with which General Paine had started to experiment several years before.

Other notable fin keelers of 1892 designed by Captain Nat were the "Handsel," thirty feet W.L., owned by Mr. J. R. Hooper at Hull, Massachusetts; the "El Chico," twenty-five feet W.L., owned by H. M. Kersey of New York, and a sister yacht to the famous two and one half-rater "Wenonah," which was owned by Henry Allen and cleaned up on the Clyde. Almost from the start of the fin keelers the Scots and English imported these Herreshoff creations, and in the next year or two they were to be the principal winners in the smaller British rating classes. Among the latter was the little one half-rater "Wee Winn," owned by Miss Cox, and she proved to be so exceedingly fast that some old-timers on the Solent are still talking about her.

Among the smaller American-owned fin keelers Captain Nat designed in 1892 were "Reaper" and "Vanessa" for the twenty-one foot class at Marblehead. But Captain Nat rather upset things that year in the twenty-one foot class, for while copies of his fin keelers were being designed and built by most everyone, amateur and professional, he came out with the centerboard twenty-one-footer "Alpha," which won fourteen firsts out of fifteen starts at Marble-head that year. (She would have made a clean sweep but was disqualified in one race.) Her name was derived from the fact that her deck plan was very triangular, her stern being al-most her widest part. The fact is that "Alpha" was quite similar to the sandbaggers of a decade before, only her bow was carried out in a graceful overhang. This sort of craft is fast, of course, in light and moderate weather with a trained crew, but I can't help thinking that in more wind and sea some of the fin keelers should have beaten her. Perhaps Captain Nat was already con-scious that the defect of the fin keeler was too much wetted sur-face, particularly for racing in light weather regions like Marble-head.

The largest sailboat the Herreshoffs built for the season of 1892 was the forty-six-footer "Wasp," owned by Mr. Archibald Rogers.

"Wasp" was very similar in rig and above water model to "Gloriana" but had her lead shaped into a true bulb keel, from Captain Nat's experience with the fin-keelers of the previous year. Her record through the year was five firsts and one second out of six starts. She seemed to beat the "Gloriana" consistently as well as the rest of the fleet, but it may not have been her bulb keel that made her win as much as the fact that she was steered in all her races by Captain Charles Barr who, a few years previously, had made a reputation for himself and the forty-footer "Minerva." "Wasp" was the first of the Herreshoff yachts that

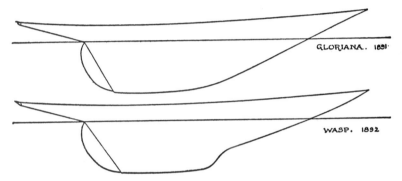

Figure 30. Comparative difference in the underwater profiles of Wasp and Gloriana.

Charlie Barr was to captain but he was to sail them almost exclusively the rest of his life, and also make a still greater reputation for himself and these yachts.

I must tell an incident that happened to him at this time. When the "Wasp" was being rigged and fitted out the little centerboarder "Alpha," that we have just spoken of, was also completed. Captain Nat had just taken her out for her trial and brought her in to the wharf near the "Wasp" where Captain Barr was greatly admiring "Alpha." Captain Nat, who was always fond of Charlie Barr, said, "How would you like to take her out for a spin?" Charlie jumped at the opportunity, and calling a couple of his crew from "Wasp," boarded "Alpha." At the time Charlie was only about twenty-four years old, and all of his experience had been in heavily ballasted Scottish cutters. He ordered one of his men to cast her off and pull the jib to windward. When this was done "Alpha" turned on her heel like a top, filled her sails, and promptly capsized. It is said she hardly went a boat's length before she was flat on her side and swamped. Of course a light boat like "Alpha" should be ballasted by her crew moving to windward, and has to be luffed or have her sheet eased in the puffs, but when properly got under way might carry her sail in a fair breeze. Captain Nat used to tease Charlie Barr about that incident in the years to come when Captain Charles Barr had become the greatest of all yacht captains.

In the fall of 1892 Royal P. Carroll, the same gentleman for whom "Gloriana" had been started, ordered an eighty-five foot cruising sloop from Captain Nat in which he intended to cruise abroad and do some racing. This yacht was built of steel and was the first metal sail boat the Herreshoff Company had built. She was named "Navahoe," and as soon as completed, early in the spring of 1893, sailed for England practically under a racing rig, commanded by Charlie Barr, and with the owner and Mrs. Carroll aboard. It is likely that Captain Barr hoped to make a record passage for as soon as he was clear of Newport and had squared away for the eastward, he clapped spinnaker and all on her, but he ran into a fog bank south of Nantucket and, strange to say, ran right into Nantucket Light Ship. His navigation must have been remarkably good considering he was on a brand new steel vessel for you might say he was less than a ship's width off the course. However, this collision sprung "Navahoe" 's mast, and she limped into Boston where a much heavier and inferior mast was put in her which was to prove a great disadvantage since the yacht lacked stability because she was too shallow. Nevertheless, "Navahoe" did fairly well abroad for she raced against a field of three or four new crack single masters of her size and did succeed in beating the "Britannia" by a matter of seconds in a remarkably hard-fought match race across the English Channel and back for the Brenton's Reef Cup. There is no doubt that "Navahoe" would have done pretty well if she had been deeper, stiffer, or had a lighter mast, and also Charlie Barr at that time was very young and inexperienced compared to the captains on the big English single stickers who were all pitted against the single American. A photo shows "Navahoe" under her original sloop rig. She must have been pretty fast for after she came back to America she won the Goelet Cup in 1894 and 1897 still under the ownership of Mr. Carroll. "Navahoe" was later changed to a yawl and went back to Europe where for a while she was owned by a Russian duke and won races in the large classes in England as late as 1902.

While I have thought it best to tell "Navahoe"'s story up to a later date, we must go back to 1892 and '93 again, for more large racing sailboats were built in these years than in any other time in yachting history. In England they built the large single stickers "Britannia" and "Valkyrie II," practically sister ships, designed by G. L. Watson; the "Satanita," designed by J. M. Soper; "Calluna," designed by Wm. Fife, Jr., while we in this country built the "Navahoe" just mentioned, designed by N. G. Herreshoff; "Colonia," designed by N. G. H.; "Vigilant," designed by N. G. H.; "Jubilee," designed by John B. Paine (son of General Paine, managing owner of "Puritan," "Mayflower," and "Volunteer"); "Pilgrim," designed by Stewart and Binney who had taken over Edward Burgess' designing business. This made a total of nine great racing cutters or sloops built in the winter of 1892 and '93. I think they were all between about eighty-four feet and eighty-seven feet water line, although they had practically twice the sail area of the recent "J" boats.

The principal reason the American yachts were built was that Lord Dunraven had challenged for the America's Cup with "Valkyrie II," and all of the Americans, excepting "Navahoe," were designed to be trial cup defenders. So, while "Navahoe" was under construction, Captain Nat received the order for "Colonia," from a New York Yacht Club syndicate headed by Archibald Rogers who had owned "Wasp" the year before. "Colonia"'s general dimensions were: L.O.A., one hundred twenty-six feet; L.W.L., eighty-five feet six inches; beam, twenty-four feet; draft, fourteen feet. This was too shallow draft for a keel sloop of that size but her owners wanted her shallow and the ways at Bristol could not handle more draft at that time. But there were some members of the New York Yacht Club who did not approve of the dimensions of "Colonia" and thought that if the

Herreshoffs could not launch a deeper yacht they at least could build a wider one to get the stability, and use a centerboard for increased lateral resistance, so they formed a syndicate headed by C. Oliver Iselin and including Captain Nat's friend, E. D. Morgan. Mr. Iselin was one of the best sailors on Long Island Sound and had started his training in the Sandbaggers where you had to fight your way for each foot of the course, and even after you had won you had to fight again to get your prize. He had owned and done well in larger yachts, particularly his seventy-footer "Titania." They ordered their sloop, which was to be named "Vigilant," about the first of 1893, which was late for building a craft of this size and kind. It seems marvelous today that Captain Nat could have designed these three great sloops—"Navahoe," "Colonia," and "Vigilant"—in a few months. However, they were quite similar in model and rig, and all three of them were somewhat the model of "Gloriana" and "Wasp," but comparatively shallower. They were, I believe, all fourteen feet deep, "Navahoe" having a rather small solid steel centerboard, "Colonia," a keel, without centerboard, and "Vigilant," which was the widest, had a fairly large built-up centerboard of bronze plates over a frame that gave trouble off and on through her life.

"Navahoe" and "Colonia" were plated with steel, but "Vigilant" had Tobin bronze and was the first vessel ever plated with bronze although every later cup defender was to be plated with bronze of some kind or another. The beams of these yachts were "Navahoe," twenty-three feet; "Colonia," twenty-four feet; "Vigilant," twenty-six feet. "Vigilant" was built wide on deck to gain stability by using a large crew. She sometimes carried seventy men while others of that size usually carried around forty, but there was no limit on crew in those days, and of course a sandbagger racer like Mr. Iselin was very conscious of the value of shifting ballast. Just before the trial races "Vigilant" was hauled out and a slab of lead nine inches deep was bolted to the bottom of her keel, and I believe her centerboard was quite heavily ballasted, so, together with her greater beam and more draft, she carried her sail better than "Colonia."

The two Boston contenders for the cup were fin keelers, and

everybody was surprised that Captain Nat had not used fin keels on "Colonia" and "Vigilant." Most of the yachting world at that time was copying the fin keelers he had brought out during the two previous years. But he realized that in the larger sizes of yachts, where the average speed was comparatively less, wetted surface resistance was a more important factor. This proved to be true, for both "Jubilee" and "Pilgrim" were dull performers in light weather although "Jubilee" showed signs of speed in a breeze, but under those conditions she usually broke down. However, she is considered by many to be the best, if not the only, large racing yacht designed by an amateur although the schooner "Sea Fox," designed by Cass Canfield, is universally considered the best all-around amateur design. Mr. John Paine I think was only in his twenties at the time he designed "Jubilee," and of course was under great disadvantage compared to Captain Nat who had much engineering data to work from and his own plant where he could have work done as he wanted it. It might interest some of my readers to know that John Paine was the older brother of Frank C. Paine who designed the "J" boat "Yankee" almost forty years later.

In the first of the trial races between "Colonia," "Vigilant," "Jubilee," and "Pilgrim," the "Vigilant" did not do particularly well with her professional captain at the helm, so after the afterguard had a conference, Mr. Iselin asked Captain Nat to take the wheel, and he handled her in all the following races of 1892, including the Cup races.

In the trial races it was soon apparent that "Vigilant" and "Colonia" were the fastest and most reliable, and "Vigilant" was chosen early giving her time to tune up for the Cup races. This was lucky for "Valkyrie II" was a fine yacht and had an able captain. In the first race "Vigilant" won by five minutes, forty-eight seconds corrected time. In the second race Captain Nat made a good start and kept "Valkyrie" covered on the windward leg, and on the reach which was in a strong breeze, "Vigilant" sailed the ten miles at the rate of twelve knots, and at the finish won by ten minutes, thirty-five seconds corrected time. The third race was on Friday, the thirteenth, and, as sailor men would expect, things happened. There was a strong east wind and lump of a sea; the course was fifteen miles to windward and return: both yachts carried working topsails over reefed mainsails. The "Vigilant"'s centerboard jammed and could not be got all the way down; otherwise she might have done better on the windward leg. This time "Valkyrie" got the weather berth at the start and in the hard two-hour drive to windward beat "Vigilant" one minute, fifty-five seconds. The run home is said by most old-timers to be the most exciting yacht race ever run, and so I will quote the account of it written by the contemporary eye witness W. P. Stephens.

On rounding the outer mark "Valkyrie" set her spinnaker after the English fashion. The sail, in a loose bunch, was hoisted from below deck and sheeted home as quickly as possible. In doing this it got caught on the bitts and was torn a little. Running in a sea and heavy wind this tear soon increased until the sail went into tatters. Another, a large and beautiful sail of light fabric (the famous muslin one of the first race), was set in its place, the work being done very smartly, but it was too light for such a breeze, and it soon went to pieces. Nothing daunted; the "Bowsprit spinnaker," corresponding to the American balloon jibtopsail, but smaller, was set as the last resort.

On board "Valkyrie" no attempt was made to shake out the reef in the mainsail or to shift topsails; but as soon as "Vigilant" was off the wind, and her spinnaker, sent up in stops in a long, compact rope, was broken out and sheeted home, the real work of the day began. Her balloon jibtopsail fouled in hoisting, and a man was sent to the topmast head, and thence down the topmast stay, to clear the sail. After this was done a man was sent along the boom, with a lifeline from the masthead about his body, cutting the reef points as he went; meanwhile a man at the topmast head was lashing the working topsail, clearing the topsail halyard, and sending it down to the deck, while another man at the gaff end was doing the same with the topsail sheet. With the working topsail still in place, the whole mainsail was shaken out, the halyards sweated up, and the small club-topsail was sent aloft. By dint of this work, such as was never before witnessed in yachting, at the imminent danger of losing the mast and the race, "Vigilant" sailed past "Valkyrie" near the finish line and led her across by two minutes, thirteen seconds, winning the race by forty seconds, corrected time.

It was an unusually fast race, as the accompanying table will show:

	Start			Finish			Elapsed Time			Corrected Time		
Name	H.	M.	S.	H.	M.	S.	H.	M.	S.	H.	M.	S.
"Vigilant"	12	27	00	3	51	39	3	24	39	3	24	39
"Valkyrie II"	12	27	00	3	53	52	3	26	52	3	25	19

"Valkyrie" had added ballast and been remeasured since the previous race, and her allowance reduced to one minute and thirty-three seconds.

It was a close shave—the closest in any Cup contest so far. "Valkyrie" had her chance, but it was not to be. If her spinnakers had stood the strain, the story would probably have been different—but, then, yacht racing is made up of "ifs."

Near the end of the race Captain Nat, who was never a strong man, became exhausted and had to ask Captain Hansen, the professional sailing master of "Vigilant," to take the helm, but it is likely the strain of sailing this large sloop before the wind in half a gale with four men up aloft changing topsails, shaking out the reef, etc., was terrific since their lives as well as the lives of the whole crew, seventy in all, might be jeopardized by the least slip of the helmsman. This feat of shaking out a reef and setting a larger topsail when running before a strong breeze shows the daring, resourcefulness, and courage of Mr. Iselin, Mr. Morgan, and Captain Nat, but they were comparatively young men then and all had a brilliant yachting future before them.

This completed the victory of "Vigilant" over "Valkyrie II" with three straight races, but as usual the English public said it was only that the challenger had to cross the ocean and the defender never could have done that, so next year, 1894, George Gould, a wealthy New Yorker, purchased "Vigilant" and commissioned Captain Nat to refit her for an ocean voyage and go to Great Britain and look after putting "Vigilant" in racing trim. So "Vigilant" was sent over under the command of the seagoing Captain Leander A. Jeffries, and this crossing has lately been well described by Hervey Garrett Smith in "The Rudder" of April, 1948. Captain Nat and the "Vigilant" 's racing skipper, Hank Haff, followed with the Goulds on their steam yacht "Atalanta." "Vigilant" made the crossing from Sandy Hook to Ireland in fourteen days, seven hours, and fifty minutes, and to Gourock, Scotland in fifteen days, nine hours which was very fast considering she was under a very short jury rig. Also these more northern destinations generally make a voyage more than a day's sail longer than the crossings to Lands End in England. On her return trip in 1895 "Vigilant," under the command of Captain Charlie Barr, made the crossing to the westward from the Lizard Point to Sandy Hook in seventeen days, nineteen hours, and fifteen minutes, making the fastest round trip across the Atlantic ever made by a sailing vessel.

The first race of the "Vigilant" abroad was certainly a memorable one. In the first place the Regatta Committee running the race notified "Vigilant" the night before the race that all competing yachts must be handled by amateur helmsmen for which "Vigilant" was entirely unprepared, but Captain Nat, being aboard, was persuaded to steer her. The start of the race was at the head of the Clyde in what is called Holy Loch, rather constricted waters for the four great single stickers, considering the high wind that was blowing, and because the starting line was crowded with spectator steam yachts. Just before the start a rain squall with considerable wind came down the Loch and shut off visibility. Captain Nat had "Vigilant" shortened down to jib and mainsail and determined to make a late start under the circumstances. Right beside "Vigilant," however, was the "Britannia," which had either thought good seamanship was the better part of valor or else she had intended to cover "Vigilant" that day. However, as the squall let up, "Vigilant" swung off for the line with "Britannia" boiling along beside her when, as the starting gun sounded, right in front of them "Satanita" collided with "Valkyrie II," cutting her down to the water line. The two big cutters swung around in a circle until "Valkyrie" freed herself, but she had by that time fouled one of the spectator steam yachts and had sunk in fourteen fathoms of water, fortunately with only one fatality. "Britannia" and "Vigilant" continued the race, and on the first leg "Vigilant" beat "Britannia" decisively in the same wind and water, and rounded the weather or outer mark nearly two minutes ahead. However, on the run home the wind became light, and although still well ahead when approaching the finish, her local pilot made Captain Nat take "Vigilant" way off shore at a point called the Cloch. "Britannia," coming up from behind, went way inshore, although she drew more water, and got a locally well-known afternoon breeze off the high land at Cloch's Point, and by steering a straighter course succeeded in winning by thirty-six seconds.

Captain Nat was much disgusted at being tricked out of this race by the English pilot, and in some pencil notes, which he has left, says, "After this I did no more racing yachts for others."

However, he did steer "Columbia" at least some of the time in her races, for Charlie Barr once said to me, "After things were straightened out" (meaning the start) "I often turned the helm over to Captain Nat for I knew he could get more speed out of her than I could." Which of course was a great compliment coming from Captain Barr.

Captain Nat says in his condensed pencil notes about "Vigilant" in England: "Short courses, light winds, and green crew all contributed to her lack of success abroad. She started in nineteen races, finishing first 7 times, second 11 times, third once. One win over "Satanita" was not allowed, making the score really six firsts, out of eighteen races." And I will add that that was pretty good for a foreign yacht racing in England where, on account of shallow water, strong tides, etc., the racing is more of a test of local knowledge than a test of the relative speeds of the competitors. But worst of all, the foreign yacht visiting England is at the mercy of the local pilot who can usually make the foreign yacht tack out into a head tide if she is ahead. This is particularly so if the foreign yacht is ahead of the yacht owned by the Prince of Wales. So a foreign yacht racing in England is under great disadvantage while the English yachts that have raced off Sandy Hook, Newport, or Marblehead have had a fair chance in these deep, unrestricted waters with negligible tides.

"Vigilant" was too long on the keel to turn quickly in maneuvering for the start in restricted waters, and her captain, Hank Haff, was no match for the experienced English captains, but probably "Vigilant"'s greatest disadvantages were that her centerboard jammed and could not be used at times, particularly in the last of the season after she had taken the ground twice; and because in the first half of the season the English sail makers would not work on her sails which had become stretched and needed alterations. A photo shows "Vigilant" and "Britannia" racing: apparently "Vigilant"'s greater beam made her stand up well in moderate weather, and the photograph shows her heading perceptibly higher. But the most interesting thing about these races was that "Vigilant" several times sailed by "Britannia" in the same wind and water, proving that an American cup defender could cross over and be faster than the best English yachts when given a fair chance. I will also note that "Britannia" was practically a sister ship to "Valkyrie II" and, being owned by the Prince of Wales, had the pick of the British Navy for her crew. She was a magnificent vessel, always well kept and, I believe, had usually beaten "Valkyrie II" when they came together.

But I am not supposed to be writing a history of yachting although I am tempted to do so someday for most of the accounts that have been handed down to us were written by reporters who were more affected by the personalities of the yacht owners, and patriotism, than by truth and logic. So I will try to stick closer to Captain Nat and his yachts.

One of the amusing incidents that is told about Captain Nat on this visit to England, which was handed down by Captain Shackford of the Gould's stream yacht "Atalanta," is about as follows. One time, when Mr. Gould was talking with the Prince of Wales, afterward King Edward VII, the Prince signified that he would like to meet the designer of "Vigilant," so Mr. Gould invited the prince aboard the "Atalanta" where Mr. Gould knew Captain Nat was at the time. But Captain Nat saw them coming and hid in the engine room and could not be found. Captain Nat certainly was a curious combination of bashfulness in personal relations and boldness in engineering designs.

Now I will ask you to bear with me while I tell a short story about Prince Edward which, though well known in yachting circles in England, may not be well known over here. You know as both prince and king Edward was the most fond of yachting of any English monarch since Charles II, but while Queen Victoria was alive he had little money of his own. However, several times after an unusually satisfying sail or race on his yacht "Britannia" he would telegraph Watson, her designer, to come to him. Then the prince would order a much larger and better yacht than "Britannia." Watson, of course, had to say, "Yes, your Highness," but after he got back to Glasgow he never did anything about it for he knew the prince could not pay for the yacht. This must have been embarrassing for Watson, and it is possible that when Captain Nat hid in the engine room, he was avoiding a similar interview.

Nevertheless, Prince Edward was the principal figure that brought yachting in the eighteen-nineties to a greater popularity than it ever had before or since, for many wealthy English and Scots took up yachting on a grand scale during his life, and even some of them like Sir Thomas Lipton, who had no particular love for it. Also the prince's nephew, Kaiser Wilhelm, had started yacht racing, and having money of his own, ordered from Watson "Meteor II," which proved one of the fastest yachts in England in 1896. Prince Henry of Battenburg owned the twenty-rater "Asphodel," and titled men from Russia to Spain were having yachts built in rapid succession.

At this time yachting was by far the most publicized sport for automobile racing had not come in, nor had baseball been organized in this country with its big league contests; the turf was practically yachting's only competitor in public interest. The newspapers at that time often devoted a whole page to a yacht race, and yachting news often got the headlines. Under these conditions it was not strange that the leading yacht designers received great notoriety, and by this time Captain Nat's only serious competitors were Watson and Fife. To give an idea how well known Mr. Herreshoff was in those days I will say that when Captain Nat was in England with the "Vigilant" he wrote a letter to his wife and simply addressed it to Mrs. N. G. Herreshoff. No doubt he intended to add further directions but had been interrupted. However, the letter came through to its destination without further address. I speak of this only to show how much the principal designers were on the minds of the general public at that time, but in these democratic times the best yacht designers' names are hardly known outside the yachting fraternity. Captain Nat returned to America before the yachting season was half over for he had much work to attend to at the Herreshoff Company.

Now I must finish up with "Colonia" and "Vigilant" for both vessels had a long and useful life. "Colonia" was changed to a schooner, and her name changed to "Corona," and she won many prizes, including the Goelet Cup in 1892 and 1896 and the Astor Cup in 1900 and 1904. She served as the flagship of the New York Yacht Club from 1900 to 1902, and the last I knew of her she was the tender for "Enterprise" in 1930, thus lasting nearly forty years and outliving all of the single stickers of her time except "Britannia," which had been periodically rebuilt.

"Vigilant," after she came back from England, served as a trial horse against "Defender" in 1895. She won the Goelet Cup in 1894 and a great many yacht club runs. She was finally broken up in about 1910 and many of her fittings and parts used on the Cary Smith-designed schooner "Enchantress."

During these years, or since Captain Nat had gone into designing the larger racing yachts, he had had trouble with the sails and sail makers. This had necessitated setting up a small sail loft to recut and alter sails at Bristol, but in 1894 Captain Nat invented the crosscut sail and, as none of the other sail makers were willing to risk their reputations on such a radical departure in sail cutting, the Herreshoff Company enlarged their sail loft and decided to make their own sails. The development of the crosscut sail entailed working out several new problems in the matter of roping, stitching, etc., and as Thomas Ratsey, the famous English sail maker said, Captain Nat worked out nearly all the methods used today in his first few years of practice in making crosscut sails.

The Herreshoff Company made arrangements with the Lawrence Manufacturing Company, makers of sailcloth, to make especially woven duck to the Herreshoff formula of selected cotton to use on crosscut sails, which was one of the problems which had to be surmounted. But later they and other mills made duck of a similar formula for other sail makers.

While a sail with the cloth running parallel with the boom had been tried on the sloop "Maria" in about 1850, it had been a failure as the strains were across the gore of the cloth, so the sail was discarded. Captain Nat was the first to design a sail with the cloths running at ninety degrees from the leach, and he worked out the formula of the cloth required, which made the crosscut sail a success. It is probable that the crosscut sail has been copied more than any of his inventions, and it is used today on almost every racing sail boat throughout the world. The first crosscut sail was made for a twenty-one foot fin keeler that Captain Nat designed for W. Butler Duncan, and the second suit went on Captain Nat's fin keeler "Alerion II" built in 1894. As we will see they almost at once started making crosscut sails of every size from cup defenders down, and I can't help thinking the crosscut sail gave Herreshoff-built yachts an advantage over others during the next few years until other sail makers were making copies.

All during this time the Herreshoff Company was making many steam yachts and launches, in fact the dollars' worth of steamers probably exceeded the sailboats, even if the sailboats did now outnumber them. It certainly is quite wonderful that Captain Nat could be designing new steam engines and developing the crosscut sail at the same time.

One of the outstanding Herreshoff yachts of 1894 was the ten-rater "Dacotah," built for the Clyde where she won twenty-five firsts, one second out of thirty-three starts. I think this was Captain Nat's first fin keeler with a topmast and three headsails, and you can see by the photo that the spoon bow was now fully developed although "Dacotah" was a few months too early to have crosscut sails. We have seen that Captain Nat considered the bulb keel the best in "Wasp," "Navahoe," "Colonia," and "Vigilant," which were designed after he invented the fin keel, but in the smaller yachts, which had comparatively greater speed, particularly in the stronger winds of Scotland and England, he was still using the fin keel with great success.

In the winter of 1894 and '95 Captain Nat certainly was busy for, beside several small sail and power yachts, he was designing the two twenty-raters "Niagara" and "Isolde" for British waters, and the new cup defender "Defender." I will describe the twenty-raters first. They were single masted with a topmast and three headsails, double planked with mahogany on the outside, finished bright as several of the smaller fin keelers had been. They were sixty-five feet O.A., forty-five feet W.L., twelve feet beam, and ten feet draft. After a trial spin at Bristol their fin keels were unbolted and they were shipped abroad on the decks of steamers. "Niagara" was owned by Howard Gould, one of the brothers who had owned "Vigilant" on her visit to England the previous year. "Isolde" was owned by Baron von Zedtwitz who was to be killed the next year in the famous "Meteor"–"Isolde" collision on the Solent. "Isolde" and "Niagara" were sister ships, but during the next few years one or the other of them was painted white at times.

The captain of "Niagara" was John Barr, the elder brother of the famous Charlie Barr of whom we have spoken. John Barr was among the best of the Scottish racing skippers and had been captain of "Thistle" in 1887 in her unsuccessful attempt to capture the America's Cup. "Thistle" was a beautiful yacht designed by Watson and was built in Glasgow by a Scottish syndicate of owners. When "Thistle" was beaten by "Volunteer" the Scots would not believe it possible so, on John Barr's return to his native town of Gourock, they blamed him so much for the failure of "Thistle" that he came to this country and settled at Marblehead, Massachusetts. (I might note that today the model and whole design of "Thistle" would appear superior to "Volunteer," but "Thistle" 's sails were altogether too flat while "Volunteer" 's sails were of the proper draft. Also "Volunteer" was faultlessly managed by General Charles J. Paine, and the management of the large yachts is most important.) At any rate, when John Barr went over as captain of "Niagara" he had an opportunity to vindicate himself and prove that he and the "Niagara" were the fastest combination in the popular twenty-rater class in England, for I believe he won a pennant in every race but one. John Barr picked up most of his crew in New England and one of them occasionally calls on the author nowadays. One of the

"Niagara"'s crew was the Norwegian Chris Christensen who subsequently went as mate with Charlie Barr for several years and eventually was captain of "Resolute." "Niagara" certainly did well for an American yacht racing in English waters. This almost clean sweep of hers must have been a great satisfaction to Howard Gould and should have made up for the rather poor showing "Vigilant" had made the previous year in British waters when owned by the Goulds.

There is no doubt that these large fin keelers were fast in a breeze, and "Niagara" once made a phenomenally fast passage between ports when racing the circuit. She had a strong, fair wind and had her spinnaker set. I am sorry I do not remember the time and distance, but I believe she made an average speed of over nine knots for some one hundred miles, which is most remarkable for her water-line length of only forty-five feet. "Niagara" did so well that even the British writer, B. Heckstall-Smith, writing about her in later years, says: "Under the length and sail area rule in 1895 Herreshoff had sent over the twenty-rater "Niagara," and it must be admitted the American designer defeated the British designers. She was not a half-measure. Herreshoff went right out for a yacht of plate and bulb type, and with her he soundly hammered the British boats."

But I credit part of the success of "Niagara" to Captain John Barr for "Niagara"'s sister ship, "Isolde," generally only finished about in the middle of the large twenty-rater class the first year, although "Isolde" did very well in the next few years after Captain Barr returned to America. In later years "Niagara" was rigged as a yawl and painted white. Under the name of "Japonica" she won the Nore to Dover Corinthian cup, the Royal Yacht Squadron handicap, the Royal Southern Handicap twice, the Weymouth Town cup twice, the Rothschild prize at Havre, and a host of other valuable and important trophies. She perhaps was one of Captain Nat's most successful designs, but because she stayed in England is not so well known over here.

"Niagara" and "Isolde" were the largest fin keelers Captain Nat designed, and perhaps the most refined. While they were designed only three years after the first fin keeler "Dilemma," the fin keelers were to go out of style nearly as quickly as they had come in for, while the Herreshoff Manufacturing Company built in all about one hundred of them, they were mostly built between 1891 and 1897. The bulb keelers were surely taking their place, both because they were faster in light weather and because the fin keeler was barred from racing in most classes after about 1897. It is said that most clubs barred them because fin keelers not designed by Captain Nat showed structural weaknesses, but I know definitely that "Niagara" and all his smaller fin keelers did not leak at all, and some would be going today if they had not gone out of style and been broken up. It certainly would be interesting to know how one of them would have acted with a high, narrow rig with its resultant higher speeds, but I fear there would be steering difficulties for the high, narrow rig definitely needs a hull that tries to head off when heeled to counterbalance the heading up tendency of a high rig. So perhaps it is just as well that the fin keelers have gone out of style.

While Captain Nat designed several other yachts, both sail and steam, for the season of 1895, by far the most important one was the cup boat "Defender," and as I believe she represents one of the greatest advances in his designs I will give her some space.

In the autumn of 1894 Lord Dunraven challenged again for the America's Cup. This time he had Lord Wolverton, Lord Lonsdale, and Captain Harry McCalmont, owner of the steam yacht "Giraldo," associated with him in the attempt. He again went to G. L. Watson for the design, but I fear Watson was too much influenced by their ideas and requests, for the "Valkyrie III," as the challenger was named, had little resemblance to a Watson yacht. In fact she was an enlarged "Vigilant" with a deep keel instead of a centerboard. She was a large yacht in every way —length, beam, draft, and sail area. The British seemed to have been impressed with "Vigilant"'s great beam and so made a wide yacht, but "Vigilant" had only been made wide because at that time the Herreshoff Company could not launch a yacht of much over fourteen feet.

But now that the ways had been changed and some dredging done around the wharves Captain Nat designed the new cup boat, which was named "Defender," with a draft of nineteen feet, and made her only twenty-three feet beam, so she was about five

feet deeper, and three and one half feet narrower than "Vigilant."
So it might be said the Americans this time had the cutter (the
narrow yacht) and the British the sloop (the wide yacht).
Some of the general dimensions of the two were as follows:

	"Valkyrie III"	"Defender"
L.O.A.	129	123
L.W.L.	88.85	88.45
Beam	26.20	23.33
Draft	20	19
S.A.	13,027	12,602
Ballast	77 tons	85 tons
Racing length	101.49	100.36

So we see the greatest difference between the two was the
amount of ballast.

To acquire this large amount of ballast "Defender" had to be
designed very scientifically: her frames were made of bulb
angles, instead of angle irons, and, although she was the first
yacht to use bulb angle frames, large ocean steamers had used
them previously. However, there were no rolls in this country for
the smaller bulb angles suitable for yacht work so Captain Nat
had to design the shapes and the Herreshoff Company paid for
making the rollers.

"Defender"'s deck beams were of aluminum, and the ones in
the widest part of the yacht were quite large—about five inches
by two and one half inches—with two smaller sizes nearer the
bow and stern. She was plated with Tobin bronze below the
water line, had aluminum topsides, and much aluminum in
the deck framing (margin plate, diagonal strapping, etc.).

"Defender," I believe, was the last of Captain Nat's cup
defenders to have a wooden deck. All later ones had metal decks
covered with either a thin layer of cork or unpainted canvas.
Apparently after Captain Nat's experience abroad racing on
"Vigilant," he was determined to beat the Englishmen this time
without any doubt. "Defender" was a very beautiful model which
has not been much improved on since although the modern
yacht has less draft and more displacement to fit the various
modern rules, and many, particularly the ocean racers, have considerably more freeboard. But in general balance of proportions

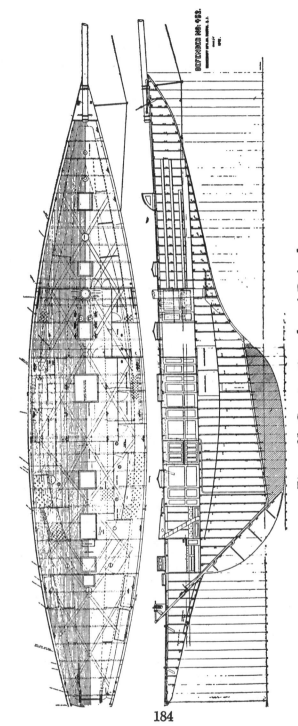

Figure 31. Construction plan of Defender.

184

she was a model that would perform well in any size from a model yacht to a ninety-footer. All of "Defender" 's rigging, spars, and fittings were very much refined and she was the first cup boat to use crosscut sails although I think a crosscut mainsail was made for "Vigilant" the same year.

"Defender" was built for C. Oliver Iselin, Edwin D. Morgan, and William K. Vanderbilt who by this time had great confidence in Captain Nat and did not interfere with the design. E. D. Morgan had been commodore of the New York Yacht Club the year before and always was a very popular man though a modest one, so there was quite a celebration at the launching of "Defender" on June 29, 1895. This was quite late for a cup boat to come out but was probably because Captain Nat had been seriously ill the previous winter. She was christened by Mrs. C. Oliver Iselin amid the acclaim of waiting thousands, who had arrived on special trains from Newport and Providence, and quite a fleet of spectator steam yachts. The *Herald* of that day says: "As she came into view outside the shop, a moving dream of white and gold, every man, woman, and child in the great crowd broke into cheers, and along the harbor shores rolled the loud boom of cannon; then as the great sloop slowly swung down the ways a sailor man on the stern flung aloft the Stars and Stripes, and the multitude cheered afresh vociferously."

But the "Defender" did not take to her element as planned for when about half way down the ways she came to a stop and could not be budged farther although one of the large steam yachts tried to start her, in fact pulled so hard that the steam yacht's towing bitts and some of her after bulwarks were torn away; but "Defender" stuck fast. When a diver was sent down to ascertain the reason for the stoppage it was found that in building these new launching ways a bolt or lag screw had been left sticking up a few inches, and when this obstruction was removed she slid down the ways with little resistance.

But I must tell an amusing incident for the benefit of those who remember the jovial Boston yachting reporter, Bill Swan. Bill had been chosen to cover this launching for one of the Boston papers, and determined to get the jump on the other reporters. After hovering around Bristol a few days he wrote up a flowery description of the launching, calling it most successful and describing how "Defender" looked afloat, etc. This story he sent to his paper a few days before the launching and asked them to hold it until he telegraphed for its release. When "Defender" started down the ways Bill started to run to the telegraph station (about three quarters of a mile away) and on arriving there quite out of breath sent the message to release his story. So the Boston paper gave the account of a successful launching which poor Bill never did quite live down.

The launching of these large or deep yachts was quite a strain for Captain Nat as he was responsible for everything: not only did he design the yacht, cradle, and ways, but he superintended the building and launching.

In the meantime "Vigilant" had been brought back from England by Captain Charlie Barr, and Mr. George Gould (now the sole owner of "Vigilant" as his brother Howard was in England racing the twenty-rater "Niagara"), spent much money to put "Vigilant" in the best possible racing trim. At great expense she had about twenty tons of her ballast removed and this was recast and bolted to the bottom of her keel which increased her draft from six to nine inches. That summer "Vigilant" was under the management of Mr. Edward A. Willard, and with her improvements and with Charlie Barr for skipper and "Lem" Miller as mate, went remarkably well, making the "Defender" appear less fast than she should have. "Defender" also had several things against her, the first of which was that her captain did not work with Captain Nat in getting her new style fittings, sails, and rigging in working shape. Her second trouble was that her mast step settled and gave trouble in the early season. While the mast step had been properly designed it seems that during Captain Nat's illness, when he could not inspect the work, several rivets had been left out in a place which could not be seen after the step structure was put in place but where there was a great strain. It was some time before the trouble was located as it was in a difficult place to get at to rerivet; it should have been done in the first place. In the meantime the press had made the general public believe the "Defender" was structurally unsound. Her third trouble was that for some patriotic reason or other she was manned entirely with an American crew, mostly Deer Islanders. While no doubt Maine fishermen are picturesque characters and good on smacks with a crew of one or two, they were not to be compared with the crews of various nationalities which had specialized in large yacht racing. To a great extent our larger yachts had been manned by Scandinavians who would obey a command promptly instead of stopping to think it over and decide whether they wanted to or not as the Deer Islanders did.

"Defender" 's fourth trouble was that the aluminum in her construction began to disintegrate which kept all hands worried. While it is true that some torpedo boats in both France and England had been built of aluminum, and while Captain Nat had made careful strength tests with aluminum, it was not then known how quickly it disintegrated when in contact with bronze and salt water. Strange to say, the aluminum often disintegrated under the paint so that "Defender" generally appears in photographs with streaked sides.

In the trial races of 1895 she raced against "Vigilant," "Jubilee," and "Volunteer," but, although she showed remarkable speed at times and, I believe, won every race, when she did not break down, she did not beat "Vigilant" materially although by the end of the season, when she met "Valkyrie III," she was undoubtedly a remarkably fast craft for her time. I should like to impress the reader with that fact on account of its connection with the Dunraven controversy which apparently sprang from that reason.

The first race between "Valkyrie III" and "Defender" started at 12:20 P.M., September 7. It was a windward and leeward race in a light breeze and a lop of a sea. The accounts of this race given by both the English and American witnesses state that soon after the start "Valkyrie" was footing the faster but that "Defender" got a lift, change of wind, which let her up and gave her a lead she kept from then to the finish. I believe the facts of the case were more as follows: Soon after the start "Valkyrie III" had to be sailed a little wide to keep her going well with her large beam in the choppy sea and light wind, while "Defender" sailed well with her sails trimmed flat, and consequently pointed high, and this had made the reporters think she had had a lift. But as the "Defender" steadily drew away from "Valkyrie" in the remaining part of the race the logic would seem that she either was considerably faster or received a succession of lifts. However, "Defender" won the race by eight minutes forty-five seconds, and it is my opinion that Lord Dunraven clearly saw in this first race that he was pitted against a definitely faster yacht. I think he saw that "Defender" with her high percentage of ballast could carry her sail well although with her slight beam she had little head-on resistance. I think he realized that "Defender" with her crosscut sails and polished bronze bottom was too fast for "Valkyrie III." Dunraven had worked very hard in building and preparing "Valkyrie," and no doubt the strain of managing her almost singlehanded was too much, for he seems to have broken down under the disappointment of this race. And then, having heard through some rumor brought to him that "Defender" had taken on some ballast after she was measured, he entered a protest against her on the assumption that her water line length had been increased since her official measurement, but when the water lines of both yachts were remeasured the following afternoon no difference from the previous measurements were found.

This incident, however, had started ill-feeling on both sides which finally was to result in a most unfortunate controversy. The rumor that "Defender" had taken on ballast arose from the fact that a few days before the race, and after she had been officially measured, "Defender"'s crew took a few pigs of lead aboard her tender to saw them into smaller blocks so the lead would stow better into the part of the bilge where they were to be carried. Originally "Defender" had all of her ballast outside but before the international races her cabin work was taken out and the pigs of lead that we are speaking about taken aboard to make up for the weight. These same pigs were aboard when she was measured but it was simply decided to stow them more compactly or in a more shipshape manner. Perhaps the only mistake was to have sawed the pigs on "Defender"'s tender instead of aboard "Defender," but no deceit was intended and perhaps that is why they did the job so openly that it was observed and the word taken to Dunraven.

But to cap the climax, in the second race three days later on

September 10, "Valkyrie III" fouled "Defender" at the start. "Valkyrie" had been a little early at the line and to use up time steered a crooked course. Being close on "Defender"'s weather quarter, as she swung, the end of "Valkyrie"'s boom caught on "Defender"'s weather topmast shroud and broke it. Fortunately the wind was quite light and the topmast did not come down and, although "Defender" was crippled, she came about so that her well side was to windward and made a start only about one minute behind "Valkyrie." "Defender"'s crew at once rigged a temporary lashing or preventer tackle to her broken shroud but she could not carry her jib topsail when on one tack. In spite of this "Valkyrie" only beat her forty-seven seconds corrected time, so we see if "Defender" had not been detained over one minute at the start she would have beaten "Valkyrie" although she was crippled, so she must have been decidedly the faster of the two.

After a protest by "Defender" the race was given to her, as it was a clear case of the weather boat coming down on and fouling a close hauled yacht under her lea. It is quite clear in my mind at least that Lord Dunraven now saw he had no chance to beat "Defender," and I imagine that if they had had ten races, "Valkyrie III" would not have won more than one or two for "Defender"'s fine model, plenty of stability, and crosscut sails made her very fast indeed. At any rate right after the start of the third race "Valkyrie III" withdrew and headed back to her anchorage, leaving "Defender" to sail alone over the course, which gave her three straight races although only one satisfactory one.

I will not dwell on the rather ridiculous controversy which continued throughout the next winter as the result of these protests by both sides, although I think the New York Yacht Club could have shown more tact at times, but will say that both before and after these races Lord Dunraven owned several of the handsomest yachts ever built. He was somewhat of a designer and had modeled the most successful of the British twenty-raters, "Audrey." It is my belief that he was broken down from overexertion in attempting to manage a cup challenger singlehanded and for a while probably was not entirely in control of his actions.

By the fall of 1895 the Spanish War was looming up on the horizon so Captain Nat had to turn to steam again for the Herres-

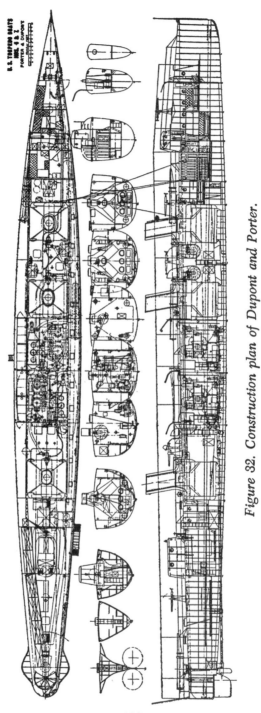

Figure 32. Construction plan of Dupont and Porter.

hoff Manufacturing Company had accepted contracts to design and build two one hundred seventy-five foot steel torpedo boats. They were alike and one was named "Dupont" and the other "Porter." These vessels were remarkably fast for seagoing torpedo boats of that time and both made speeds of approximately thirty-one miles per hour. The design of vessels of this kind perhaps calls for more work if not more skill than a cup defender, and in this case almost every part of these vessels—boilers, engines, and all—had to be designed special so Captain Nat was extremely busy, even too busy to take time off for his usual Saturday and Sunday sails in the summer of 1896, but he certainly turned out some remarkable designs in this time. They were double enders at the water line and below, and certainly were fast, good sea boats. I believe they cost more to build than their contract price but at that time the Navy Department gave a large bonus for each quarter mile that a vessel exceeded her contract speed, and that was what Captain Nat was aiming at in this design. As they exceeded their contract speed quite a lot this speed bonus, besides covering building losses, made the Herreshoff Company a reasonably good profit.

At that time one of the great difficulties the torpedo boats had throughout the world was vibration from what then were considered high-speed engines. The usual torpedo boat engine was quite long, as it had the valves between the cylinders, and, although the whole mass of moving parts could be somewhat counterbalanced, the ends of these engines gyrated considerably around the center of weight; in fact it was on account of the vibration trouble of the reciprocating engine that the turbine got its first start, and that, in turn, before the reduction gear was used, had serious propeller vibration trouble. For the "Dupont" and "Porter" Captain Nat designed remarkable engines which were almost completely balanced both statically and dynamically. These engines were four cylinder, triple expansion with two of the cylinders above so that, together with its valves and valve gear at the side, the overall length of these engines was less than half of other engines of their class and horsepower, and as the two end crank throws were opposite each other the pistons and reciprocating parts counterbalanced each other.

The moving parts were extremely light; the crankshaft was hollow at both the main bearings and at the crankpins. These engines weighed 18,750 pounds apiece and developed approximately 1,700 horsepower apiece. But the best thing about the

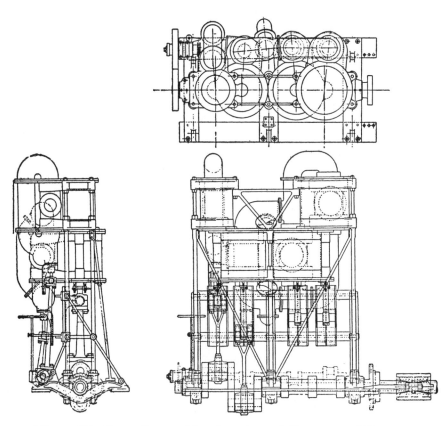

Figure 33. General assembly of engines of Dupont and Porter.

engines was that they ran approximately twenty years in naval service without major repairs.

The boilers of the "Dupont" and "Porter" were of the type known as Du Temple, an arrangement of tubes and drums first used by the French engineer, Captain Du Temple who had spent most of his fortune and life in trying to develop a flying machine driven by steam. He brought out this type of boiler in 1873, and it can be said that this was the first of the so-called express type of water tube boilers and the one from which the Normand, Thornycroft, Yarrow, and Herreshoff boilers descended. Each of these two torpedo boats had three boilers, and each boiler had a grate area of 53½ feet, and a heating surface of 2,710 feet. They carried a boiler pressure of only a little over two hundred pounds, and it seems remarkable today that these torpedo boats made such great speed, for today boiler pressures of over a thousand are quite common. Some of the weights of these vessels were:

Hull	56.5 tons
Propelling machinery	76.8 tons

They carried about twenty tons of coal and other naval equipment on their trial runs, and had bunker capacity for sixty tons.

The "Dupont" and "Porter" saw active service in the Spanish War as they were at the naval battle off Santiago when Admiral Cervera's Spanish fleet was destroyed. Right after the battle the "Dupont" carried the dispatch announcing this victory to the mainland for the telegraphic cables had been cut. It is interesting that in making this run "Dupont" exceeded her trial speed.

In 1896 the Herreshoffs built the "Morris," U.S.N.T.B. No. 14 as well as the "Gwin" and "Talbot," U.S.N.T.B. No. 15 and No. 16. "Morris" was one hundred forty feet long and the sister ships "Gwin" and "Talbot" one hundred feet long.

I must now tell why the Herreshoff Manufacturing Company stopped building for the United States Navy. When the Navy decided to build several torpedo boats in 1895 the Navy Department designed, I think, all that the Herreshoffs did not build, and some of these designs were rather poor as can be seen in looking at their plans which are in the 1897 year book of the Transactions of the Society of Naval Architects. Some of the personnel of the Navy Department became jealous and caused annoyance to the Herreshoff Company with their inspectors. Among other things the Navy inspectors condemned the piston rod guides on the "Dupont" 's engines and said they were made of the wrong kind of steel. Now these piston guides on a four cylinder engine were quite a job to make as they must be all hand fitted and scraped, like the ways of a lathe. It was not the expense that Captain Nat objected to; rather it was to be compelled to make them of metal that his experience had shown was not satisfactory. Well, when the "Dupont" started to run her trials, these new guides heated up so that she could not run well and when she was limping back

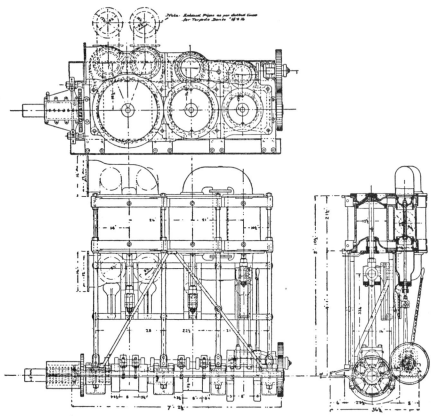

Figure 34. Engines used in Morris, Gwin and Talbot.

to the building yard Captain Nat, although very mad, asked very respectfully if the original guides could not be temporarily put in place to complete the trials. Fortunately this was allowed and she ran her trials without any further trouble, but Captain Nat and J. B. were so mad about this incident that they shook hands

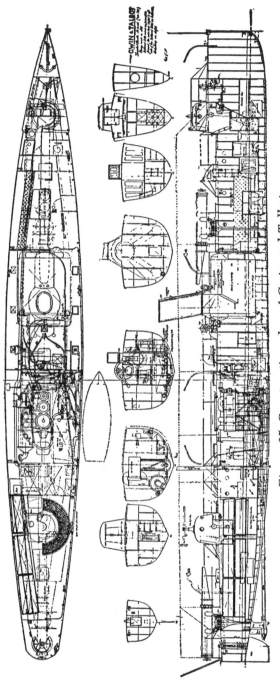

Figure 35. Construction plan of Gwin and Talbot.

195

in the office and agreed not to build any more vessels for the Navy Department after they finished their present contracts.

This, of course, made it very nice for some of their competitors of that time who have since built many millions of dollars' worth of destroyers for the Navy, but on the other hand one of the builders of the torpedo boats was in litigation with the Navy some thirty or forty years before they were completely paid.

I have said before the Herreshoffs lacked tact, and no doubt a little tact would have managed the inspectors, for some of the other builders so entertained the inspectors with wine, women, and song that most anything passed. However, it was hard to have unqualified inspectors, who themselves could not design anything, condemn the work of a man who at that time was one of the world's greatest authorities on light steam engines. Maybe the Herreshoffs were right in preferring to deal with civilians for in the next few years among their clients were the Morgans, Vanderbilts, Belmonts, and perhaps one hundred other leading families. These men seemed to understand and appreciate good design and honest workmanship, and it must have been pleasant for Captain Nat to have his designs fully appreciated while Uncle Sam neither understood nor cared, and generally gave his plums to political grafters. I must add, however, that some of the Navy personnel who manned these early torpedo boats were much liked at Bristol, and two of the officers who commissioned these early torpedo boats were polished gentlemen of great ability who later became admirals in the United States Navy.

Captain Nat designed most of his fin keelers before the Spanish War, and, as we have said before, he considered the bulb keel the fastest with the large yachts but designed many fin keelers for the smaller classes. By 1897 the fin keel was barred in this country by some clubs while in England in 1896 they had adopted a measurement that included the skin girth of the yacht below water at the midships section. The rule was roughly: Length and Beam and 75 per cent of girth and $.5\sqrt{SA}$ divided by 2 $\dfrac{L + B + .75G + .5\sqrt{SA}}{2} = $ Rating. This rule and later ones that measured girth in different ways penalized fin keelers so severely that few were built after about 1897.

Even before 1897 Captain Nat was designing a few bulb keelers in the small classes and was beginning to consider the bulb keel the fastest in all sizes. But because lately there has been rather a revival of interest in fin keelers I will say something about one of the last of Captain Nat's boats of this type. She was "Vaquero II," built for Herman P. Duryea, one of our best amateur helmsmen in the eighteen-nineties, who took her to England and raced with fair success. "Vaquero II" was built in 1895, was thirty-nine feet O.A., twenty-six W.L. In some ways she would appear very modern with her small sail area and forestay inboard. Mr.

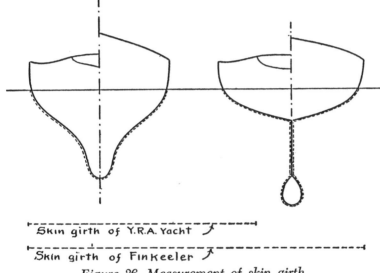

Figure 36. Measurement of skin girth.

Duryea thought a lot of this "Vaquero" and after her return from abroad she was stored at the Herreshoff Manufacturing Company for about a quarter of a century.

Perhaps the most notable of the late fin keelers were the so-called Newport one-design Thirties. They came out in 1896 and were forty-two feet O.A., twenty-nine feet six inches W.L., eight feet four inches beam, and seven feet one inch draft. They cost $2,850 complete, including one suit of sails and this was considered expensive then, but it is doubtful if any builder could duplicate one of them today for $25,000. They were beautifully built, double planked with mahogany over cedar, and each frame was steamed over a separate mold so that many consider them the first really one-design class with perhaps little or no variation in their speeds, weights, or dimensions. I speak of this because today there is considerable variation in the boats of many so-called one-design classes, many of which are built by different builders, and in the case of the numerous Star Class there is allowed quite a variation in shape, construction, and size. I think there were ten of the Newport Thirties which are listed below:

"Vaquero III"	H. P. Duryea
"Dorothy II"	H. P. Whitney
"Wawa"	J. A. Stillman
"Puck"	E. D. Morgan
"Hera"	R. N. Ellis
"Carolina"	Pembroke Jones
"Esperanza"	A. S. VanWinkle
"Musme"	J. McDonough
"Veda"	Cornelius Vanderbilt
"Mai"	O. G. Jennings

These owners were wealthy men with summer homes at Newport, and the class was raced very hotly with from forty to fifty races a season for the first few years, and many of them had new sails often, sometimes a new mainsail each week! There were many valuable prizes offered for the class, and some bets at rather high stakes between the owners, but they were good sportsmen, and good feeling generally prevailed with few protests. It was in the Newport Thirties that some of our best sailors, both amateur and professional, got their training, and some of both afterward graduated into the New York Yacht Club Seventy-foot Class. Some of the professional captains of the Thirties were:

"Ed" Willis of "Vaquero III"
Capt. Wilkey of "Wawa"
Capt. Holmes of "Esperanza"
Sam Seaman of "Carolina"
Clayton Haff of "Veda"
James Barr of "Musme"

Capt. Bird of "Hera"
Capt. Anderson of "Dorothy II"

Many of these men were captains or mates on later famous yachts, and "Ed" Willis was perhaps our best professional small boat sailor between 1900 and 1910.

While the Newport Thirties raced some on the Sound, and occasionally in the ocean, most of their racing was in Narragansett Bay near Newport where there are many ledges and islands, together with some flow of tide, so that to a great extent working the tides by tacking close inshore was necessary. While this no doubt added much to the excitement of the racing, the Thirties often struck bottom very hard, but their hulls were so light and scientifically built with the weight mostly in the lead that the concussion was absorbed in the denting of the lead at the bottom of their fins.

The Thirties could turn very quickly and were wonderful boats to maneuver so they could approach dangers more closely, and sail in closer formation, than most any other class of yachts either before or since. This ability to turn quickly brings to my mind an amusing story which Captain Nat told me about one of them. I have said before that most of the Thirties had able captains, but it happened that one of them was taken away from Bristol by two men who had only sailed on heavy, slow-turning smacks like the Friendship sloops. Soon after this yacht got under way she made a couple of circles, came about, and jibed over, whereupon the captain hurriedly dropped anchor, got into the dinghy and rowed ashore. He went to the office and reported that there was something radically wrong with his Thirty as she could not be managed at all, so Captain Nat went out with him to see what was the trouble.

After they got under way the Thirty seemed to handle and balance perfectly like all the others of the class so Captain Nat said to the captain, "Now just tell me what happened when you tried to sail her."

"Well," the captain said, "we got under way all right and when I got ready to tack ship I sent the man forward to back the jib to windward, then I put the helm hard down, but before you could say Jack Robinson she went into a spin and nigh cast the man forward overboard. Then she turned on her heel and went into a jibe afore I could call the man aft to tend the backstays."

Captain Nat then showed the captain how slowly she could be brought into the wind if desired, and as she shot to windward how she could be brought from one tack to the other, back and forth, before her momentum was used up. Then, bringing her off before the wind, he showed the captain how, by her quick turning, one could prevent a jibe even after the leach had started to jibe over.

This anecdote will not seem so amusing to the younger generation who mostly have known nothing but quick turning sailboats, but perhaps Captain Nat's fin keelers of the eighteen-nineties were the quickest turning of any sail boats that had moderate displacement. The reasons for this were that they had short keels nearly amidships, together with very rounding sections forward and aft, and because they had good-sized balanced rudders which could be put hard over instantly with little effort. Altogether the Herreshoff Manufacturing Company built about a hundred fin keelers in a little over six years. They ranged between fifteen and forty-five feet on the water line and, though they all had rather low and wide gaff sail plans, there is no reason to suppose that they were not as fast as some of the much advertised and exaggerated fin keelers built recently and which fit no measurement rule.

At the present time the young exaggerators and exhibitionists use the word "planing" in the case where the older sailor would have used the words "sailing at a good clip," and have succeeded in making many think they had invented a new type of vessel whereas the fin keeler was at its best soon after Captain Nat invented it in 1891 which was several years before most of the present exhibitionists were born. If the only object of a sailboat was to acquire maximum speed under perfect conditions, a strong breeze wind on the quarter, of course the unballasted scow like those used on inland lakes has the highest maximum speed of the single-hulled craft. But the object of the racing yacht in all sizes and classes is to make the best average speed, that is, to be fast in prevailing conditions, for a race won in a light head wind and choppy sea will count as much as the race won when planing in a quartering wind. So among the smaller yachts without restrictions the fastest type is the centerboarder with very light hull and large sail plan whose stability is acquired by a trained team of athletes that can hike out to windward.

In the larger classes the bulb keeler with her smaller wetted surface is decidedly the fastest, but there may be some sizes, say two hundred square feet sail area, where the combination of fin

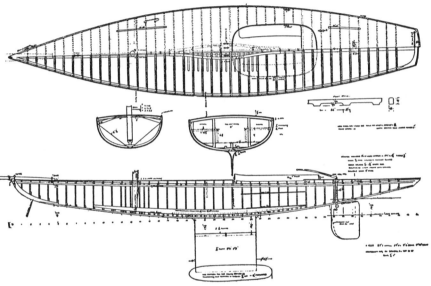

Figure 37. One of the last of Captain Nat's fin keelers.

keel and human shifting ballast would go well in moderate weather, but the properly sailed centerboarder will beat her in a breeze, and the bulb keeler will beat them both in light weather. However, the properly designed fin keeler is slightly cheaper and they will last a long time for there is no large wood keel or deadwood to rot, shrink, and swell.

The last of Captain Nat's fin-keelers were proportioned as in Figure 37, and the medium-sized ones had fins made of three plates as follows: The lower section of this fin was one thickness of bronze plate while from there up the fin was in two thicknesses which were somewhat spread at the upper middle part with the entering and trailing edges riveted together. The upper edges flanged outward and allowed the attaching bolts to be well spread. These bolts went up close to floor timbers and passed through hard wood stringers which rested on top of the floor timbers and made the floor timbers into pure unpierced cantilevers so the strains from the fin had no tendency to strain the keel or garboards; in fact the keel amidships was little thicker than the planking. Many of Captain Nat's fin keelers did not leak a drop, but the workmanship of that time was at a very high standard, and the yachts were all double planked with the two layers cemented together with thick shellac which in some ways is superior to modern, quick drying adhesives. Many of the fin keelers were finished in bright, high-grade mahogany with the planking of each side from the same log so as to match perfectly in color. Some had mahogany decks also, and altogether, with their neat rig and special bronze fittings, they were far superior to any fin keelers of today. They were a better model, of more scientific construction, and of vastly superior workmanship, but the later bulb keelers were to beat them under any measurement rules that we have since had.

So the fin keelers went out of existence for about forty-five years, or until they were nearly forgot, and that is the reason I have given them so much space. However, by 1897 Captain Nat had considered them passé and from that time on only designed bulb keelers, bulb keel centerboarders, and pure centerboarders. Several of his small bulb keelers of the modern type were fifteen or sixteen footers built to race at Larchmont. These had a full spoon bow, large sail area, bowsprit, and deep keel. Later the Newport fifteen-footers were made from this model; then from the same molds but with a shallower keel and centerboard the first of the Buzzards Bay Fifteens were built and, although they were from one of Captain Nat's early models of that type (I think made in 1896), the Buzzards Bay Fifteens remained popular for some forty years with perhaps a hundred and fifty or so being built, and these at the present time command a high price.

The famous twenty-one-footer "Cock-Robin," the construction plan of which is shown in Figure 21 came out in 1897. She was one of Captain Nat's first attempts at bulb keel on small racers, and she was soon followed by the raceabouts "Cockatoo," "Fly," "Fancy," "Sally II," "Sintram," etc., until several other designers

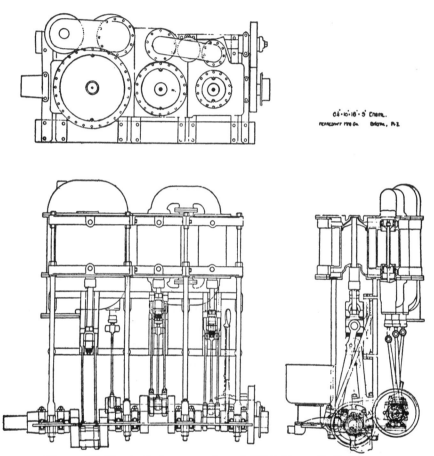

Figure 38. Typical steam engine of 1896 Herreshoff design.

began to turn out similar but more extreme models. It is surprising that between 1890 and 1900 Captain Nat brought out many patterns of marine hardware and deck fittings. Many of these were designed in several sizes and included blocks, turnbuckles, winches, flange eyes, and many bronze castings to use in connection with hatches, skylights, gangways, etc.—perhaps two hundred different items many of which have never been equaled by other makers. One experienced yachtsman has said lately that there is hardly a thing on a yacht today that Captain Nat did not originate, improve, or perfect, and, while it is true many of his fittings were not understood or appreciated for many years, still at the present time about the only useful fittings on the market are imitations of his original models. The fittings alone that he designed would have been a creditable lifetime work for a designer. I say it is surprising that he brought out all these fittings in these ten years because at the same time he was designing several models and sizes of steam engines and sailboats, literally in all the sizes between sailing dinghies and cup defenders.

One of the remarkable small sailboats of the late eighteen-nineties that Captain Nat designed was the racing catboat "Wander," twenty-one feet nine inches water line, built for Mr. E. T. Bedford. She had quite large overhangs and low ends and proved most successful in racing on the Sound where she had to compete with some very fast cats that had descended from the sandbaggers and were hotly raced.

An interesting medium-sized yacht, designed by Captain Nat in 1897, was the ocean cruiser "Spalpeen," seventy-three feet O.A., fifty-six feet W.L., twelve feet beam, eight feet draft. She was a ketch and when she came out had a small auxiliary steam engine which was taken out after a few years. From then on she cruised under sail only. Her construction plan shows that she was very similar in model to the yawl "Dorade" that was to make a great sensation some thirty-four years later. "Spalpeen" was built for Mr. R. M. Riddle of Philadelphia, who was a very remarkable and likable man and a particular friend of Captain Nat and his whole family. In his youth Mr. Riddle had had a severe sickness which left him entirely deaf so that, not being able to hear his own voice, he had lost the power of speech; and to add to this, one time when he was working on the "Spalpeen"'s steam engine a monkey wrench slipped out of his hand and hit him in the eye, so that the rest of his life he was deaf and mute and blind in one eye. Mr. Riddle took several long cruises in the

"Spalpeen" and consequently did much night sailing. Unfortunately one night "Spalpeen" was run into by a steamer which struck her a very hard glancing blow with such a loud noise that the crew and guest of "Spalpeen" thought she would sink at once. As the steamer came alongside again the crew and the guest, Mr. Riddle's nephew, attempted to board the steamer but the nephew fell overboard and was drowned. It was found "Spalpeen" was not leaking at all so the steamer put the crew aboard again and she sailed to Bristol. I am only telling of this collision because of its interesting structural effect for the "Spalpeen" was literally bent sideways, or her center line had become curved. After she was hauled out in the shop and some of her deck removed and the fastenings in other parts of the deck loosened, she sprang back into perfect alignment. The collision had actually bent the whole panel of the deck sideways which must have required a great force as "Spalpeen" was a flush decked yacht. The rest of her hull was intact except, of course, where the steamer had made contact.

Another interesting yacht built in 1899 was the yawl "Petrel," seventy-six feet O.A., fifty-six feet W.L., fourteen feet beam, nine feet draft. You can see that she would look very modern today although designed more than fifty years ago.

Of course the most important design of Captain Nat's in the late Gay Nineties was the cup defender "Columbia." She was built for a syndicate, headed by J. Pierpont Morgan and C. Oliver Iselin. Mr. Morgan was the principal owner, I believe, and as he was commodore of the New York Yacht Club that year a great deal of interest was taken in "Columbia." When she was launched on June 10, she was christened by Mrs. Iselin and it was an evening launching for her great depth required high tide to float her off the cradle. As she appeared outside the construction shop calcium lights were played on her so that her polished bronze bottom glistened like gold while her white topsides reflected the strong light so brightly that the assembled thousands broke into a cheer that could be heard for miles. As she took the water an immense silk yacht ensign was raised on a staff aft, followed a few moments later by a jury mast stepped in her mast hole flying the private signals of Mr. Morgan and Mr. Iselin.

"Columbia" was the first of the cup boats to be launched on a marine railway that had its cradle mounted on wheels, so it took seventeen minutes for her to run the length of the track into water deep enough to float her. She was a majestic sight as she slowly emerged from the construction shop into the June evening, and the thousands of spectators were well repaid for coming to see this spectacle. She was lowered down the ways by a wire rope connecting her cradle to a drum which was geared to a steam engine, and she could only go as fast as the steam engine paid out the wire cable, probably at the rate of about one mile an hour, and she could have been stopped instantly if things had not proceeded as they should.

"Columbia" is often considered the best of Captain Nat's designs, or at least the best of his cup boats, but as a matter of fact she was not a radical improvement over her predecessor, "Defender," for she was much the same model and construction. However, she did have a hollow steel mast, gaff, and boom, and her plating was bronze below water and steel above. To be sure "Columbia" had longer overhangs and no rocker at the bottom of her keel. She was really a refined and perfected "Defender." Her framework and general construction were the same, and her general dimensions were:

L.O.A.	131 feet
L.W.L.	89 feet 8 inches
Beam	24 feet
Draft	19 feet 3 inches
S.A.	13,135 square feet
Lead	90 tons

The real secrets of "Columbia"'s success were her captain, Charlie Barr; her managing owner, C. Oliver Iselin; and her principal owner, J. P. Morgan, who had perfect confidence in Captain Nat, Captain Barr, and Mr. Iselin, and would back them up and never interfere with them. This was Mr. Iselin's third campaign in the afterguard of a cup defender, and he was a resourceful and capable man. "Columbia" was also Captain Nat's third cup boat and by this time he had acquired a great deal of data on this type of craft, so, together with his experiences in sailing on "Vigilant" and "Defender," it is not strange that he designed a hull that never showed structural strains. And, too, there is no doubt that "Columbia" was a good job of building as the Herreshoff Manufacturing Company by that time had considerable practice at building metal racers of this size, "Columbia" being the fifth metal racer of about ninety feet water line. During the first of the season she did, however, have some difficulties with her spars and rig, and once carried away her mast and messed things up in general.

"Columbia" was the only new boat in the trial races that year, and her only competitor was "Defender" with Uriah Rhodes for captain and W. Butler Duncan as manager. "Defender" had been rejuvenated with a hollow steel mast to replace her original Oregon pine mast which, I believe, allowed her to take on over a ton of extra ballast and still float the same. The two boats raced many times that season but "Columbia" proved the faster so was chosen to defend the cup.

The challenging yacht was the first of Sir Thomas Lipton's "Shamrock"'s and a very fast yacht. She was designed by William Fife, Jr., of Scotland but was built in England by the famous torpedo boat builders, Thornycroft & Company. Every effort was made to have her construction light and scientific; her bottom plating was manganese bronze while above water her plating was an aluminum composition which, I believe, stood up better than the aluminum plating of "Defender." Nevertheless, this "Shamrock" was the last yacht to use aluminum in any quantity in her construction. Her mast, boom, and gaff, like "Columbia," were of steel but they gave trouble and did not stand well, otherwise she might have been very difficult to beat for she certainly had great speed-giving qualities. "Shamrock"'s captain was "Archie" Hogarth, who, like Charlie Barr, was a comparatively young man at the time, but it was the custom on the challengers to have a second captain who gave advice when required. The second captain of "Shamrock" was Robert Wringe, and I will mention that Captain Nat considered both of these men as particularly able and perhaps better than any we had in this country. This was quite natural for the English at that time were racing large yachts much more than we were. It is only fair to say that Captain Nat acted as second captain on "Columbia," as he had on "Vigilant" and "Defender," and actually steered her part of the time.

The cup races that year were very late, the first one scheduled for October 3, but, though several starts were made, fog and light wind prevented the finish of a race until October 16. This race was in a moderate but steady easterly breeze with light fog at the start and a short chop of a sea. It was a windward and lee-ward race, and although "Shamrock" was over the starting line first it was found that her rather flat bow did not slip through the chop as easily as "Columbia" so that soon after the start "Colum-bia" got the weather berth and rounded the weather mark with a lead of about nine and one-half minutes. On the run home "Columbia" increased her lead and won the race by ten minutes, eight seconds corrected time.

The second race was the following day as the regatta commit-tee was endeavoring to complete the series before cold weather. This time the race was over a triangular course; the wind was still east and had made up quite a chop of a sea. Both yachts went over the line almost together and, although "Shamrock" was slightly ahead, she was also to leeward. The first twenty-five min-utes the race was very close, and after they had both tacked ship, "Columbia" was close to leeward but with her wind free. Just as she drew ahead of "Shamrock" the latter's topmast collapsed and her club topsail and all its gear came down nearly where "Colum-bia" had been a few minutes before. "Shamrock" withdrew and "Columbia" continued in what must have been a pretty good breeze, for she completed the course of thirty or more miles in three hours and thirty-seven minutes.

The next race was not sailed until October 20. It was a cold, clear day with half a gale of wind blowing from the north which at times got up to over thirty miles per hour. It was a windward and leeward race, the first leg being downwind. "Shamrock" got the start by about a minute, both yachts carrying only their three lower sails, but on the run to leeward Captain Barr succeeded in setting a spinnaker and working topsail so that at the lee-ward mark "Columbia" led by seventeen seconds. The following fifteen-mile beat back was one of the most magnificent thrashes to windward ever witnessed in the larger classes. Perhaps the principal reason "Columbia" went better was that she had cross-cut sails while "Shamrock" had sails with up-and-down cut. Near the end of the race "Shamrock" set a club topsail in a desperate effort to catch "Columbia," but this only made her heel exceedingly without increasing her speed so that "Columbia" won the race by six minutes and thirty-four seconds, corrected time—taking three straight races.

As I have said, it was a cold day, and after the joyous excitement of winning this final race Mrs. Iselin, who raced on "Columbia" throughout the season, persuaded Captain Nat to take a drink, and it is told that this was the only time in his life that he tasted liquor. A photograph shows "Columbia" winning this race and the crew waving their caps and jumping for joy. On the first day that a race was scheduled there was a record fleet of steamers to watch the race but that year revenue cutters and torpedo boats under the command of Captain Robley D. Evans patroled the course so strictly that the excursion steamers were kept about a mile away. After the first few days the fleet dwindled down to a small fleet. No doubt, on account of postponing the races from day to day, many were discouraged. But it always had been the custom for the steam yachts to race back to New York after the finish of the final race, and this time the little "Vamoose," designed by Captain Nat eight years before, led the fleet so Captain Nat was first with both sail and steam.

During these races Mr. Fife, the designer of "Shamrock," was confined to a New York hotel by sickness where Captain Nat called on him to pay his respects. The races had caused unusual public interest, perhaps because in those days there were few other exciting events, as this was before automobile racing and before the American public at large took much interest in horse racing. It is likely also that such picturesque men as J. P. Morgan and Sir Thomas captured the imagination of the average man, for J. P. was one of our greatest Americans since Lincoln and Sir Thomas was an almost mythical figure whom you might say lifted himself with his own bootstraps from a grocery clerk to the owner of an English concern operated along the lines of the original Atlantic and Pacific Tea Company. He was a lieutenant of the

City of London, had been knighted for his charities in London where he supported hospitals for the poor, and was a favorite of King Edward. Those were the days when men could do things and the public gloried in the exploits of these heroes.

At any rate the papers gave the "Columbia" several full pages and many headlines during her building and trials; *The Rudders* of 1899 had many full page pictures of her together with long articles, and the public was worked up to a high pitch of interest. When the telegraphic news of her victory was received in the little town of Bristol where "Columbia" was built, the whistles and bells rang gayly and the citizens were filled with pride at the handiwork of the old town. It probably gave them as much satisfaction as had the return of one of the Bristol Privateers from a successful cruise nearly a hundred years before.

Soon after Captain Nat returned many of the citizens and employees formed a sort of street parade and serenaded the residences of Captain Nat and his brother John. Captain Nat at that time was living at his place called The Farm about a mile out of town, and when the people gathered on the lawn in front of the house, he stood to receive them on a stone step at the front door of this ancient farm house with his youngest son on his shoulders and waved and nodded to his admirers, but his modesty prevented him from making any sort of speech. This serenade was a surprise to Captain Nat but some of the females of the family knew of it and had a barrel of cider on hand at the back of the house to respond with some cordiality to the people who had walked way over from town; and I remember the barrel was empty the next morning.

While this serenade in no way compared with the ovation the city of Boston tendered to General Charles J. Paine and Edward Burgess in ceremonies at Fanueil Hall after they had defended the cup three times, still it was a spontaneous expression of the townspeople's esteem for Captain Nat for his having defended it three times. But he was to go on and successfully defend it three times more as we shall see in succeeding chapters.

That winter about Christmas time the employees of the Herreshoff Manufacturing Company presented Captain Nat with a silver loving cup, so the last months of the nineteenth century certainly were busy and exciting, not only for Captain Nat but, as a matter of fact, for the whole town, which shared in the general acclaim that came to the Bristol builders by whom so many of the townfolk were employed.

CHAPTER ELEVEN

Designs from 1900 to 1910

THE YEAR 1900 certainly was a busy one for the Herreshoff Manufacturing Company, and in some penciled notes that Captain Nat has left he has said: ". . . this was the busiest year of the company." It is true, however, that they had employed more men at times in previous years. I believe somewhere around 1878, when most all of the work was done by hand, they employed around three hundred, and when the steel torpedo boats for the Spanish War were building they employed about two hundred and fifty. But, though the employees in 1900 and the next few years were usually less than two hundred, the production was great. This was because the company had developed certain methods of building that were particularly efficient, and because the works were especially well managed. It seems remarkable today that fifty years earlier such a small crew of men could turn out so much work. You must remember, however, that things were quite different then: the men went to work at seven in the morning and, excepting for the noon hour, worked right through to six at night. I well remember the appearance of the works lit only with open gas lights on the long winter evenings. There were fewer holidays then for the workers of the Herreshoff Manufacturing Company, and as I remember it they were New Years, Fourth of July, Labor Day, Thanksgiving, and Christmas. Of course they worked all day Saturday.

The men of those days were strong and tough; sometimes after this ten-hour day they would work overtime at a slight increase in pay, and I recall one man who worked twenty-four hours straight. This was a sparmaker, Jim Davidson, who made a new mast for one of the Newport Thirties which had carried hers away in a race and wanted a new spar for the next race with, I think, only a day between races. Many of the men neither smoked nor drank and were as hard and muscular as athletes in training. They were able to work hard, and liked it; they could saw or plane continuously for hours without stopping to rest, and that is one of the reasons they built so many yachts in 1900 with a small crew. But they also had the know-how and made every stroke count. They gloried in accomplishing a good day's work, and I glory now in having known and seen these Samsons and Vulcans at work, but I fear the mold they were cast in is lost and that we will never have such accomplishment again.

The workmen at this time were paid less than fifty cents an hour, generally, although the Herreshoff Company at that time was noted for its high rate of pay.

Many of these workmen owned their homes and had good wholesome home-cooked food such as beef stew, salt-fish dinners, boiled dinners, etc. They seemed very happy and certainly liked their work. In the summertime many would arrive at the works an hour beforehand and impatiently wait for the seven o'clock bell, or on Sundays would at times wander down to the works hoping that that boring day would soon pass so that they could get back to the work they liked.

Even though we are able to account for the manner in which the workmen built their yachts so fast in those days, I fear no one will ever account for how Captain Nat got the designs out for them for he certainly designed more yachts than anyone had before or has since, and went into much greater detail. As an example of his great productiveness, at the last of his life the Herreshoff Manufacturing Company had on file about eighteen thousand drawings for most of which he had drawn or laid out the principal proportions in pencil, and he often kept three or four draftsmen inking in his drawings. The models he made would have been a creditable lifework for anyone in quantity alone leaving aside the quality. Although we know that for many years he worked twelve hours a day and most Sundays and holidays, still his accomplishments were amazing. These eighteen thousand drawings of the Herreshoff Manufacturing Company are now at the Massachusetts Institute of Technology, but it is only fair to say that a thousand or so of them were originated by Captain Nat's oldest son, A. Sidney DeW. Herreshoff, and perhaps a hundred or so by others.

In looking over Captain Nat's drawings one cannot help but be impressed with the amount of calculation and concentrated thought that went into them. The cast parts are the best shape for casting, and the forged parts of such shape that rod and plate could be upset or folded into. It is no exaggeration to say that most all of them are extremely ingenious and could have been made only by a person of much experience who could concentrate steadily on his work, and who lived a very long life. After looking over these drawings anyone who can understand them will spontaneously say that Captain Nat deserves even more renown than his reputation has given him.

Among other things the Herreshoff Company was producing many sails at the beginning of the century for they were the principal makers of crosscut sails then. You must realize that they were building many yachts I am not mentioning, for every year they built many small craft, both sail and steam, and some sizable steam yachts which probably would not interest the average reader today, and, besides, I am only telling about the principal yachts that made an impression on my youthful memory—those that had some interesting story connected with them during their life.

The first sizable sailboat turned out in 1899 was the seventy-foot water-line sloop "Athene." She was an able, wholesome yacht which lasted in use about forty years and I believe made a world cruise when she was nearly forty years old. She went in a remarkable race, however, when she was brand new. This was the Puritan Cup Race off Marblehead on June 30, 1900. It blew a living gale from the northwest that day, and when it was time to start, only six yachts showed up with no competitor for the hundred and seven foot water line "Constellation" in the schooner class, so the Regatta Committee started her with the sloops and the race turned out to be a knockdown, drag-out contest between "Constellation" and "Athene." The first leg of the course was from Marblehead to the buoy off Minot's Light, and "Constellation" going down wind wing and wing with her hundred and seven feet of water line left "Athene" behind. The next leg was close hauled to Graves' Whistler and "Athene" passed "Constellation," rounding the buoy several minutes ahead. The last leg was a reach back to Marblehead, and "Constellation" drew ahead again. Twice around the course they went, thirty miles in a howling northwest gale. "Constellation" parted a halyard and "Athene" broke her gaff jaw but they carried on and finished with "Athene" winning seven minutes boat for boat and twenty-four minutes corrected time. As "Athene" approached the finish line she got a heavy knockdown and became partly unmanageable. Although her topmast was housed and she was under jib and mainsail, the water came way up to her hatches; they could not get at the jib sheets to let her up in the wind and had to chop them with an ax. There was a remarkable photograph taken of "Athene" in this race, and no doubt some of the readers have seen it at the Eastern Yacht Club. Although this race was half a century ago, I occasionally talk to two of "Athene"'s crew in that remarkable race. One of them is Llewellyn Howland of Padenarum, who was in the afterguard, and the other is Jonathan Mason of Marblehead who was mastheadsman on "Athene."

Soon after "Athene" in 1900 the Herreshoff Company turned out the one design class of New York Yacht Club seventy-footers. They were:

"Mineola"	August Belmont
"Yankee"	H. P. Whitney and Herman Duryea
"Rainbow"	Cornelius Vanderbilt
"Virginia"	W. K. Vanderbilt

The Seventies' dimensions were:

L.O.A.	106 feet
L.W.L.	70 feet
Beam	19 feet 8 inches
Draft	14 feet
Measured sail area	6000 square feet

They had about forty tons of lead on their keel and carried a crew of fifteen besides the afterguard.

They were practically the size of the "J" boat of the nineteen-thirties but of course were much shorter on the water line as they were built under the old rule where water-line length was the most important factor in the rating. However, their length from the end of the bowsprit to the end of the main boom must have been some twenty feet longer than the length overall of the "J" 's.

The Seventies raced very hard indeed the first year, and it was rough most of the time with hard breezes off Newport so that they got some hard pounding. One of the reasons they were raced hard was that two of them had imported English captains and crew which put the Yankees and Scandinavians of the other two yachts on their toes. "Mineola" had Captain Wringe of the "Shamrock" with an English crew. "Rainbow" had Captain Parker who had been second captain of "Shamrock," also with an English crew, while "Virginia" had Captain Hansen who had been captain of "Vigilant" with a Scandinavian crew. "Yankee" was handled by Herman Duryea, one of her owners and about our best amateur helmsman of the time. She, I believe, had a crew mostly composed of Yankees and did fairly well, but "Mineola" was launched first so Captain Wringe had two or three weeks to get her in trim before "Rainbow" came out. "Virginia" and "Yankee," which came even later, were under still more of a handicap for time to shake down.

During the first season "Mineola" started in thirty-two races, many of which were before the other Seventies came out. Of the twenty-seven races for Seventies she came in first thirteen times; second, eight; third, three; fourth, once. "Rainbow" started in twenty races, was first eight times; second, seven; third, six; fourth, five. "Yankee" started in nineteen races, was first five times; second, six; third, five; fourth, three. "Virginia" started in twenty-one races and was first once; second, six; third, six; fourth, five. I believe at the end of the first year their points figured out: "Mineola," 50; "Yankee," 49; "Rainbow," 45, and "Virginia," 31.

Several of the owners and afterguard of the Seventies, as well as some of the crew, got their training in the hot-racing Newport Thirties, and I can assure you that the Seventies were raced very hard. They were the largest size yacht we have ever had in a one-design class, and it is strange that so few people know about them today. The Seventies have been criticized by some writers of that time as being unsound, of poor design and inferior workmanship, because they sprung out of shape and leaked some, but the truth of the matter is that all yachts built under the old water-line and sail area rule that had long overhangs were difficult to hold in shape, and the Seventies were among the largest of the water-line rule boats that were planked with wood. Such later yachts as the cup boats "Constitution," "Independence," and "Reliance" had complicated internal bracing to hold them in shape. But don't for a minute think the Seventies were of inferior workmanship for they were perhaps among the finest constructed yachts ever built and vastly superior to anything being built today. Their trouble was their long, flat ends. As a result of the structural trouble of the Seventies, which came from their model alone, the New York Yacht Club decided to formulate a new measurement rule which would allow longer water lines and discourage flat ends, so in a way the Seventies were the cause of the New York Yacht Club sponsoring the Universal Rule, which was got up by Captain Nat at their request.

Wire rope trusses were put in the Seventies when they were straightened out and strengthened in the winter of 1900–01. The two trusses were of seven eighths inch plow steel wire and attached to the stem, went under the mast step, then through holes in the floor plates, and finally swung up to attach to the rudder and stern posts. I believe these trusses held the bows of the Seventies down in place after this but they were only raced a few years after and then mostly on Long Island Sound and New York Yacht Club cruises.

After the Seventies Captain Nat on composite yachts always used belly bands, or straps running from bow to stern each side of the keel, although all of his later composite yachts built under the Universal Rule were of a model that had inherent fore and aft stiffness. In fact in smaller yachts of more modern shape the bow is apt to sag and the sheer raise amidships, a condition exactly the opposite to what happened to the Seventies.

Before finishing with the seventy-footers I will mention that they once sailed one of the fastest triangular races ever recorded for yachts of any size. This was off Newport in heavy weather on July 21, 1900, when they covered a triangular thirty-mile course with an eleven-mile beat to windward in two hours and forty-five minutes. Surely the Seventies were raced hard. An amusing story is told about Captain Nat at this time as part of a conversation with Mr. Gay, owner of "Athene." She was built just before the Seventies, or in the fall of 1899. She was a centerboarder of about eleven-feet draft, and a good wholesome yacht with bulwarks around her deck, and not an extreme racer, while the New York Yacht Club Seventies were out-and-out racers which drew perhaps fifteen feet of water. Well, Mr. Gay said to Captain Nat, "Mr. Herreshoff, isn't there some condition when the "Athene" could beat the new Seventies?," to which Captain Nat replied, "Yes, where there is less than fifteen feet of water." In other words "Athene" did not have a ghost of a chance, and I only tell this to show how short spoken Captain Nat was and to show that his few words were at times combined with some humor.

This same year Captain Nat designed a quite remarkable small steam yacht for August Belmont to act as a tender to the "Mineola." She was named "Scout," and eventually the Herreshoff Company built seven of these fast steamers which were generally referred to as the Scout Class. They were all built on the same molds and had the same power plants but varied in length some fourteen feet, and, as I recall it, varied in speed from about twenty to twenty-one and a half miles per hour. They were as follows:

1900	"Scout"	81 feet	August Belmont, tender to "Mineola"
1900	"Mirage"	81 feet	Cornelius Vanderbilt tender to "Rainbow"
1901	"Tramp"	81 feet	William O. Gay, tender to "Athene"
1901	"Zinganee"	81 feet	William H. Moore
1901	"Stroller"	81 feet	G. T. Rafferty
1901	Niagara II	81 feet	Howard Gould
1902	"Express"	89 feet 3 inches	M. F. Plant; afterward named "Mermaid" and owned for several years by J. P. Morgan, Jr.
1906	"Sisilina"	95 feet	Nathan Straus

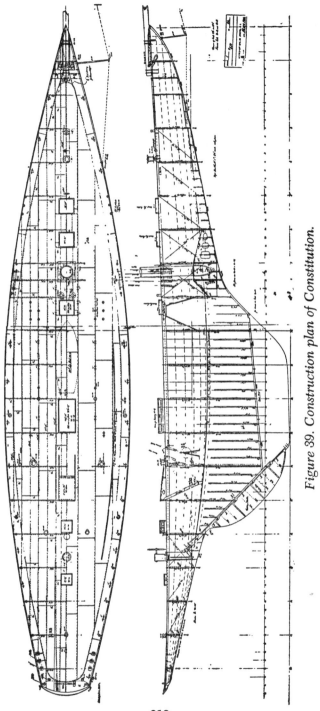

Figure 39. Construction plan of Constitution.

219

These were extremely smooth running yachts that were fine sea boats and economical in fuel consumption. Some of them lasted quite a long time and they were the forerunners in construction and general arrangement of many gasoline launches built by several builders.

Captain Nat also designed the two sister yachts "Shark" and "Altair" in 1900. They were seventy-four feet overall, forty-five feet water line, fourteen feet three inches beam, and ten feet four inches draft. They were very similar in model and sail plan to the Seventies, but smaller. The spreaders of these yachts were well below the gaff jaws, a feature adopted later on some English yachts, for this supports the masthead better.

The next year, 1901, Captain Nat designed a very similar yacht named "Humma." She had two sets of swinging spreaders, one supported the masthead and the other the topmast. She was a very handsome boat and was sometimes called the "Little Constitution," for "Constitution" also had the same spreader arrangement and was built the same year. "Humma" was built for J. Rogers Maxwell but was afterward owned by R. W. Emmons and was a remarkable boat of her day.

In the fall of 1900 Sir Thomas Lipton again challenged for the cup, so soon after a syndicate headed by August Belmont and including Oliver H. Payne, F. G. Bourne, James Stillman, and Henry Walters ordered a new cup boat from the Herreshoff Company. This yacht, which was named "Constitution," was one of Captain Nat's best designs and the first yacht, or, for that matter, vessel, that was built with the so-called longitudinal form of construction, which means she had her frames running fore and aft. This longitudinal framing is supported, or held in place, by deep web frames which, of course, hold the vessel in perfect shape as far as her sections are concerned. This is the lightest known system of framing because the continuous longitudinals make a bridge structure or girder of the hull, while the deep section web frames will resist athwartship strains far better than numerous shallow frames, and these are the reasons why, fifty years after the "Constitution," almost all scientifically built steamers are constructed this way. It would be no exaggeration to say the bodies of all large airplanes, wood or metal, are now of the same construction. Captain Nat's later cup boats "Reliance" and "Reso-lute" also had longitudinal framing.

While the greatest advances in the design of "Constitution" were structural, her model, as we look at it today, would appear also better than "Reliance" for light and medium weather, par-ticularly if there was a choppy head sea. While the public and all writers of that time think Captain Nat made a failure in "Consti-tution" because "Columbia" was chosen to defend the cup in 1901, Captain Nat always thought "Constitution" the best of his large cup boats—better than "Columbia" or "Reliance"—and the general public has overlooked the fact that "Constitution" easily beat "Columbia" in 1903 when both "Columbia" and "Constitu-tion" were trial horses for "Reliance." The fact remains that Charlie Barr was captain of "Columbia" in 1901 and captain of "Reliance" in 1903, but it is my opinion that if he had been cap-tain of "Constitution" either of these years she would have won out and perhaps defended the cup twice. "Constitution" also had many refinements in rig, including worm gear backstay winches worked from below deck.

Butler Duncan was in charge of "Constitution" and had been in charge of "Defender" in 1899 when she had been trial horse for "Columbia." Mr. Duncan was a thorough seaman with a Navy training, but perhaps not as mechanically minded as was best on a bag of new tricks like "Constitution," although he was one of the best all-around sportsmen and sailors we ever had. "Constitu-tion" also had for captain Uriah Rhodes, who had been captain of "Defender" in 1899, while "Columbia" that year had the almost unbeatable combination of J. P. Morgan and E. D. Mor-gan for owners, E. D. Morgan as manager, with Charlie Barr for captain, and a remarkably well-trained crew, many of whom had been with him on "Columbia" in the previous cup races.

While the only close racing that year of 1901 was between "Columbia" and "Constitution," the Boston millionaire Thomas W. Lawson built from B. B. Crowninshield's design the trial cup boat "Independence" which raced in eight races, six against "Columbia" and "Constitution," and two against "Columbia" alone. The "Independence" came in last every time because she was slow in light weather and broke down in a breeze, although the Bostonians made quite a noise because she once sailed one leg of a course in better time than her rivals. During the season "Columbia" and "Constitution" raced together twenty-two times but only eighteen of these races were finished within the time limit, and each yacht won nine times. Because "Constitution" had done poorly in the last of the season the cup defense committee decided to choose "Columbia" as the most dependable yacht, in which case they were quite right, but undoubtedly if the whole crew and afterguard of the two yachts had changed at the beginning of the season things would have been quite different.

In the middle of that season both "Columbia" and "Constitution" ordered new mainsails from the Herreshoff Company, but as they could make only one of the large sails at a time, and because there was no other sail loft at that time that could make a suitable crosscut sail of that size, the brothers J. B. and N. G. Herreshoff had an embarrassing decision to make. On the one hand naturally Captain Nat favored making the sail for his new boat "Constitution," and on the other hand he did not want to turn down his old friend, E. D. Morgan. Also it was not tactful to disappoint J. P. Morgan, but the sail or sails were made for "Constitution" notwithstanding, and partly as a result of this J. P. a few years after encouraged or arranged with Ratsey to open a loft in this country which perhaps on the whole has been a good thing.

But to go back to "Constitution" and her new sails. Butler Duncan had persuaded the Herreshoffs to make them of heavier sailcloth than the first suit and they proved too heavy and dead and that, together with the "Constitution" carrying away her mast and making her crew jumpy afterward, accounted for her going poorly in the last of the season. The strangest and most unfortunate part of it was that "Columbia," when she sailed in the final cup races against "Shamrock II," had only old stretched-out sails and she nearly lost the last race as a result of this for on this day there was a dry, light northerly wind and the head of "Columbia"'s sail had stretched out longer than the gaff. But Captain Charlie Barr and the sail maker from Bristol, Mr. Hathaway, were up very early that morning and had seized the peak of "Columbia" 's sail as far out on the gaff as was possible, while, I believe, at the throat they puckered or made a fold in the headrope.

Now I must say something about "Shamrock II" for she was considered a very fast boat and a remarkably good design which is no wonder as she was designed by George Watson who was the best designer in Europe, if not the world, and if Captain Nat did usually beat him with racing sailboats, Watson certainly was supreme with the large steam yachts. Although this was a long time ago "Shamrock" 's model, or development models, were carefully tank tested. "Shamrock" was plated with a then new alloy called "immadium," which was very light for its strength. She had rather a flat model with a deep keel and large sail area, fourteen thousand square feet or more. Her dimensions compared with "Columbia" were as follows:

	"Shamrock II"	"Columbia"
L.O.A.	137 feet	131 feet
L.W.L.	89 feet 3 inches	89 feet 8 inches
Beam	24 feet 6 inches	24 feet
Draft	20 feet	19 feet 3 inches
Sail Area	14,027 square feet	13,135 square feet

The two yachts rated nearly the same with "Shamrock" allowing "Columbia" less than a minute over a thirty mile course. The two captains of "Shamrock" were Wringe and Sycamore. Wringe had been on "Shamrock I" and Sycamore on "Valkyrie III." They were both able, experienced men who had raced over the Sandy Hook courses before.

The first race was started on September 26, 1901 but called off on account of lack of wind with "Columbia" about a mile in the lead. The second attempt was made on September 28 in a moderate breeze of approximately ten or twelve knots and smooth sea with the course a windward and leeward one. After some jockeying before the start, the two yachts went over the line almost together, "Shamrock" having a lead of only two seconds for Charlie Barr had now met his match and could not fool with "Shamrock II" as he had with "Constitution." The beat to the windward mark was extremely close and exciting with "Shamrock" rounding the weather mark forty-one seconds ahead, but much to the surprise of every one "Columbia" passed her rival on the run to the finish and beat her thirty-five seconds boat-to-boat, thus winning without time allowance one of the most interesting races for the spectators ever sailed. Another attempt was made on October 1 but the race was called off for lack of wind.

On October 3 they were sent over a triangular course in a breeze of twelve or more knots at the start, and for some reason "Columbia" made a very bad start, being one minute and thirty-four seconds behind "Shamrock II," but during the first two legs of the course "Columbia" gained slightly so that at the second mark she was only forty-two seconds behind. On the last leg, which was to windward in a good breeze of fifteen or more knots, Charlie Barr and "Columbia" did some remarkably good sailing so that "Columbia" crossed the finish line one minute and eighteen seconds ahead of "Shamrock."

The next and last race was a windward and leeward one in a moderate offshore breeze, the first leg being to leeward so that both yachts hung back at the start each hoping to blanket her rival on the first part of the run, but "Shamrock" went slightly the best to leeward and rounded the mark forty-nine seconds ahead. The beat back to the finish line in a dying breeze was extremely close and as they approached the finish line the two yachts were actually lapped making the closest finish perhaps that had ever been witnessed in the larger classes over a long course. "Shamrock" was two seconds ahead boat-to-boat, but as she had to allow "Columbia" forty-three seconds, the latter won by forty-one seconds, taking three straight races in the closest contested match that had ever been held for the America's Cup.

This made the fourth time one of Captain Nat's yachts had defended the cup but it was too close to be much of a victory over George Watson. Of the ninety miles the yachts had raced, not counting the crooked courses in tacking to windward, "Columbia" only covered this distance in three minutes and thirty-six seconds less time than "Shamrock II." Some of my young readers might like to know what Watson's excuse was for not winning, and I must say he expressed it in a few words when he said, "Herreshoff did not have a test tank." Apparently "Shamrock II"'s wave action and behavior was different from what the tank tests had indicated, or perhaps he meant that if he had not wasted time fooling around with tank tests but had devoted the effort to improvements in construction and rig he would have been further ahead. It is said that Watson tested no less than eleven models in Denny's tank at Dumbarton where the "Shamrock" was built, and made about sixty changes in shape while developing the lines for "Shamrock II." But I never knew Captain Nat to make more than one model for his larger yachts and when he was cutting the model, which he always did very quickly, he seemed to know exactly what shape he desired, and I believe this knowledge all came from his observations of full-size craft.

There is no doubt "Columbia" would have done better if her sails had not been old and overstretched, but one of the things Charlie Barr was most proud of in after life was that he had defended the cup in 1901 so economically. He used to say, "Yes, Mr. Morgan and I defended the cup in 'Columbia' the second time for much less expense than it had ever been done before or since." You see Captain Barr had laid the "Columbia" up in 1899 and, when in 1901 he fitted her out with many of the same crew, there were no changes or alterations found necessary. Charlie Barr was a sober, canny Scot who always looked out for the interest of his owners, and besides, when "Columbia" needed new sails, she could not get them so they undoubtedly went through the season with very trifling expense for such men as J. P. and E. D. Morgan. Possibly the cost was some twenty thousand dollars and much in variance with what some people think it costs to defend the cup.

I must say Captain Barr was much impressed with J. P. Morgan. Although he had been captain for several other remarkable men and raced against Prince Edward and Kaiser Wilhelm, he thought Mr. Morgan much the largest caliber of them all. When J. P. Morgan's name was mentioned he would say, "There; there is a man for you." I believe J. P. Morgan had a kindly glint in his burning, diamond eyes for those who did things well. For Mr. E. D. Morgan Captain Barr had that great respect and affection that comes between people who have succeeded in a great accomplishment.

As for J. P. Morgan and Captain Nat, well, a short time before Mr. Morgan's death, or in about 1912, J. P. invited, or perhaps ordered, Captain Nat to come down to see him. When in after years I questioned Captain Nat about that interview about all he would say was, "Mr. Morgan was such a strong-minded man that the doctors did not mind telling him he had but a short time to live, so he had me down to talk over old times." I can imagine, however, the conversation was not very lively as neither of them was ever a talkative person, and the subject of how the "Columbia" beat the "Constitution" was never a popular one with Captain Nat.

Mr. E. D. Morgan was of about the same age as Captain Nat and lived nearly as long so that they were close friends for almost half a century. There have been few handsomer or more kindly men than E. D. Morgan; not only was he our number one yachtsman of all time, but also a most sincere friend to all his large number of acquaintances.

Most people now considered Captain Nat the premier yacht designer of the world. He had led in America since Edward Burgess' death in 1891, and now that he had beaten Watson three times and Fife once he had defeated the best that Europe or Scotland could offer. When one considers the success Captain Nat had in all sizes from small centerboarders to torpedo boats, and realizes that he designed the power plants for all his steamers, it would seem that he justly deserved that title.

While most of the yachts built by the Herreshoff Manufacturing Company in 1902 were steam or rather small sail yachts, they did build the one-design class of Buzzards Bay thirty-footers. There were twelve of these and their dimensions were: L.O.A., forty-six feet six inches; L.W.L., thirty feet; beam, ten feet ten inches; draft, five feet four inches; weight of lead about ten thousand pounds; S.A. one thousand three hundred and twenty-five square feet. They were centerboarders for the shallow waters of Buzzards Bay, and originally set a small club topsail from their masthead which was run up a little above the peak halyards and jib stay. They may be distinguished from the Bar Harbor Thirties by this peculiarity. Some of the Buzzards Bay Thirties are still going and make good cruisers with their shallow draft if the rig has been reduced and modernized.

Two other fine little racers built that year were the almost sister ships "Bobtail" and "Alert," both bright mahogany and very pretty excepting they had rather short sterns, as the name "Bobtail" suggests. They both won many important races during their lives. "Bobtail" was built for Edgar Scott, and "Alert" for J. W. Alker.

Two other fine, wholesome sailboats of 1902 were "Trivia," built for Harold S. Vanderbilt (the first yachts of his that I remember having built at Bristol), and "Azor," built for J. M. Forbes, which made her home port Naushon Island in Buzzards Bay for several years.

Another nearly identical yacht, "Nellie," was built for Morton F. Plant in 1903. Their principal dimensions were L.O.A., forty-six feet; L.W.L., thirty-four feet; beam, twelve feet three inches; draft, six feet; and these three were among the nicest all-around sail boats of their size ever built. I believe one or two of them are still sailing now, nearly fifty years later, "Nellie" afterward having the names of "Ishkoodah" and "Butterfly."

Captain Nat's own ninety-four foot steam yacht "Roamer" also came out in 1902, a picture of which I have shown in Chapter VII. And this reminds me to say something more about his steam engine designs. At about the turn of the century, or perhaps between 1898 and 1904, he brought out several sizes of very compact steam engines, partly in an effort to keep the engine room on a steamer as small or short as was possible with the internal combustion engine, which was just coming into use. These engines were what were called triple expansion steeple engines and had the low pressure cylinder above the high pressure and intermediate cylinders. Not only in this way was he able to make the engine extremely short, but by having an uneven spacing of the crankpins, he was able to make an engine that was almost perfectly balanced. In fact these engines were nearly vibrationless.

When some of the first of these engines were made they were set up in the machine shop on a bed or mattress of coil springs. By having a paper mounted on a disk at each end of the crankshaft when the engine was run under steam at various speeds, by bringing a lead pencil in contact with the paper disks, a perfect record was made to show which side of the crankshaft needed correction in counterbalance. One of the remarkable features of these engines was that the crankshaft was of cast steel with hollow

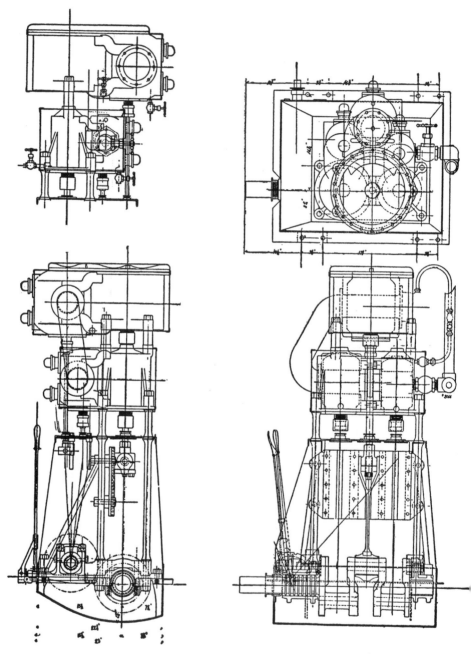

Figure 40. Triple expansion steeple engine.

crankpins, and the counterbalance weights cast on—a system now being adopted by the builders of many automotive engine. I think all engines built by the Ford Company are that way now, or half a century later than the engines of which I am speaking.

Of course these engines had the valves at one side, actuated by a separate crankshaft, as his earlier engines were arranged. This was a feature that made this short-coupled arrangement possible as well as greatly simplifying the reverse mechanism. Not only did the extreme shortness of these engines save space and make the solution of the vibration problem possible, but the length of the receiver pipes that conducted the steam from

Figure 41. Hollow cast steel crankshaft with counterbalances, thrust bearing and drive gear integral.

one cylinder to the other was so shortened that much loss of heat was prevented and the engine room was consequently much cooler.

These engines had enclosed crank cases with splash lubrication, and many novel and ingenius features that simplified the casting, machining, and setting up of the engines, which were made in at least four sizes. Captain Nat was fifty-two years old in 1900 and perhaps nearly at the peak of his genius, but still adding to his knowledge through his own experiments and experience with the engines and yachts of his own design.

In those days the challenges for the America's Cup came in rapid succession, and Sir Thomas challenged again on October 7, 1902, two years and five days after his previous challenge and approximately four years after his first. Sir Thomas certainly must have spent a lot of money in those days but we must remember the average shipyard worker in Scotland was only paid about a pound a week then, while over here the pay was probably three times as much. This time Sir Thomas switched back to Fife as designer, and the new challenger was named "Shamrock III." She was built at the Denny yard in Dumbarton, as "Shamrock II" had been. Denny was a good size shipyard in those days and employed about four thousand workmen. They had become famous for building fast passenger steamers, and they made their own power plants. They also built ocean steamers, but on account of shallow water in the proximity of their yard did not build steamers of the largest class. They had, I believe, the first privately owned model test tank, which along with its apparatus had been designed by no less a person than the eminent Professor William Froud and built about 1880. This test tank was three hundred feet long, twenty feet wide, and ten feet deep, and although most of its recording apparatus is ingeniously simple I doubt if any later tank has given more accurate indications.

However, Fife did not use the tank much in developing "Shamrock III," but rather depended on his experience with past full-size yachts. Though, as a matter of fact, he had not had as much experience as Watson with the larger yachts, nevertheless, all of the Fifes were among the world's best designers. Denny had been building steamers since 1814, and by 1900 was building the fastest cross-channel steamers, some of which went well over twenty-four miles per hour, and they were the first builders of turbine-driven steamers, the "King Edward" and "Queen Alexandria," which came out in 1901. Denny had recently built James Gordon Bennett's three-hundred-foot steam yacht "Lysistrata," generally considered the finest yacht ever built, or likely to be built while this present leveling process continues.

So the little Herreshoff Manufacturing Company, with its perhaps two hundred workers, a drafting force of four, and only one real designer would appear like David tackling Goliath. But we will see how Yankee ingenuity made up for the difference in might.

"Shamrock III" in model resembled an enlarged "Columbia," although being painted differently may appear quite different to the uninitiated. She undoubtedly was a fine job of building but lacked almost entirely the sail-handling devices so numerous on "Reliance" and which were to make the reporters of that time think the English crew slow in handling her sails. "Shamrock III" was plated with steel, both above and below water, and this may have been a handicap to her as few anti-fouling paints can be rubbed down to as hard and smooth a surface as polished bronze. No doubt "Shamrock III" was a fast yacht and might have beaten an enlarged or improved "Columbia." She proved to be very fast in the trial races she had with "Shamrock I," and all of Great Britain was very enthusiastic about her, and even over here many people thought Sir Thomas would win the cup this time.

As for "Reliance," as the new cup defender was named, she was ordered in time enough so there was no particular hurry in her building. She was ordered by a syndicate of New York Yacht Club members, including Elbert H. Gary, Clement A. Griscom, James J. Hill, C. Oliver Iselin, William B. Leeds, Norman B. Ream, William Rockefeller, Cornelius Vanderbilt, Henry Walters, and P. A. B. Widener, all very well-to-do men. Although Captain Nat thus had almost unlimited financial backing, I believe "Reliance" only cost about $175,000. I doubt if she could be duplicated today for a million, for she was very intricate and special all over.

Mr. Iselin was selected to be manager of "Reliance" and he tried to persuade Captain Nat to make her an out-and-out scow as that type was becoming successful in the smaller classes under the length on water-line and sail-area rules, but Captain Nat compromised in developing a model that was as long overall as the scows but had finely modeled, graceful ends so that her mid-body gave the stability to carry an extremely large rig while her ends seemed to allow her to slip along easily in light weather. I remember well watching my father cut this model and he did most of it in two evenings, but he was an extremely fast worker. He seemed to have no hesitancy about shaping the model and seemed to know beforehand exactly what shape was wanted to best do the job, which is quite in contrast to some later designers who seem to be feeling around in the dark as they have made and tested various models of quite different shapes.

But although I think the model of "Reliance" is the finest and most highly developed of any water-line and sail-area yacht, still

I cannot help feeling her very scientifically constructed hull and its ingenious fittings, together with the amazingly light spars and rig, contributed most to her speed. If the British designers were using test tanks Captain Nat certainly was using testing machines for proving the strength of materials. He had at his disposal three —one small one in the model room of his home, the medium-sized one in the machine shop, and a large one in a building near the machine shop. Many of the fittings for "Reliance" and some of the rigging, after it was made up, were proof tested, but the knowledge gained by Captain Nat in testing parts to destruction during many years armed him with a knowledge that was ever so much more definite than the vague indications of the test tank.

It may interest some of my readers to know how he gauged or measured the strains that were developed in the rigging of "Reliance" when she was sailing. Well, he had two clips clamped on the wire or shroud that he wanted to test; the clips were about six inches apart, and by measuring the change in distance between them he could calculate the strain that was on the wire for he had previously tested that wire, or a piece of it, in the testing machine and recorded its stretch under different strains. Of course the measuring was done with a micrometer. He had to be held in place while making these measurements when the yacht was heeling much or it was rough for it takes both hands to use the micrometer. Of course today the Navy and Air Force have strain gauges that were developed when the dirigibles were being built around 1925, but there is no doubt that Captain Nat had more data on the strains that were developed in the large racing yachts than anyone.

"Reliance" was launched on the afternoon of April 12, being christened by Miss Nora Iselin, daughter of Mrs. C. Oliver Iselin who had christened "Defender" and "Columbia," so that if "Reliance" were to be the fourth cup defender Captain Nat designed she was also to be the third christened by and managed by an Iselin. As "Reliance" went down the ways she nearly filled the doorway of the building shed. Her bow had been decorated with festoons of holly and carnations, and at the very stemhead was a large stuffed American eagle.

This premeditated and practical early launching of a new cup boat gave more time for practice races than usual and the summer of 1903 saw more races of the large sloops than has ever been witnessed in America before or since for, besides "Reliance" with Charlie Barr as Captain and Mr. Iselin as manager, there was "Constitution" with Captain Rhodes, and Mr. Belmont as manager, while Mr. E. D. Morgan very sportingly fitted out the old "Columbia" with "Lem" Miller as captain.

In these days, it would be impossible to find a crew suitable for one of these large sloops, and even in 1903 there were hardly enough trained and experienced men to go around, but Captain Barr with his reputation was able to gather together a crew of Scandinavians who were remarkably good, and under his mate Chris Christensen were soon trained to act almost like a machine. While "Reliance" was building, Captain Barr studied her construction and watched her many winches and fittings as they were being made in the machine shop so that he knew how to use them and tried hard to use them in the way that they were intended to be used, which was quite different from some other captains who have tried to use new devices as older ones had been used.

A great deal of "Reliance"'s gear was worked from below deck and, besides a very remarkable mainsheet arrangement, she had, I think, about nine winches below deck including two jib sheet winches, two fore staysail sheet winches, one topmast hoisting winch, two lower backstay winches. Some of these winches were extremely ingenious: they were two speed and self-releasing for the wire sheets or backstays wound directly on drums in these winches. In their construction Captain Nat used worm gears, multiple disk clutches, and ball bearings, and you must remember this was when the automobile industry was in its infancy and such things were not at all common, and of course had to be designed special throughout. They were self-releasing by simply reversing the direction the cranks revolved. It may interest my readers to know that some of these self-same winches which were made for "Constitution" and "Reliance" were afterward used on "Resolute," "Enterprise," "Rainbow," and "Ranger," as well as some duplicates made by the Herreshoff Manufacturing Company for "Vanitie" "Yankee," and "Weetamoe," and no one else has yet equaled their design.

"Reliance" also had an ingenious rudder and steering gear. The rudder was plated of thin bronze sheets over a frame, but at its lower part there was a small hole which let water in or out of its interior. Her rudder post was hollow, or had a hole through it, so that by having a valve at the head of the rudder post air could be forced down into the hollow rudder blade with a foot pump similar to the ones used to inflate pneumatic tires. With this arrangement the water could be forced out of the rudder or let in as occasion required. If she steered hard, water was let into the rudder blade so its weight relieved the steering; but if she had a tendency to head off, then more air was forced into the blade.

"Reliance" had two wheels on her steering gear so if necessary the helmsman could be relieved by one or two people without interfering with one another. She had a very effective and neat brake also on the steering gear that was operated by the foot of the helmsman pressing on pedals located on either side of the steering gear, and that is a great relief to a helmsman in a long race, for after he has turned the wheel he can hold the helm almost automatically by foot pressure and still instantly release it.

"Reliance"'s topmast when housed ran clear to the mast step through her hollow steel mast, and when hoisted in place was held at the heel by several steel ratchets which automatically fell in place as the topmast reached the proper level. But to describe all of her unique construction, fittings, and rigging would take many pages.

You must remember that "Shamrock III" and "Reliance" were the last of the great single stickers built under the length and sail-area rules, and they were nearly the last large racers built without any scantling restrictions, or restrictions on construction, so that Captain Nat had full opportunity to go to the limit in light construction. Many people say "Reliance" was the most scientifically designed sailing vessel ever built and that some of her parts compare in strength for weight with the best aeronautical practice of today. It is very probable that "Reliance" had

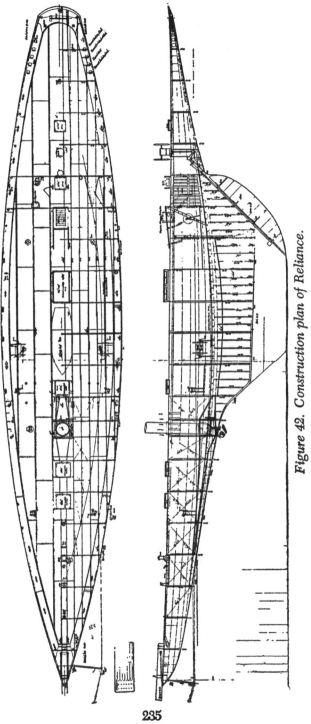

Figure 42. Construction plan of Reliance.

the lightest rig for her sail area of any boat ever built, but nevertheless with Captain Barr as her captain she went through the season with no other structural trouble than the topmast settling a little in its socket which was easily and quickly corrected.

During the season of 1903 the three big sloops, "Columbia," "Constitution," and "Reliance" raced together many times for they were all in commission early, but during the summer the races ended in tiresome monotony with "Reliance" first, "Constitution" second, and "Columbia" last, which, besides making "Reliance" an easy choice as defender for the year, definitely showed that "Constitution" could beat "Columbia" regularly when Captain Barr was not aboard "Columbia," conclusively proving that "Constitution" was a great improvement in design over "Columbia," and vindicating Captain Nat's claim that the "Constitution" was the better boat. Most writers of yachting history have overlooked the results of 1903 when "Constitution" definitely beat "Columbia."

I give you below the length and sail area of the cup boats since "Puritan" as an example.

	L.W.L.	S.A.
"Puritan"	81.01 feet	8,000 square feet
"Mayflower"	85.06 feet	8,600 square feet
"Volunteer"	85.11 feet	9,271 square feet
"Vigilant"	86 feet	11,272 square feet
"Defender"	88.05 feet	12,602 square feet
"Columbia"	89.08 feet	13,135 square feet
"Reliance"	89.08 feet	16,160 square feet

During the season of 1903 the three big yachts had one race in heavy weather with quite a sea running: this was off Newport on July 1. The three started on the windward leg under lower sails only, but on this leg the gaff of "Constitution" collapsed leaving "Columbia" and "Reliance" to fight it out. "Reliance" turned the weather mark only about two minutes ahead of old "Columbia." On the next leg Mr. E. D. Morgan very sportingly set a topsail and was running up a jib topsail when "Columbia" suddenly ran her bow under taking green water on deck which washed four men overboard. Then with remarkably good seamanship "Columbia" maneuvered around and picked up three of the men. The fourth man was never seen again, and this so upset Mr. Morgan that he raced "Columbia" rather halfheartedly the rest of the season. And I must say it was wrong to race these big racing machines in such weather for, while a wave can sweep a knockabout without much danger or inconvenience, it is quite another matter at the speed of the larger yachts, and these yachts without bulwarks or other protection are very dangerous under these conditions. At any rate "Reliance" was chosen to defend the cup, and on account of coming out early and racing in many races, she and her crew were in remarkably good condition to do the work.

We shall now turn to "Shamrock III." As I have said before, Sir Thomas brought over "Shamrock I" to act as a pacemaker, so that the two "Shamrock"s could practice and train in the waters off Sandy Hook, the race course. Sir Thomas must have spent much money that year for, besides towing "Shamrock III" over with his large steam yacht "Erin," he had "Shamrock I" towed over by the large English seagoing tug "Cruizer," so that he had under his pay quite an armada with these crews. Besides, "Shamrock II" was still in storage at Erie Basin, so we might say he had five large yachts and vessels in America then. In their races "Shamrock I" and "III" were reported to make phenominal speed, and at the time of the final cup races it is said "Shamrock III" went to the line in perfect shape, so that it was expected to be a close contest although it turned out otherwise.

The first race of the international series was called off on account of light weather after the yachts were some halfway around the course, but on the twenty-second of August—the anniversary of the day on which "America" had originally won the cup —the two yachts started in a good southwest breeze and clear sky. The course was a windward and leeward one of fifteen miles and return. At the start there was a breeze of fifteen or sixteen miles per hour and both yachts had medium club topsails and baby jib topsails set. For the first hour of this race the two yachts were remarkably close with "Shamrock III" going to windward unusually well in the choppy sea and rather strong breeze. The strength of the wind can be gauged by the fact that both yachts took in their jib topsails on the first part of this weather leg, but when they rounded the weather mark "Reliance" had a lead of approximately three minutes. "Reliance" seemed to go well down wind with her large spinnaker and balloon jib set, so that she crossed the finish line nine minutes ahead and beat "Shamrock" seven minutes and nine seconds corrected time in the first race.

The second race was a triangular one sailed also in quite a fresh southwest breeze which at one time on the first leg had both yachts' rails under. At the first mark "Reliance" was a little over one minute ahead, but on the next leg, which was a reach, she gained more than another minute. On the last leg, as they were approaching the finish, "Reliance" ran into light weather and it looked for a while as if "Shamrock III" would catch her, but she in turn slowed down near the finish line so that "Reliance" was able to beat her with corrected time of one minute, nineteen seconds. Although both yachts were almost becalmed near the finish this was an unusually fast race with both yachts covering the thirty-mile triangle in about three hours and a quarter. After this good showing of "Shamrock III" many people looked forward with great interest to see the next race with betting again quite even.

The first attempt at the third race failed on account of dying wind with "Reliance" crossing the finish line six minutes and thirty-seven seconds after the time limit had expired. She had, however, a very big lead, perhaps quarter of an hour over "Shamrock." For several days after this the races were held up by an easterly storm and thick weather which brought with it a heavy ground swell, but at the first opportunity, when it had cleared, another attempt was made. The wind again was too light so that the race was called off with "Reliance" miles ahead. The next two days proved thick fog with no wind, so that the cup contest had dragged on so long the crews and afterguard of the two contending yachts were almost distracted by the tension they were under waiting in the fog and dreary weather back of the Horseshoe at Sandy Hook. Finally there came a day with a moderate southwest wind and fair visibility at the time of the start, and although there was quite a slop of a sea running, which was a disadvantage to as flat a model as "Reliance," still she succeeded in beating "Shamrock" about eleven minutes to the first mark of this windward and leeward course.

On the run back to the finish line the wind remained light, but about half an hour after "Shamrock III" rounded the mark a thick fog settled on the race course so that both yachts were shut off from view of the spectator fleet. However, "Reliance" was rapidly leaving "Shamrock" behind when last seen, and both yachts were rolling considerably in the cross sea and light wind that was not strong enough to keep spinnakers and mainsails full. After a while the yachts at the finish line began to hear the rattling of light sails and suddenly "Reliance" appeared out of the fog headed exactly for the finish line. She was carrying her balloon jib and appeared like a gigantic pyramid as fog shrouded her hull and lower parts. She crossed the finish line the winner, four hours and twenty-six minutes after the start, but poor "Shamrock III" somehow or other was lost in the fog. She did not appear again until about half an hour after "Reliance" had finished when she showed up several miles to the northeast of the finish line where her tender, the tug "Cruizer," took her in tow and she never crossed the finish line at all. Thus ended the International races of 1903 with "Reliance" winning three straight races—in fact "Reliance" was practically an unbeaten yacht for I believe she won every race that she started in excepting one when she dropped out because of topmast trouble. This made the fifth time that one of Captain Nat's yachts had defended the cup; it was the fourth time that Mr. Iselin had managed a cup defender, and the third time that Charlie Barr had been captain of a defender, and the experience of all these men contributed to the remarkable record of "Reliance" going through the season with no breakdown or accident. Captain Nat sailed on "Reliance" in the final races and he and his family lived aboard his steam yacht "Roamer" which stayed at Sandy Hook during this long drawn-out series of races.

As "Shamrock III" and "Reliance" were the largest sloops, or single-masted vessels ever built, I will give some of their dimensions which will seem strange to some of my younger readers who never saw the yachts of forty or more years ago.

	"Shamrock III"	"Reliance"
Length on water line	89.78 feet	89.66 feet
Length over all	134.42 feet	149.68 feet
End of bowsprit to end of main boom	187.54 feet	201.76 feet
Racing length or rating	104.37 feet	108.39 feet
Measured sail area	14,154.23 square feet	16,159.45 square feet
Number of crew	56	64

"Reliance" 's spinnaker boom was 83.75 feet long which certainly must seem strange to many sailors of today who are used to spinnaker poles of six or eight feet. Her mainsails, of which there were six made (four of triple 0 duck, and two of four 0 duck), were the largest single sails ever made of heavy hand-stitched duck, although lighter sails, such as spinnakers and balloon jibs, which were sewn with sewing machines, have had larger area. The dimensions of "Reliance" 's mainsails were, luff, seventy-two feet three inches; head, sixty-nine feet four inches; foot, one hundred and twelve feet; leach, one hundred and thirty-nine feet seven inches. These mainsails were made of duck twenty-two inches wide, and as each seam was double sewn besides all the reinforcements around the edges there must have been several miles of hand stitching on each sail. It is likely that one of these mainsails would cost, in 1950, around twenty thousand dollars apiece. Four 0 duck was the heaviest sailcloth made and the weight used on the six-masted coal carriers of that time whose largest sails, nevertheless, were only perhaps one quarter the area of "Reliance" 's mainsails.

"Reliance" 's jib was one hundred and twenty-six feet on the luff, ninety-one feet on leach, fifty-four feet on foot, and used a three quarter inch plow steel luff rope strong enough to lift out of the water a whole fleet of the modern democratic yachts. Her balloon jib was made of only six and one quarter ounce Wamsutta twill, forty inches wide, which seems remarkably light for such a large sail measuring one hundred and sixty-six feet six inches on the luff, one hundred and forty-seven feet on leach, and one hundred and five feet on foot. The spinnaker was also of six and one quarter ounce Wamsutta twill, forty inches wide and measured as follows: luff, one hundred and seventy-nine feet five inches, leach one hundred and fifty-nine feet, foot one hundred and three feet four inches.

"Reliance" was undoubtedly the largest and most scientifically designed sailing machine ever built, and probably the fastest single-hulled yacht ever built. It is said she got up to sixteen miles an hour at times, but her average speed certainly was not great compared to her size or compared to the more modern yachts with less wetted surface and high narrow sails. However, it is difficult to compare her speed with the modern yacht because at that time the marks of the race course were laid out each day by seagoing tugs which apparently dropped the mark buoys at least two miles farther apart than was intended. This was because the tugs did not stream their logs until they had straightened out on the course and because apparently the captains of the tugs seemed to want to give good measure. But if you place two buoys on a triangular course some two miles farther apart, instead of the length of the course being thirty miles it has become some thirty-six miles, and this would bring the recorded speed of the ninety-footers up to speeds comparable to that which the wave formation in many photographs would indicate. I will state that both Captain Barr and Captain Nat have told me that the markers of the courses in those days were often two miles farther apart than had been expected. I will also say I have several times seen the ninety-footers leave all but the fastest steam yachts behind, and have no doubt they often went fifteen miles per hour on a reach with a steady twenty-mile breeze.

I must not neglect to speak occasionally of the small steam yachts that were built by the Herreshoff Manufacturing Company for, if they were less sensational than the racing sailboats, it is probable that they represented at least half of the production of the company between 1890 and 1905, and, while the Herreshoff steam yachts were small and not particularly handsome, they were economical, reliable, and quiet.

Just before 1890 Captain Nat had developed a type particularly for cruising that had small, compact machinery with very little fuel consumption. Several of these were of about eleven feet six inches beam and of different lengths on the same molds. Among the first of this type were "Judy," built in 1890 for F. T. Howard, and "Tranquillo" built the same year for E. D. Morgan. These little steam yachts ranged in length from a bit over one hundred feet down to the cute little "Reposo."

They were all very similar in appearance with clipper bows and overhanging sterns. "Reposo" was seventy-three feet on deck, sixty-eight feet water line, eleven feet six inches beam. In many ways these yachts were superior to anything we have today: they were remarkably good sea boats, in fact one of them went through the tail end of a hurricane off Cape Hatteras in about 1895 when she was under the command of the late Bristol captain "Bill" Torrey. These little yachts usually kept sails bent and often carried sail on long trips.

They were altogether remarkably comfortable little ships, entirely free from the danger of fire, and made runs about as long as the modern power craft. They usually could maintain a speed of ten miles per hour. Because sailing on them was so very restful they often ran ten or twelve hours a day whereas the modern cruiser, while it may be capable of fifteen or twenty miles per hour, still it is usually slowed down to ten or twelve miles when in a seaway, and on account of the tiresome noise, smell, and vibration usually does not run more than eight hours a day. So I must tell some of the younger generation that ladies and gentlemen cruised more comfortably around 1900 than the so-called cruisers do today. They went just as far, and often made a longer day's run, and personally I think they had ever so much more real pleasure.

The little "Reposo" was owned for several years by a lady who cruised in her quite extensively and some years went along on the New York Yacht Club cruises. No doubt some of the youngsters today will laugh at the appearance of "Reposo" with her awnings full length and her hanging side curtains to screen the sun, but the woman of today is as different from the lady of 1900 as the yachts of these periods differ, and I must say I prefer the yachts and ladies of 1900 even if some of the women now can stand as much sun as a Bahama pirate.

As time went on the type of clipper-bowed steam yacht built at Bristol developed into something like "Wana," one hundred and thirty-two feet long built for S. R. Van Duzer in 1903. She had one of the triple expansion steeple engines that I have spoken of before, and was a sweet-running yacht that could maintain a speed of something like twelve miles per hour under most any condition, yet had very comfortable cruising accommodations and plenty of safe deck room, which latter the modern yacht does not have. At about this time the Herreshoff Company also built three other quite similar yachts with similar power plants: they were "Quickstep," built for Frederick Grinnell in 1902, one hundred and twenty-four feet long; "Parthenia," built

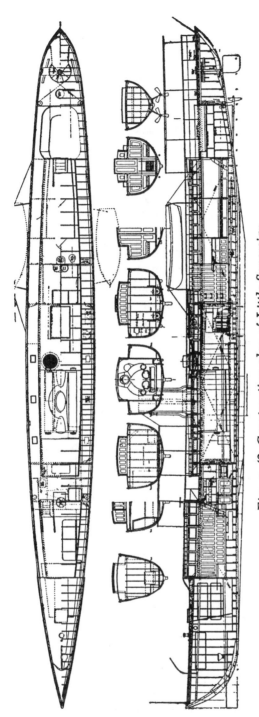

Figure 43. Construction plan of Little Sovereign.

243

for Morton F. Plant in 1903, one hundred and thirty feet long; and "Eugenia," built for J. B. Herreshoff in 1904, one hundred and thirteen feet long. These yachts were of very similar model but had different cabin arrangements and quite different deck houses. There were a great many others of this what we might call "cruising type" of steam yacht designed by Captain Nat during this time, but to my young eyes at that period the faster steamers seemed more interesting, and one of them was the "Little Sovereign," built in 1904 for M. C. D. Borden. She was one hundred and twelve feet long and only eleven feet six inches beam, ran mostly in Long Island Sound, and made many trips between Narragansett Bay and New York. I do not remember exactly her speed but I think it was around twenty-six miles per hour, which was remarkably good for her power. She was not by any means the fastest yacht of her day, but I think I am right in saying she was one of the most efficient steamers ever built and ran during her life at more nearly her trial speed than other fast steamers.

"Arrow," designed by Mosher, for instance was said to have run a mile once at the rate of forty miles an hour, but in use I for one, and I saw her many times, never saw her go over twelve or fifteen miles per hour. There were several other large commuters around New York that were credited with extremely high speed but I doubt if any of the time of "Little Sovereign" had as high average speed, or as great day-after-day reliability. This was principally because "Little Sovereign" 's speed came from having a proper beam length ratio and because she was of extremely light construction. It is very doubtful if there has ever been another yacht that carried her accommodations as fast with so little cost of fuel. So, altogether, including model, structural design, boiler, and engines, she was a designing triumph and I am very sorry I do not have a photograph of her for she certainly was a handsome yacht.

In 1904 Captain Nat designed two very remarkable sister steam launches. One was named "Mist," built for Edward Morrell, and the other "Sunbeam," built for J. L. Hutchinson—both fifty-nine feet long and eight feet six inches beam. They had small triple expansion steeple engines which developed approximately

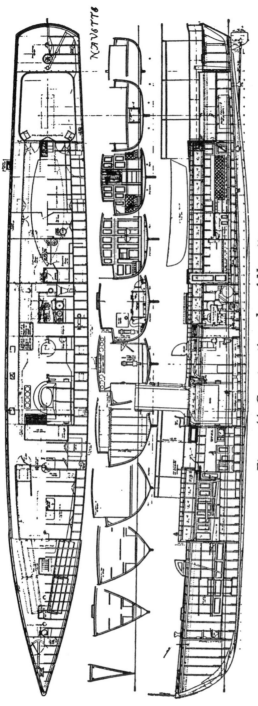

Figure 44. Construction plan of Navette.

245

one hundred and twenty-five horsepower, and when new these launches could attain a speed of twenty-two miles per hour. I speak of them now mostly because they were of the finest workmanship throughout that I have ever seen: they were double planked, and the mahogany for each side and the deck was sawn from separate logs so they matched perfectly. The boiler was entirely enclosed in a polished brass casing; the cylinders had brass lagging, and the lower part of the engine, which was enclosed, had a casing of polished blue Russian iron.

During this time the Herreshoff Company built many steam launches to be hoisted up on the davits of the large steam yachts of that time, some of the yachts even having two steam launches, and there is no doubt that these launches were the lightest, strongest and fastest launches of their time to be had. While I can only enumerate or speak of a very small percentage of the steamers built in those years I will finish up with them by skipping to 1917 when Captain Nat designed the last of his high-speed steam yachts, although as a matter of fact she was not particularly high speed. This was "Navette," length, one hundred and fourteen feet, beam, fourteen feet three inches, built for J. P. Morgan, the son of the J. P. who had owned "Columbia." "Navette" was twin screw and had rather a flat, wide stern; her construction plan is shown in Figure 44. Mr. Morgan used her in commuting between Long Island and New York City up until about 1931, and I think she was the last of the steam commuters. She was not designed as much for speed as some of Captain Nat's previous steamers, but she did have good accommodations for her crew. She had a large, roomy after cockpit and, of course, was a safe, reliable and quiet craft. As Mr. Morgan had used the Herreshoff-built steamer "Mermaid" for this purpose before, I think I am right in saying he commuted between his home on Long Island and New York City during the summer months for some twenty-five years in these two Herreshoff yachts.

While the Herreshoff Company built several steamers after 1917, and particularly during World War I, these vessels were designed principally by Captain Nat's oldest son, A. Sidney DeW. Herreshoff, who was a talented steam engineer and developed some improved types of oil-burning boilers. But even to the last the main engines of all steamers built at Bristol were designed by Captain Nat. I believe Captain Nat enjoyed designing the steam yachts and their power plants, and throughout his life devoted many more hours of work to these than to the sailing yacht.

Now I should tell about some of Captain Nat's powerboats or gasoline launches and his early dislike of them. When internal combustion engines first came into use on the water, before 1900, most of them were extremely noisy, and for some reason or other they all smelled terrible and were most unreliable. Captain Nat's very sensitive nature just could not stand the sharp noise of the exhaust, and he always was much affected by disagreeable odors. In fact his home was built with the kitchen separate so that the smell of cooking could not enter the main house. The smell of tobacco smoke was so obnoxious to him and his brother John that their later steam yachts were built with the forecastle, or crew's quarters, aft so the crew's tobacco smoke blew astern rather than running the length of the yacht, and I must admit that some forecastles in those days gave off remarkable odors. Some of the crew used the same brand of tobacco for both smoking and chewing, and some of the cheaper cigars and cigarettes of those days had odors which I hope never to smell again.

Some people have supposed that Captain Nat disliked the gasoline engine because it was taking the place of steam—his own sweetheart—but I really believe his early dislike of gasoline was mostly from the noise and smell it made in the early launches, and at that time he even disliked having noisy and smelly launches come alongside his yacht when at anchor. For these reasons his yacht "Roamer" and many of the steam yachts built at Bristol around 1900 had electric launches, and while the batteries of those days were heavy, and the charging took time, still these electric launches were absolutely noiseless, clean, and reliable. And I should say a very nice electric launch could be built with present-day batteries which are lighter and cheaper than formerly.

Captain Nat also did not like the internal combustion engine on shore so all of his early automobiles were either electric or steam, and while he owned later gasoline automobiles he never drove one himself though he had no objection to his family using them, and his sons had motorcycles and gasoline launches. In his old age he told me that he had made a mistake and should have designed or developed a high-grade gasoline marine engine to be built by the Herreshoff Company.

But to get back to powerboats he designed. The first one was the double-ended fifty foot launch "Express" built for Morton F. Plant in 1903. I think J. B. took the order for her when Captain Nat was away on a cruise; otherwise they may not have built a gasoline launch for some time to come. This launch was built on the molds originally made for the steam launches "Our Mary" and "Jersey Lily" built in 1888, also Captain Nat's own steamer "Squib" built in 1898, but whereas these earlier steamers had plumb bows and square sterns, the "Express" was built with a slightly over-hanging bow and a canoe stern. "Express" had a four-cylinder heavy duty Standard engine and was a great success in every way so that eventually there were four of these launches built:

"Express"	1903	Morton F. Plant
"Helvetia II"	1903	C. O. Iselin
"Adrienne"	1903	Adrian Iselin
"Sarah Webb"	1908	G. H. Webb

One or two of these launches, I believe, are still running.

Soon after this the plumb bow and square stern launches "Waneeche," for Butler Duncan, and "Seashell" for H. L. Maxwell, were built so that the Herreshoff Company began building launches of most every size powered with engines of various makes.

One of the most interesting of the smaller gasoline launches was the "X P D N C." She was built for Frank H. Croker in 1904 and might have had a great racing career had Mr. Croker not been killed that winter in a racing automobile at Ormond Beach. However, in 1905, when owned by Siegel and Gilligs, she won the National Trophy in a series of races on the Hudson on September 14 and 16, which consisted of three thirty-knot heats in which she made the average speed of about twenty-eight knots; and, if I remember right, she made a record between New York City and Poughkeepsie which stood for several years. Although "X P D

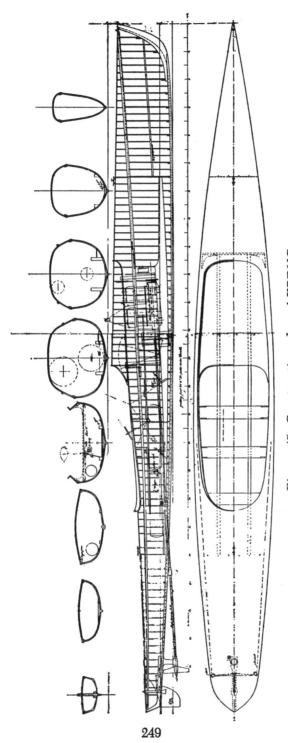

Figure 45. Construction plan of XPDNC.

N C" proved to be one of the fastest launches of her time it is very interesting that her model had been made in about 1878 for a steam torpedo boat which was not built. But what is even more remarkable is the fact that some of the latest torpedo boat destroyers—those now in use—are very similar in underwater shape, and when the destroyer finally gets to this exact model, it will be nearing perfection.

The Herreshoff Company built three launches in all from this model, and the writer had occasion to run one of them quite a little in comparatively rough water and can say that this model goes very smoothly and evenly in a choppy sea and is not slowed down by waves of a size that make the more modern shapes jump and pound seriously. To the writer, at least, it seems remarkable that Captain Nat developed this shape over seventy-five years ago.

However, in the next few years after 1905, Clinton Crane and his brother, who developed the engines, made an unbeatable combination and, although Mr. Crane's "Dixies" and "Challengers" were the fastest launches of their time, they were not of a model that was as comfortable if caught in rough weather, or perhaps as easily driven. For the "X P D N C" went surprisingly well for her horsepower which was then rated at seventy-five while most of the later and faster racing launches had double this horsepower. Captain Nat later designed many gasoline yachts, including the eighty-one foot "Vasanta" built for George Pynchon in 1920. One of the fastest gasoline yachts he designed was the sixty-six foot "Mary Ann" built for Henry Lippitt in 1919. This yacht went about thirty miles per hour and set the style in model and construction for many motor yachts designed by several designers.

While Captain Nat did not like gasoline yachts he did make several contributions toward their improvement. Perhaps the most important of them was the reduction gear. Of course the reduction gear had been used with steam turbines for some time, but about 1912 the Herreshoff Company began building reduction gears from his design that were used on many of the yachts the company built after that, and some of these gears are still in use.

Before finishing with Captain Nat's experiences with gasoline

I will say that about 1904 he designed an experimental compound gasoline engine. I think his principal object in this design was to make an engine that had a quieter and cooler exhaust. This engine had three cylinders of which the forward and after ones were perhaps one-third the volume of the middle cylinder; the crankshaft was arranged so that when the two end pistons were up the middle one was down, so the engine was nicely balanced. The two end cylinders were of the four-stroke cycle, so timed that one after the other exhausted into the middle cylinder. This engine proved to be smooth running and quiet. It probably had about forty-five horsepower and drove a launch slightly faster than other engines of its time and weight, but Captain Nat became disgusted with it because twice the cylinder block cracked near the exhaust valve. With a little more patience undoubtedly an engine could have been worked out that had a slight increase in economy over the usual gasoline engine together with quietness and a cooler exhaust. It is too bad that this engine discouraged Captain Nat for the Herreshoff Company had a very good machine shop for that time and could have easily jumped into the gasoline engine business. For instance, the Lathrop Engine Company, only about fifty miles away, had less advantages at the start but is now in the third generation of ownership making some of our best marine engines, both gasoline and diesel.

In speaking of the compound gasoline engine I do not want to give the impression that it was an invention of Captain Nat for at about that time others, both in Europe and over here, had experimented with compound internal combustion engines, and somewhere around 1904 there was an automobile named The Compound made in this country. But I should tell of another incident that turned Captain Nat against gasoline. Somewhere around 1905 he and his oldest son, Sidney, had arranged a boiler from a Stanley steam automobile together with a Herreshoff engine on the chassis of a Renault automobile which had had the engine removed to put in a launch built for Robert Goelet. Well, one Sunday, when the workmen were out of the shops, Captain Nat and his son got up steam in this automobile, which had recently been assembled, when suddenly the whole machine was enveloped in a very hot flame which only lasted for an instant. This was caused by the bursting of a small expansion tank that was connected to the Stanley gasoline burner. The tank had a relief valve which was intended to keep the gasoline fuel at a certain pressure, but in the assembling of the piping to the burners this relief valve had unfortunately been put on the wrong way around, so that it did not relieve the pressure that was pumped into the tank by the pump attached to the engine. Fortunately this expansion tank did not hold much more than a tumbler full of gasoline, but when the tank burst it discharged into the atmosphere an atomized spray which went in all directions and at once turned to flame. Captain Nat and his son were close to the tank and were very painfully and severely burned while this writer, who was on the other side of the machine, only sustained slight burns on face and hands. The backs of Captain Nat's hands were so deeply burned in this accident that they never entirely healed and were mottled the rest of his life.

Captain Nat had been very friendly with the Stanley twins who built the Stanley steamer and had suggested to them several improvements which they adopted, one of which was to use an electric galvanized steel boiler in place of the copper one they had formerly used. At the time of this accident the Herreshoff Company was building an experimental steam engine for an automobile. It was a "V" engine of six cylinders of the single-acting type and very much resembled the gasoline engine of today. The engine was of a variety called a poppet valve uniflow engine, that is, it had valves like the usual gasoline engine but the steam only went one way in the cylinders. It entered through the inlet valve at the top of the cylinders and exhausted through the cylinder walls at the bottom of the stroke, an arrangement that has certain thermal advantages.

However, after this accident Captain Nat did not experiment further with this engine although it was run some connected to an electric dynamo. It was, I believe, the last steam engine that Captain Nat designed. But we must go back to the sailboats he designed between 1900 and 1910.

At the turn of the century the New York Yacht Club was becoming very much disgusted with the yachts that were being turned out under the length-on-water-line and sail-area rule of measurement, so on February 13, 1902 a committee was formed, including some of the racing members of the club, to look into the matter. S. Nicholson Kane, who had been on the regatta committee for several years and had been commodore in 1877–79, was the chairman of this committee, and George A. Cormack, the secretary of the New York Yacht Club, was also secretary of this committee. No yacht designers or yacht builder was on the committee but one of the first moves of the committee was to send letters of inquiry to the most prominent yacht designers of the United States, Canada, Australia, France, Germany, England, Denmark, Norway, and Sweden, asking for advice in forming a new measurement rule that would produce or encourage a more wholesome type of yacht. The response to these letters was voluminous and thus the committee had the co-operation of the leading designers of the world, several of whom gave the matter much thought and time, and sent to the committee a great amount of figures, drawings, and diagrams, while some even appeared before the committee, which tells us today what a great general interest was created by this effort to produce a more wholesome type of racing yacht.

However, the consensus of opinion of these designers was that length, sail area, and displacement should be measured factors in the new rule, and as the rule suggested by N. G. Herreshoff in its first simple form was length times the square root of sail area divided by the cube root of displacement the committee adopted this general formula and requested Captain Nat to complete the rule in detail and bring the resultant sum down to a figure to be used with the existing time allowance tables which give the number of seconds per mile that a larger yacht allows a smaller one. With the first factor—length—which for many years had been measured in several ways he adopted a measurement which was later called "quarter beam length" and which took the length of the yacht at the water line, not at the center line, at a line parallel with the center line halfway out to her greatest beam at the water line. As this distance out is one quarter of the yacht's total beam, it is generally called the quarter beam measurement. Captain Nat adopted this measurement as he felt that it gave a truer gauge of the yacht's real sailing lines than the previous center-line measurements, all of which had proved unsatisfactory one way or another. With the second factor—sail area—he used the area's square root as this changed area to a linear measurement; and with the third factor—displacement—he used the cube root as this also brought volume down to a linear measurement.

Captain Nat's original scheme was to play length and sail area, which are speed-giving dimensions, against displacement, room below the water line, for he believed that a yacht of liberal displacement was a more wholesome yacht. So in the formula the speed-giving dimensions are multiplied by one another and the resulting sum is divided by a linear dimension representing the displacement. Thus, as displacement is the division in the rule, the large displacement or roomy yacht would rate low and have an even chance with her leaner sisters who would rate higher although they may be of the same length and sail area. To bring the resulting figures of this formula down to a figure to be used with the existing time scales for yacht racing, 18 per cent of the resulting figure was taken, and this, with the yachts of that time, generally resulted in a rating not very different from their waterline length.

We will not go into the various changes that were made in the rule, both during its formation and later, but by 1903 the rule was in use by the New York Yacht Club, and by 1904–05 it had been adopted by nearly all of the prominent yacht clubs along the Atlantic coast and the Great Lakes. As it had promise of becoming quite universal it was called the Universal Rule. Ever since about 1905 most of our sailing yachts have been built to this rule, and it is no exaggeration to say they include the finest racing sailboats ever built. The effect of the Universal Rule on yacht design was marked and sudden for, in place of the short water-line, wide yachts with large sail area that were in use in 1900, the yachts became almost at once wholesome, roomy vessels with moderate sail area. If their maximum speed was somewhat less than the older yachts their average speed was considerably more, so that the "J" boats of the nineteen-thirties had higher average speed than the large cup boats of before 1900 although the "J" boats had less than half the sail area and nearly as much displacement.

The working up of the Universal Rule was one of Captain Nat's great contributions to yachting, and in recognition of this, and in appreciation of his work in defending the America's Cup five times, the New York Yacht Club made him an honorary member of the club. This was a very great honor for, excepting several ex officio members such as the President of the United States, the Secretary of the United States Navy, Secretary of the Treasury, etc., the only other permanent honorary members at the time were H.M. King Edward VII, H.R.H. the Prince of Wales, H.I.M. Kaiser Wilhelm, Sir Thomas J. Lipton, and the Hon. Elihu Root. So Nathanael Greene Herreshoff was the only untitled honorary member of the New York Yacht Club for many years. The Seawanhaka Corinthian Yacht Club soon followed suit and made Captain Nat an honorary member of that club for they much appreciated what he had done for yacht measurement. In fact the Seawanhaka had always been foremost in developing and experimenting with improved methods of measurement and, if I remember right, they adopted the Universal Rule at the same time as the New York Yacht Club. The Bristol Yacht Club, the club of his home town, then made him an honorary member, so, as the Boston Yacht Club conferred the same honor on him in January 30, 1877, he was an honorary member of four yacht clubs, and it is doubtful if any other untitled man has enjoyed this privilege. The Boston Yacht Club had honored him in 1877 for getting up the tables called "Time Allowance Tables for One Nautical Mile in Seconds and Decimals," which are the tables today found in the back of most yacht club books throughout the world. It is these tables which have made it practical to race yachts of different rating together with what is called time allowance. I remember that when we were cruising on Captain Nat's steam yacht "Roamer" between about 1905 and 1910, we were very particular to hoist the proper yacht club flag for the region we were in, for there seemed to be some responsibility in being an honorary member of so many clubs.

About this time a very remarkable man began visiting the Herreshoff Manufacturing Company at Bristol. He was Morton F. Plant, and he had been the principal owner of a line of steamships which, when in middle life, he decided to sell and which it was said netted him forty million dollars in cash, and you could do quite a lot with a million dollars in those days. There were of course several other Americans who were wealthier but few, if any of them, could or were willing to spend their fortunes so freely. Well, in a few years he had built at Bristol five yachts, the most important of which was the eighty-six foot water-line steel schooner, "Ingomar," and the "Ingomar" was the first of a remarkable line of nine steel schooners which Captain Nat designed. Mr. Plant must have had some strong power of persuasion for not only did he persuade Captain Nat to design the first gasoline launch that the Herreshoff Manufacturing Company built, but it took some persuading to get him to design a schooner, for at the time Captain Nat very much disliked the rig and said it was too complicated and costly, and that it had too much wind resistance. He had not designed a schooner since about 1870, although before that he had designed three or four small wooden schooners that J. B. Herreshoff built.

However, "Ingomar" turned out an unusually fine vessel and probably would have had a long racing life if she had been built to fit the Universal Rule, but she was built to race under other various rules. "Ingomar" came out in the season of 1903, but as that was the year of that remarkable creation, the "Reliance," her construction and first year's performance are so overshadowed by her more racing sister that few people remember her in 1903. "Ingomar" was built in the north shop and so had to be launched on greased ways. She took the water at good speed, perhaps ten miles an hour or more, and, after performing a graceful circle in the harbor, returned to nearly where she was launched still running stern first, and ran her stern up on the north wharf but did little damage to either herself or the wharf.

In her first season she won nearly every race in Class B, the largest class for schooners. She won every yacht club run, and the Astor Cup of that year, but "Ingomar" is best remembered for the season of 1904 when she went abroad with Charlie Barr as captain, who had of course been captain of "Reliance" the previous year, 1903. "Ingomar" was fitted out at Bristol with an ocean-going rig in the spring of 1904; during the winter her centerboard had been removed and her draft increased by adding a slab of lead about two feet deep to the bottom of her keel. I believe she did not have any inside ballast. For the trip across she had a shorter bowsprit, shorter topmasts and gaffs, and a shorter main boom, her racing spars being shipped over by steamer, and, of course, smaller sails although they were crosscut. Her masts and shrouds were her regular racing ones. I give you here some of her dimensions: L.O.A., one hundred and twenty-two feet; L.W.L., eighty-six feet; beam, twenty-four feet; draft, sixteen feet three inches. The diameter of the main mast at the deck was eighteen and one half inches; the main truck was one hundred and twenty-three feet above deck; the main boom, seventy-five feet; the spinnaker boom, sixty-seven feet; sail area eleven thousand eight hundred and eighty square feet.

Her crew consisted of Captain, First Mate, Second Mate, first steward, second steward, first cook, second cook, and sixteen men in the forecastle besides the crew's fox terrier mascot—making in all twenty-five mouths to feed. She left Bristol bound for Southampton promptly at nine in the morning April 30, 1904, in a strong nor'wester which blew so hard and turned so cold that she practically had to lay-to the first day, and a few days later encountered a southeast gale so that her passage across was not extraordinarily fast, but as it is recorded from Bristol to abreast the Lizard it is hardly comparable with recorded passages from sight to sight of shore. It took her sixteen days from Bristol to the Lizard.

"Ingomar" raced very successfully in England and Germany. While in Europe she sailed twenty-two races, winning twelve firsts, four seconds, and one third. But in England she was given an arbitrary handicap which made it very difficult for her to win. To quote from the British yachting writer, B. Heckstall-Smith:

An American schooner, the "Ingomar," visiting our waters in 1904, found no British yacht which could compete against her on Y.R. time. The races were not sailed according to a fixed scale of time allowance, but merely by a rule-of-thumb method of allotting each yacht a handicap upon her merits. The "Ingomar" was sometimes penalized to give the English yachts nearly three times the actual allowance she would have been obliged to concede according to a time allowance scale based upon measurement.

Now I will quote another noted British yachting historian whom I will not name. He says:

"Ingomar" was a fin keel vessel drawing seventeen feet of water, and had a very large sail area. Many people consider that she was much too leniently treated by the handicappers throughout her visit. However, not an undue share of first prizes were awarded her in British waters.

He later adds the typical British remark: "Taken altogether, this season was singularly uninteresting and uneventful." But I am sure that if the British had had a schooner that could have occasionally beaten "Ingomar" on even terms they would have considered the season exciting enough.

"Ingomar" also had her difficulties in German waters for apparently the German yachts felt that they had the right of way under all circumstances through some eminent right of domain, but they were up against the wrong man when they had Charlie Barr to contend with, and at least twice he ran into them when they tried to force him when he had the right of way. It must have been very trying for Captain Barr to be racing against several large steel schooners which apparently thought he had no rights.

Most of the racing there was in shallow waters or channels through sandbanks, and Captain Barr did his own navigation to a great extent as local pilots, as a general rule, are not so good out of the regular channels used by steamers. The racing also was in unusually strong winds and tides which, of course, make the worry of collision and grounding much greater. Besides, "Ingomar" was of too great draft for the German waters, or England for that matter. Nevertheless, she did so well in Germany that the Emperor looked her over once or twice and admired her so much that he ordered a larger schooner from Captain Nat, which seems surprising as the Emperor's fine schooner "Meteor III," one hundred and twenty feet water line, designed by A. Cary Smith and built in the United States of America, was only two years old.

Captain Nat started to design the new schooner for the Kaiser with much enthusiasm for she was to be a large vessel and the

Kaiser had plenty of money in his own right, which was not the case of some other monarchs and princes of that day, but soon after the model was made the Kaiser cablegrammed to know what dimensions Captain Nat had chosen for the new yacht. On receiving the reply, the Kaiser ordered some of them to be changed, whereupon Captain Nat cabled back what amounted to the following: If you want the yacht as I designed her you can have her, but I will not design a yacht for anyone of dimensions my experience shows are not suitable. Here was a case of two men of stubborn natures coming up against each other and, as neither of them was used to being dictated to, work on the new yacht stopped at once. Later, however, I believe the Kaiser tried again to have Captain Nat design him a schooner but to no avail. I think the principal thing that the Kaiser and Captain Nat disagreed about was draft, but at that time Captain Nat thought considerable draft was necessary for consistent winning with the large sail areas then in vogue. Below is a copy of a letter to Captain Nat written aboard "Ingomar," the flagship of the Larchmont Yacht Club, by Captain Barr nearly fifty years ago.

Flagship Ingomar
Ryde, I. W. 9th Aug. 1904

N. G. Herreshoff, Esq.

Dear Sir,

I have just received your letter regarding the "Ingomar," and am very much pleased to hear that you are likely to build the Emperor a schooner. She will be a fine ship.

1st. The Ingomar" is as good a cruising yacht as you will find anywhere, the only drawback being the draft which keeps you out of some of the harbors. We could only go in Dover with springs, and at Southampton we have to be a long way off. I understand, however, that the present "Meteor" draws nearly as much.

2. In the race at Cuxhaven, where it was blowing very hard and a nasty sea caused by the tide, the port bow at the water line was dented in between four frames—that is three dents. There was a butt between two plates where the middle dent was, and that leaked. It was nothing very serious as we did not have it repaired till we got to England.

In the collision with the "Navahoe" we struck her almost at right angles and did not start a thing except the bowsprit, and were going about 9 knots by the wind. I think this shows she is strong enough.

3.   I understand that the bulwarks are not high enough for yachts built now, and because we had more deck erections (hatches, skylights, steering gear, etc.) than 175 cubic feet, we had to carry in addition to our regular outfit 75 fathom of 3/4 chain cable, and 50 fathoms 5 inch rope, and an anchor weighing 880 lbs. They said at one time that we would have to carry 7/8 chain but I told them we could not use it on our windlass so they compromised on this. We never could find out exactly what we lacked, as they said many different things about it. We received a certificate in the end after putting the extra cables etc. on board.

4.   I think the steering gear is very satisfactory, and it has never shown any signs of weakness. We had the rudder stock twisted 5/8 of an inch at Southampton by the boat sitting back on the rudder in the mud berth and forcing it hard over against the brakes.

We had to take the quadrant off, and cut a new keyway. The steering gear was one of the things the Emperor took the most interest in.

5.   I think the same type of steering gear would be suitable for a larger boat.

6.   We had very strong winds in Germany, although we never reefed. Both "Meteor" and "Hamburg" reefed several times against us, also the old "Yampa." I understand however that these strong winds are somewhat unusual. The extra chains etc. did us no harm in Germany, but of course we put them on shore as soon as we left. She was too stiff in light winds but now she can do any of the boats we race against in the lightest winds. There is no opportunity to put anything out here so you have to count on carrying the whole equipment.

7. 8. The sails you made for "Ingomar" were the best you ever made, and there has been nothing done to any of them except the jibs and forestaysails. We have used and sent on shore to be cut, both sets of headsails you made, and also those made by Ratsey & Lapthorne. We have also condemned the No. 2 maintopmast staysail you made because it was so wide that it trimmed against the spreader close hauled, and we are using the one made by Ratsey. These are the only Ratsey sails we have used but we carry his spinnaker in case of accidents.

The mainsail is as good now as the first day it went up, and the foresail very nearly so. The topsails are all good. The clubtopsail spars are too light, and do not weigh half as much as those on some of the small yawls we sail against.

All the schooners here use a triangular staysail on a stay and have double triatic stays which they slack up and set up every tack. They get their staysail drawing much quicker than we do, but the "Meteor" carries three men aloft, two on the fore and one on the main, to overhaul the gear. Theirs is the best sail for close hauled work, but it seems to carry a lot of gear with it.

I think the balloon maintopmast staysail should have a cringle and strengthening piece on the foot to haul down to the foreboom end.

I had to have a strut and stay put on the mainmast, which buckled badly, and a foreboom horse made 3 ft. 9 in. long. I also think the main topmast stay could be made fast aloft, as ours cut off at the block on the way across.

With best regards, I remain

Yours respectfully

CHARLES BARR.

"Ingomar" had gone abroad principally to try to regain the Cape May Cup, which had been given by James Gordon Bennett in 1872 and had been raced for by our larger schooners several times, until Sir Richard Sutton's "Genesta" had taken that cup and the Brenton's Reef Cup away from us in 1885. The Brenton's Reef Cup had been regained by the "Navahoe" in 1893 in one of the closest races ever sailed, which I told about when writing of "Navahoe." But a few days later when Charlie Barr and Aubrey Crocker sailed "Navahoe" against "Britannia" for the Cape May Cup, she was beaten about half an hour by the "Britannia" in a fluky cross-channel-and-return race in light weather. So, naturally Captain Barr was anxious to have another try for that cup, but strange to say after the "Ingomar" challenged for the cup it could not be found. According to the deed of gift the cup was to be held by the yacht club to which the winning yacht belonged, but as the winning yacht had been "Britannia" the Royal Yacht Squadron had let her owner, the Prince of Wales, take it away. In the meantime the prince had become King Edward VII. His Majesty had Windsor Castle ransacked in vain to find the cup, and a scandal was about to break when fortunately the Cape May Cup was unearthed at Sandringham Palace. It was discovered by that time that the deed of gift also stated that if the yacht holding the cup was sold out of the club the cup must be returned to the New York Yacht Club, and as King Edward had sold the "Britannia" out of the club the cup was returned to the New York Yacht Club where it now is. Hence "Ingomar" could not race for it after she got abroad. The cup returned to America before "Ingomar," in fact was raced for over here on September 10, 1904, by the schooners "Atlantic," "Endymion," and "Vergemere," the "Atlantic" winning.

Much of this is not connected with Captain Nat's life but I have thought it necessary to explain why "Ingomar" did not race for the Cape May Cup in England for which she principally went over.

If I remember correctly "Ingomar" originally cost $115,000, and this seems amazing today, for it is doubtful is she could now be duplicated for half a million. In fact it is doubtful if she could be duplicated at all for there were hundreds of bronze castings on her which were of unmachinable shape so had to be finished by hand. In fact the whole yacht, to a surprising extent, was handwork, much of which, particularly the forgings, would have to be made by men of greater skill in handwork than the workman of today.

It is amazing that Captain Nat could design "Ingomar" the same winter as "Reliance" when probably no one alive today could do the work he did on "Reliance" alone in one winter. But most surprising is the fact that he also designed the Bar Harbor thirty-one-foot one-design class and several other smaller yachts the same year—1903.

Although by 1904 Captain Nat had acquired almost every laurel that a man of his profession can win, had been presented with numerous diplomas of merit by the colleges of mechanical arts, as well as engineering societies, and was doing very well financially, still he was an unhappy man. This was because his wife was seriously sick and continually suffering with cancer. At that time, fifty years ago, the medical profession had not developed the modern techniques of dealing with this disease so the patient often suffered considerably for a year or more, and during this time Captain Nat continued to have hope of her recovery and spent a small fortune in a futile attempt to save her life or reduce her suffering. She was operated on twice and in the summer of 1904, during a temporary recovery, went for a cruise on Captain Nat's steam yacht "Roamer" attended by a trained nurse. By the fall of 1905, however, she passed away leaving a void in Captain Nat's household never to be quite filled again.

The death of Mrs. Herreshoff was a great setback to Captain Nat for she had managed his home and other family responsibilities so skillfully that he had previously been able to devote himself almost entirely to his work. Mrs. Herreshoff had also acquired the esteem of Captain Nat's early clients, many of whom visited his home during the construction of their yachts. She was always loved and respected by the workmen in the Herreshoff Company, most of whom she knew, and would stop to speak with, inquiring for their families. If some of the workmen or their families were sick she would remember them with jars of preserves, wine jelly, or flowers, so that as a matter of fact she was more popular among the workers in the boat shop than Captain Nat himself, and no doubt added much to the general feeling of good will that prevailed throughout the works at that time.

It is often said that some great sorrow has enabled artists, composers, and even actresses to do their most notable work, and while no doubt a great disappointment has some ripening and sobering effect on the intellect it is very doubtful if sorrow in any form is beneficial or stimulating to a yacht designer, and in Captain Nat's case he withdrew from most human interests and became partly estranged and almost severe with his immediate family. Perhaps if he had had a stronger faith he would have been relieved of some of his sorrow, but with his mechanical mind he turned to mechanical things instead.

He had in his model room a very fine Precision Bench Lathe made by the Rivett Lathe and Grinder Company of Boston. It was their model 608, and was one of the most versatile bench lathes made in the world at that time. With its many attachments it could be set up to do almost any conceivable light machine work. It was placed before a double window which overlooked

Bristol Harbor, and the shining bay. This lathe was to give Captain Nat many hours of relaxation during the next thirty-five years. Mr. Rivett, the inventor and builder of the lathe, was a close friend of Captain Nat, and they seemed to enjoy each

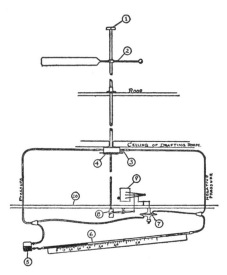

Figure 46. Diagram of Captain Nat's Recording Anemometer. 1. Head with orifice to windward for pressure, with orifice to leeward for negative pressure. 2. Weather vane. 3. Mercury sealed valve allowing upper pressure tubes to revolve. 4. Compass dial and indicator. 5. Bottle partly filled with colored liquid. 6. Gauge glass with scale for wind velocities. 7. Diaphragm to actuate velocity pen. 8. Spiral to actuate direction pen. 9. Drum of recording barometer with barometric pen. 10. Mantel of fireplace.

other's company very much; in fact the last long trip undertaken by Captain Nat was to visit Mr. Rivett.

Among the things that Captain Nat made on this lathe was a recording anemometer that not only gave a continuous record of the wind velocity but also recorded the direction of the wind. This was done by arranging two extra pens on a recording barometer, one giving the velocity and the other the direction of the wind, so that together with the barometric pen he had a very complete record of atmospheric conditions as each pen recorded with a different color ink.

He had for many years, perhaps fifty altogether, recorded the weather each night for the weather bureau so had a rain gauge and a recording thermometer. In his old age he was a most remarkable weather prophet, and, although he seldom made verbal predictions, still you could tell by the arrangements he made from time to time that he knew almost exactly what was coming and made his plans accordingly for rain, gale, cold wave, or calm. I must note here that Captain Nat did not think the wind velocities recorded by the usual revolving anemometer were correct, and that the velocities recorded by the weather bureau were considerably below what they should have been, and his contention was substantiated several years later when recording instruments were used on airplanes that had to record wind velocities that agreed with their speed between places. Since that time the weather bureau has used a calibration that corresponds to the velocities Captain Nat used in calibrating his recording anemometer which he obtained in the following way.

He made a very exact metal true screw, or wind mill, which was mounted on nearly frictionless bearings of the two-disk type such as are used in mounting a hand driven grindstone. The shaft of this screw was connected to easily motivated clockworks which reduced the revolutions so that the last gear in the train revolved once as some known fraction of a mile of wind passed. This last gear made an electric contact at each revolution, and wires led to either a light or buzzer within the home so that by timing with a stop watch he could calculate the exact velocity. His recording anemometer was actuated by wind pressure which came from a small tube mounted well above a weather vane that kept the face of the tube to windward. To do away with any back pressure there would be in the tubing, as the wind pressure varied, he also arranged another tube to lead to the leeward side of the tube that had collected the oncoming air. These two tubes led down to a glass tube that was partly filled with colored liquid and fastened to the wall on a slight angle with the pressure tube attached to the lowest end while the negative pressure tube was attached to the upper end of the glass tube, so that, as the wind velocity or wind pressure varied, the colored liquid in the tube rose or fell. Then, by using his other anemometer that recorded electrically, he was able to make spots on a strip of paper placed back of the glass tube that represented the height to which the liquid would rise at various wind pressures.

With this accurate calibration he worked up a scale that was permanently mounted back of the tube and that was graduated to read in both knots and statute miles and their fractions, so that by glancing at the tube one could tell instantly exactly what the wind velocity was at that moment, and it was a very interesting thing to watch in stormy or puffy weather. Often I have seen it register over sixty miles per hour in the puffs of a northwest gale. Living in the house with such an instrument soon accustomed one to judge wind velocities as one also becomes able to judge temperatures if he lives in a house with a thermometer.

Captain Nat was also very fond of working on or improving clocks, and he had two with what are called seconds pendulums; that is, they had pendulums one meter long that made one swing over and back in one second. These clocks had very fine movements made by the Howard Clock Company. One clock he had bought with part of a gratuitous present made him by the owners of the cup boat "Columbia," and the other from part of the appreciation the owners of "Reliance" had given him. To improve the time-keeping ability of these clocks he made compensating pendulums of his own design which amounted mostly to a pendulum rod of nickel steel with a very accurate coefficient of expansion with changes in temperature, while the bob or pendulum weight was made of zinc which had an expansion compared to its length that mathematically kept the center of weight of the rod and bob combined at exactly the same distance below the hanging point at its upper end.

While a compensating pendulum was by no means a new thing, the ones Captain Nat made were beautifully simple and capable of being more mathematically correct than other ones of that time through a range of temperatures. This, of course, was before Invar metal was procurable in this country, or perhaps even before it was invented in Europe. However, Captain Nat succeeded in having these two long case, or Grandfather, clocks run with an error of about two seconds a month which is quite remarkable, for to get great accuracy it is necessary to have a pendulum clock mounted on a very heavy or firm foundation so that the pendulum cannot set up sympathetic vibration at its upper end.

Captain Nat made many things on his Rivett lathe including some very accurate patterns for small propellers which were milled out to an exact true screw. He worked on this lathe until he was about eighty-eight years old, and I occasionally use some special drafting scales he made for me on it when he was about that age. But we must get back to the yachts he was designing at that time.

The next yacht of importance that Captain Nat designed was the steel schooner "Queen" built for Mr. J. Rogers Maxwell, which came out in 1906, with dimensions of L.O.A., one hundred and twenty-six feet; L.W.L., ninety-two feet six inches; beam, twenty-four feet; draft, fourteen feet ten inches; and she had a small centerboard. It was a great honor to get an order from Mr. Maxwell for a large yacht for he had previously designed most of his own. Mr. Maxwell was probably our best amateur designer of those times, and thus also our greatest connoisseur of yachts. He was a man of ample means and had owned many yachts, large and small, and raced them with great success. It is interesting that when Mr. Maxwell ordered "Queen" he simply wrote Captain Nat a short note stating that he wanted a schooner for Class B, and that he considered Captain Nat could work her out best without any suggestions, which seems amazing when of late years most owners so confuse the designer with conflicting requirements that the designer has great difficulty in producing even a mediocre yacht.

Although Captain Nat was working on "Queen" 's designs when Mrs. Herreshoff died, still "Queen," in my opinion, was about his finest design. She was an able yacht with moderate overhangs, and his first large yacht built under the Universal Rule of measurement. But the workmanship on "Queen" was perhaps her most outstanding feature for those who were qualified to judge the matter have said she was the fairest and smoothest metal yacht ever built.

At that time the Herreshoff Company did not have much heavy metalworking machinery, and so most of "Queen"'s plates were shaped up by pounding them with sledge hammers on an iron slab which is extremely hard and noisy work. At that time there were still some of the crew who had worked on "Reliance," "Constitution," and "Columbia," so that each plate fitted almost perfectly before it was hung. After she was riveted up she was very carefully gone over with dolly irons and metalworking hammers so that at the completion she was nearly as fair as the shell of an egg. After cementing and painting, her underbody and topsides presented a sight that would cause envy to any shipbuilder in the world and was quite in contrast to the welded shell-plating jobs of today.

"Queen" also had metal disks that fitted in each porthole to make her topsides perfectly smooth while racing. Her bronze deck fittings were particularly well finished as at that time there were men skillful at that work which is mostly done by hand. Her spars, most of which were solid, were some of the finest sticks I have ever seen, but "Queen" is particularly remembered for the arrangement of her main topmast staysail which was arranged to be left set when tacking ship. This was accomplished by leaving off the fore topmast backstay and holding the head of the fore topmast aft with a stay between the topmast heads. You will note early in the chapter, in the letter from Captain Barr, that he speaks of the complicated rig the European schooners were using to accomplish the same results. Right after this most American schooners adopted this rig and it has since been called the Queen Staysail Rig.

"Queen" had a very good captain and crew and I believe was the best kept large yacht I have ever been on, and I have been on some fine ones including the "Britannia." I raced on "Queen" a couple of times and I shall never forget the sight looking forward along her spotless deck, polished bright work, and handsome spars. And Mr. Maxwell, her owner, was a fine, polished gentleman of the old school. She also had beautiful sails, some made by the Herreshoff Company and some by Ratsey, and while "Westward" and "Elena" were larger yachts, "Queen," to me, will always seem the queen of all sailing yachts both before and after her time. Unfortunately "Queen" had a rather short life: Mr. Maxwell sold her to E. W. Clark, who renamed her "Irolita," but Mr. Clark was not then a hot racing man. The third or fourth "Irolita" (ex Queen) was destroyed in the fire at City Island about 1910 when many other fine yachts met their end.

Another yacht of Captain Nat's design that came out in 1903 was the first "Irolita" built for E. Walter Clark. This one was seventy feet O.A., fifty feet W.L., fifteen feet four inches beam, and only six feet ten inches draft. She was afterward changed to a yawl, and under the name of "Polaris" is said by some to have been one of the most desirable cruisers ever built, for she was roomy and able though of shallow draft. The next "Irolita" designed by Captain Nat came out in 1906 as a sloop and was changed to a schooner, ninety feet O.A., sixty-six feet W.L., eighteen feet beam, and eleven foot draft. She afterward had the names of "Virginia," "Princess," and "Saraband," and was considered one of the handsomest schooners on the Sound for a few years after World War I.

In 1905 Captain Nat designed the fifty-two-footer "Sonya" for Mrs. Turner-Farley of Falmouth, England. "Sonya" was built to fit the British Y.R.A. rule then in force, which heavily penalized girth. Thus, like others in her class, she had great slope to the bottom of her keel. "Sonya" did not do particularly well in the class in 1905–06, coming in somewhere in the middle of the class, which very much pleased the British yachtsmen who had been so thoroughly trounced by Mr. Herreshoff's "Niagara" some ten years before. Perhaps one of the reasons "Sonya" did not do particularly well was that she carried away her mast twice in the first year, and besides this, which naturally made her crew jumpy, no doubt she was not able to enter some of the races. She also had very stiff competition, being up against some of the best yachts and helmsmen of the time.

About this time Captain Nat also designed a sloop of about forty-five feet W.L. for another European rule. If I remember right she went to Germany, but I do not recall her name or the name of the owner. However, this yacht and "Sonya" were shipped abroad on the decks of steamers, and these two yachts I believe were the first Herreshoff yachts to use Merriman blocks, although the Herreshoff Company continued to make their own small blocks and all other deck hardware.

In 1907 Captain Nat designed the one-design class of N.Y.Y.C. fifty-seven-footers which were remarkably handsome vessels. They were eighty-five feet three inches O.A., sixty-two feet eight inches W.L., sixteen feet beam, and ten feet ten inches draft, and listed below are the names of the yachts and owners:

"Aurora"	Cornelius Vanderbilt
"Winsome"	Henry F. Lippitt
"Istalena"	George M. Pynchon

As they came out they were able, easily handled sloops, but their owners, who were used to more comparative sail area with yachts built under the old rule decided to have the sail area increased. This jumped their rating up to 65, and besides making it harder for them to save their time on other yachts, in my opinion it made them less desirable yachts. The "Winsome," now rigged as a yawl, is still in commission, and in 1950 was the handsomest yacht that visited Marblehead Harbor during the year.

The same year, 1907, Captain Nat designed the sloops "Avenger" and "Adventuress." Although they were smaller than the fifty-seven-footers, they were of composite construction as were the Fifty-sevens. But "Avenger" and "Adventuress" had all hollow spars excepting the bowsprit, while the Fifty-sevens had solid mainmasts. "Avenger" was built for R. W. Emmons and was seventy-four feet nine inches O.A., fifty-three feet W.L., fourteen feet six inches beam, and nine feet two inches draft, and rated at the very bottom of the class in which the Fifty-sevens raced. As the three fifty-seven-footers rather interfered with one another in luffing, the "Avenger," with her lighter spars, usually slipped in and beat them with time allowance. In fact the "Avenger" was one of the most successful yachts Captain Nat designed, and besides winning the Astor Cup four times she won countless other large and valuable trophies. The author raced on "Avenger" many times and was in her afterguard twice when she was winning the Astor Cup.

"Adventuress" was built for C. C. Rumrill. She was sixty-seven feet O.A., forty-five feet six inches W.L., thirteen feet beam, and nine feet draft, and was one of the prettiest yachts of her time. While she did not race much under her original rig, she did win the Puritan Cup twice. She was used for many years and sailed with a leg-o'-mutton rig under the names of "Kalinga" and "Riptide," so that at one time or another Henry Maxwell owned both of these yachts—"Avenger" and "Adventuress"—and it is safe to say he has also owned more Herreshoff yachts, large and small, than any other man.

Of the smaller sailboats built by the Herreshoff Company during these years were the sonder boats "Skiddoo," built for Herbert M. Sears; "Alarm," built for Max Agassiz; "Toboggan," built for R. W. Emmons; and "Bibelot," built for Harry Paine Whitney. The latter was taken to Germany and, when sailed by R. W. Emmons, won the Kaiser Wilhelm cup for sonder boats and is considered the fastest sonder ever built in any country. "Bibelot" was left in Germany and up until about 1935 was used by the sea scouts at Kiel.

The "Q" boats "Dorothy Q" and "Eleanor" came out in 1907, and the "Eleanor" proved to be the fastest boat in this class, and among other prizes won the principal cup offered at the race given in honor of the Jamestown Exposition. "Eleanor" not only was a beautiful little yacht with her bright mahogany topsides and varnished soft pine deck, but she was about the first of the modern shaped yachts and very similar to the later "P" boats designed by Gardner and George Owen. In fact right down to the time of "Ranger" there has not been a great variation from this model, although some designers born since the time of "Eleanor" would try to make us believe this model was the result of tank testing. Apparently Captain Nat's reasoning powers were some thirty years in advance of tank development. "Eleanor" was remarkably well kept, and, although only twenty-six feet three inches W.L. had two professionals: her captain was Frank Martin, one of our best professionals at the time, and the sailor man was Sorenson who later became famous on the North Shore and was captain of several of Frank Paine's winning yachts. No doubt these men contributed to "Eleanor" 's enviable reputation.

In mentioning the smaller yachts of that time I must not fail to speak of the N.Y.Y.C. thirty-footers which came out in 1905: they were the fourth class of one-design thirty-footers Captain Nat designed, the other classes being the Newport Thirties, 1896; Buzzards Bay Thirties, 1902; Bar Harbor Thirties, 1903. The N.Y.Y.C. Thirties, I believe, were the first one-design class built by any one under the Universal Rule, and they were safe, sane, able craft making comfortable cruisers for their size, and a few of them accompanied the N.Y.Y.C. on its cruises during the next several years. Their principal dimensions were L.O.A., forty-three feet six inches; L.W.L., thirty feet; beam, eight feet ten inches; draft, six feet three inches. They had about one thousand square feet of sail area, and cost $4,000 complete with eighty-eight separate items of equipment, which seems amazingly cheap today, but these Thirties were probably the first boats built with a carefully planned system of quantity production. There were eighteen of them and they were built in what was called the middle shop of the Herreshoff Company, which was a new shop then, and that winter was given over entirely to building these Thirties. There were generally three of them side by side in this production row, the first one upside down over her molds being planked; the next one turned right side up having her deck laid and interior built; while the last one had been set on her lead and was being finished off and painted. After they really got in production these boats shifted along in this production line at the rate of one a week, or in other words one was completed each week and was taken away to the storage yard on a special wide-wheeled low gear hauled by four horses. Of course most all the parts of these boats were prefabricated, and there was a pattern for each plank and other principal parts which were gotten out about eighteen at a time. These Thirties were double planked with cypress inner planking and yellow pine outer planking set in shellac which seems to be a very good combination; while cypress is not often used for inner planking on account of its weight, it is a wonderful wood to resist rot.

When these Thirties were rigged I happened to be working with the rigging gang and remember well that we rigged one in seven minutes, which was done as follows. As the Thirty came down the track in her cradle to be launched we had her mast, with all its rigging attached and stopped down, hanging from a derrick right over where she would be as she floated off the cradle. Her boom, sheets, and other parts were on a scow alongside. When the Thirty moved under the derrick her mast was lowered in place and about six men leaped aboard, each knowing exactly what to do as we had previously rigged several just like her. Every part fitted perfectly, and after the pins of the turnbuckles were in place we rove off her sheets and halyards as if we were setting a spinnaker in a race. Those were the days when men knew how to do things and did them.

The New York Yacht Club Thirties had a remarkable queue of owners, many of whom had had much larger yachts. They were:

"Minx"	Howard Willets
"Pintail"	August Belmont
"Maid of Mendon"	W. D. Guthrie
"Neola II"	George M. Pynchon
"Phryne"	Henry Maxwell
"Cara Mia"	Stuyvesant Wainwright
"Alera"	A. H. Alker
"Atair"	Cord Meyer
"Linnet"	Amos T. French
"Nautilus"	Addison G. Hanan
"Adelaide II"	G. A. Adee
"Anemone"	J. M. Mitchell, Jr.
"Tobasco"	Henry F. Lippitt
"Banzai"	Newbury D. Lawton
"Ibis"	O'Donnell Iselin
"Dahinda"	W. Butler Duncan, Jr.
"Oriole"	Lyman Delano
"Carlita"	Oliver Harriman

It would be hard to get together at any time a class of better sailor men and they raced the Thirties very hard and had few protests. Soon after they came out it was found that it never paid to reef in a race, and the Thirties were certainly great sail luggers;

they often carried full sail in winds of forty-five miles per hour.

This class is said to have raced more than any other. As they raced very actively the first ten years and fairly regularly the first thirty years, this statement is probably true. They are now forty-five years old and appear structurally sound with the topsides nearly as smooth as when new. These boats no doubt have given more fun for the money than any boats ever built for their annual expense has been small as they have required almost no repairs or alterations.

The Thirties were almost exactly alike when new and it was told that the one that came in last at the end of the first year came in at the head of the class some subsequent year. Many different ones have won the season's championship in their turn. Many one-design classes have come and gone since the New York Yacht Club Thirties were built, but none of them has begun to hold its popularity over as great a term of years. These New York Thirties are a monument to Captain Nat's genius in construction, and it is very likely that if any of their parts had been either larger or smaller, or of different material, they would not have stood so many years of hard driving.

In 1904, just before the New York Thirties, Captain Nat designed two Thirties for a rule then in use at Marblehead. These yachts were the "Wasaka" and "Chewink IV," the latter with Mike Into, the man who invented the Into hook, as captain winning the championship in the class. These boats were quite wide and had a deep keel, and proved capable of being driven very fast in strong breezes. They were among the last boats that Captain Nat designed for the length-on-water-line and sail-area rules although he did continue to design Buzzards Bay twenty-one-footers for a few years more.

Another interesting yacht of his design that was kept at Marblehead for some time was the "Cock Robin II" built in 1904 for Mr. C. S. Eaton, who had had several Herreshoff sailboats built, including the twenty-one-footers "Cock Robin" and "Cockatoo," and the "Little Robin" and "Mimosa III." The "Cock Robin II" was designed to be just a good sailboat and not fit any particular rule. It is a good example of a model about halfway between the Universal Rule boats, with their short quarter beam and rather large displacement, and the older types, with long lines to sail on and no pot belly. There was another yacht built on the same molds but longer—"Suzetta III"—which went to Blue Hill, Maine. These two boats were somewhat under-rigged but fast sailers on a reach in strong wind.

Among the medium-sized racers of that time was the "P" boat "Seneca," which I think was the first "P" Captain Nat designed. She was only thirty-two feet W.L. but a very pretty yacht of almost the same model as the "Q" boat "Eleanor." If I remember right, she successfully represented the United States in the races against Canada on the Great Lakes.

This brings us up to about 1910, but you must not suppose that these were the only yachts Captain Nat designed in these years. They are simply the ones that made the greatest impression on my memory, and as there were many of them it has been hard to choose the most interesting ones. You will note that I have grouped them more according to their type and size than in chronological order, but the Herreshoff Manufacturing Company was still producing nearly as many dollars' worth of steamers and powerboats at that time. At the end of this book will be an alphabetical listing of yachts built by the Herreshoff Company.

CHAPTER TWELVE

Captain Nat's Designs Between 1910 and 1920

HE "Westward" was the most important of Captain Nat's yachts to come out in 1910, and she came to be built as follows. Alexander S. Cochran had owned the famous sloop "Avenger" in 1909, when Charlie Barr was her captain. Although Mr. Cochran had not been a very enthusiastic yachtsman, after winning the Astor Cup that year and listening to the stories Charlie Barr told of racing "Ingomar" abroad a few years before, he decided to have a schooner that could make the crossing and make a good showing when she got there. So he asked Captain Barr how it could be arranged and Captain Barr told him, "All you will have to do is run up to Bristol and tell N. G. Herreshoff you want a yacht for that purpose and be sure not to tell him how to design her for if you do he probably will not take the order. You may have to show him some credentials for he doesn't like to design a large yacht unless he thinks the owner can afford it."

So one day late in the summer of 1909 Mr. Cochran ran up to Bristol in his steam yacht and called on Captain Nat. He must have furnished good credentials for Captain Nat started at once on the design of a ninety-six foot water-line steel schooner for him, and she was at the time the largest sailboat the Herreshoff Company had made. She was named "Westward" and came out

276

early in the season of 1910, with general dimensions of: L.O.A., one hundred and thirty-six feet; L.W.L., ninety-six feet; beam, twenty-six feet eight inches; draft, seventeen feet. She was modeled somewhat to fit the measurement rules then in use in Europe which, among other things, took in a girth measurement so that "Westward" had some drag to her keel and the lead was rounded off to make her girth less. "Westward" also was partly built to Lloyd's rules for construction although Lloyd's inspectors did make some concessions to the improved constructions that Captain Nat had developed, including an improved layout of rivets that weakened the plating less.

After a few trial sails under her racing rig "Westward" was refitted for the ocean crossing with sails of less area, working gaffs, etc., and set sail for England under the command of Captain Charlie Barr with her owner, Mr. Cochran, aboard. Mr. Cochran was an inveterate cigarette smoker and had purchased a large quantity of cigarettes to last him on this trip even if it were prolonged by light weather, but when the "Westward" had cleared Newport and had squared away on her course for England Mr. Cochran stepped to the lee rail and, to break his smoking habit, gave all his cigarettes a sea toss knowing that even with all his millions he could not purchase another cigarette in the next three thousand miles. "Westward" did not make a remarkably fast crossing for she had unsuitable weather with head winds, etc., but after reaching the other side she proved to be remarkably fast and was undoubtedly the most successful foreign yacht that had ever raced in England and Germany.

As I write this I have before me a letter from Captain Barr to Captain Nat written aboard the "Westward" on July 16, at the middle of the racing season, in which he says among other things; "She is a splendid boat. Crossed over with some rather rough weather and got no water on deck, and practically on an even keel. She has not shown the least sign of strain and made no creaking inside, which I think is a rare thing in a boat crossing the Atlantic. She has started nine times and won eight without time allowance and one with the time allowance." I must note that after the middle of the season "Westward" was given an arbitrary handicap and had difficulty in winning. I believe this arbitrary handicap was so raised that on the day of the last race "Westward" lay at anchor believing the handicap too great to give her a chance. Although this would seem very unfair to a visiting yacht it is an automatic testimony that "Westward" could beat all the English and German yachts when rated by measurement.

However, Mr. Cochran and Captain Barr had a wonderful time beating all the largest yachts in Europe; in fact Mr. Cochran was so enthusiastic over this yachting experience that in the next few years he was to have the three-masted schooner "Sea Call" built, as well as the cup candidate "Vanitie." Perhaps if Captain Barr had lived to handle the "Vanitie," she might have been difficult to beat, but that winter when "Westward" was laid up at Southampton, Captain Barr died suddenly of a heart attack so that "Westward" was the last command of this greatest of all professional yacht captains.

The "Westward" was to live a long time, however, and have an interesting history. In the spring of 1911 she was brought back to this country under the command of Chris Christensen who had been her mate under Captain Barr; in fact Christensen had been crew or mate with the Barrs, John and Charles, for about seventeen years. In the seasons of 1911 "Westward" raced against the new schooner "Elena," which I will speak of presently, and "Westward" won the Astor Cup of that year. In about 1912 or 1913 she was sold to German owners, and while in Germany had some quite heavy and elaborate cabin work put into her, including a grand piano. The German designer, Max Ortz, had designed a German-built schooner that was very much a copy of "Westward" but larger, and there probably would have been some hot racing in the large schooner class in Germany if the war had not started in 1914. "Westward" was in England in August of that year, probably for Cowes Race Week, and at the very sudden commencement of the war was laid up in England where she was later seized by the English. In later years she was owned by T. B. Davis who made his home port the Channel Islands of Jersey and Guernsey where "Westward" was annually stored and overhauled including the work on her spars, rigging, and sails. Manned with a Channel Islands crew she raced quite regularly, and after "Britannia" was perhaps the most popular of the large British yachts.

When the English had adopted the Universal Rule for rating the larger classes, she was always a potential winner with a strong beam wind, and on August 9, 1935, the last day of the Royal Yacht Squadron's Regatta, beat everything including the large "J" class sloops "Velsheda," "Yankee," "Candida," "Endeavour," "Shamrock," etc. Although these large sloops had fresh jibs and gigantic spinnakers the "Westward"'s model allowed her to leave them all behind on a reach. Of course she was a much more sensible, safe and comfortable yacht than her competitors, in spite of being then twenty-five years old. Mr. Davis was very fond of "Westward," and requested that when he died she should be taken to sea and sunk, but the British authorities objected to this waste of material and I do not know her final disposition. However, she was probably the most successful of any American-built yacht that raced in foreign waters, not excepting "America" and "Sappho," for "Westward" raced successfully for many years against many highly developed yachts. While she is not so well known in this country she probably was one of the greatest racing sailboats of all time.

But we must go back to 1910 again for late that winter, after "Westward" was well under way, Harold Vanderbilt, who was then a student at Harvard Law School, ordered from Captain Nat a small composite-built schooner which was completed very rapidly. I think she was put together in about two months although she lasted well. This was the first "Vagrant" whose general dimensions were: L.O.A., seventy-six feet; L.W.L., fifty-six feet; beam, seventeen feet six inches; draft, ten feet six inches. At that time Harold Vanderbilt was not much of a racing man and he used her mostly for cruising, but right after World War I, when owned by Nathaniel F. Ayer and under the name of "Queen Mab," she came out with a new rig designed by Captain Nat that had a leg-o'-mutton mainsail, and I believe was about the first American schooner with track and slides on the luff of mainsail, although of course there had been many leg-o'-mutton sails and trisails that ran on hoops or used lace lines before that, including the Chesapeake Bay "Bugeyes," Connecticut "Sharpies," etc. However, Captain Nat was the first to develop a satisfactory track and slide for a vessel of this type, and "Queen Mab" did very well in racing for the next few years although originally she had been built mostly for cruising.

In 1911 Captain Nat got the order for "Elena," and I must tell something about that incident for it will seem very strange to modern ears which are used to much salesmanship, bickering, and endless estimates in connection with ordering a new sizable yacht. Well, then, Morton F. Plant, who was to be "Elena"'s owner, used swear words when talking to men (although he was a most kindly man to children). At any rate, one evening after a good dinner he called Captain Nat on the telephone, and their short and sweet conversation was about as follows:

Plant speaking:	Is this N. G. Herreshoff?
Capt. Nat:	Yes, I think so.
Plant:	I want a ——— ——— schooner for Class B, and I want her to be ——— ——— good.
Captain Nat:	Humph, all right.

Of course Mr. Plant had done business with the Herreshoffs before and had had "Ingomar" built only a few years previously, and Captain Nat knew that Mr. Plant was good for most anything he might order. In other words they both had complete confidence in each other, but it is interesting how some of the men of that time did business. No doubt signed contracts followed this conversation, and when "Elena" was tried out, Mr. Plant was as much interested in every detail as could be but he did not in any way interfere with the design. "Elena" was almost a sister ship to "Westward" and had the same general dimensions, but the shape of her lead was different for, as I said before, "Westward" was designed to partly fit some of the European rules where a girth measurement was taken, but in "Elena"'s case the forward end of the lead was deeper, and the keel at its lower edges was not rounded off so that "Elena" had the center of her ballast lower, and if I remember right she had a little more sail area than "Westward." However, "Elena" and "Westward" went at it hammer and tongs in the season of 1911; while "Elena" should have beaten "Westward," I believe they were quite evenly matched.

The captain of "Westward" was Chris Christensen, and the captain of "Elena" was Bill Dennis, that adroit skipper who had done so well with the two schooners "Elmina" which between them had won the Astor Cup seven times. After this training with the racing of "Westward" and "Elena" these two captains were chosen as sailing masters of the cup candidates "Resolute" and "Vanitie" that came out a few years later.

In both 1912 and 1913 "Elena" won the Astor Cup, but then, owing to World War I and Mr. Plant's death, she was laid up for several years. However, in 1928, when owned by Mr. William B. Bell, she entered the transatlantic race to Santander with John Barr as captain. This John Barr was the son of old John Barr and nephew of Charlie Barr. "Elena"'s sails were very old and many of them gave out in this race, but she succeeded in winning in the large class nevertheless, and got the King of Spain's cup.

Among the smaller yachts of this time that Captain Nat designed were the "P" boats, "Corinthian" built for the Sewanhaka Corinthian Yacht Club; and the "Joyant," built for W. H. Childs of the famous Childs's restaurants. At the time Gardner had designed several handsome "P" boats that were more or less copies of the earlier "P"s that Captain Nat had designed, and there was considerable rivalry in the class for some important cups were offered for their competition. Captain Nat designed "Joyant" much larger than other "P"s of that time: she was about thirty-five feet six inches W.L. while the Gardner "P"s were about thirty-two feet five inches. "Joyant" had around two hundred more square feet sail area than the others, for Gardner never seemed to work out boats that rated low under the Universal Rule, and this was later to be the principal trouble with "Vanitie." However, "Joyant" eventually did so well that she nearly broke up the "P" class so Gardner, whose boats had been beaten, brought power to bear to have the measurement rules so changed that the displacement and sail area under the Universal Rule were kept within certain proportions of the waterline length. "Joyant" also had some reverse curves in her forward and after overhangs, so at the same time rules were made which prevented this peculiarity from reducing the rating. "Joyant" is notable for having caused the present limits to proportions now in the rule.

Another yacht built in 1911, the same year as "Joyant" but of very different model, was "Flying Cloud," built for Francis and Lawrence Grinnell. She shows how versatile Captain Nat was, for while most other yachts of that time had long, narrow bows and sterns, "Flying Cloud" had a very small amount of overhang. However, she was a smart sailer and one of the smallest yachts the Herreshoff Manufacturing Company built of composite construction. She was only fifty-eight feet O.A., and although in 1950 she was thirty-nine years old she is sailing with a leg-o'-mutton rig, and is owned by F. M. Temple of Toledo.

Things were a little slack at the Herreshoff Company in the winter of 1911–12 and Captain Nat had the little centerboard sloop "Alerion" built for his own use at Bermuda where he was for the next few years to spend part of his winters. "Alerion" has lasted a long time and her owner in 1950 was Isaac B. Merriman of Warren, Rhode Island. In a letter to me he said, "I think she is one of the finest boats that was ever built," and he ought to know for he has had some of the best of them.

For the season of 1913 Captain Nat designed the steel schooner "Vagrant" of eighty-five foot rating for Harold S. Vanderbilt. This was the second schooner this owner had had named "Vagrant," and her principal dimensions were, L.O.A., one hundred and nine feet; L.W.L., eighty feet; beam, twenty-four feet ten inches; draft, fourteen feet ten inches. "Vagrant" was built to Lloyd's rules of construction as a 100 A-1 vessel so was comparatively heavy, but though not particularly handsome, on account of her rather straight shear; she nevertheless proved to be so well liked that there were eventually two others like her built. They were the "Mariette," built in 1916 for J. F. Brown of Boston (afterward named "Cleopatra's Barge") and the "Ohonkara," built in 1920 for Carl Tucker of New York. These three steel schooners were particularly able and comfortable and had a lot of accommodation. It might be said that Harold Vanderbilt first took to racing seriously when he owned this "Vagrant," and he won the Astor Cup with her in 1921, 1922, and 1925, as well as the King's Cup in 1925, and many other yacht club runs.

But the most important work of the Herreshoff Company for 1913 was the one-design class of New York Yacht Club Fifties for there were nine of this one-design class built that winter, which seems strange these days when a yacht of the same overall length recently built cost over two hundred thousand dollars. Although the Fifties were of about the best material and workmanship that ever went into yachts of their size, they were so efficiently built that it is said they only cost approximately seventeen thousand dollars apiece in 1913. The general dimensions of these Fifties were: L.O.A., seventy-two feet; L.W.L., fifty feet; beam, fourteen feet six inches; draft, nine feet nine inches. Their original owners and names were:

Name	Owner	Later Name
"Acushla"	G. M. Heckscher	"Revery"
"Barbara"	H. P. Whitney	
"Carolina"	Pembroke Jones	
"Grayling"	J. P. Morgan	"Ibis"
"Iroquois II"	Ralph Ellis	"Chiora"
"Pleione"	H. L. Maxwell	
"Samuri"	W. Earl Dodge	"Andiamo"
"Spartan"	Edmund Randolph	
"Ventura"	G. F. Baker, Jr.	"Venture"

Although "Pleione" was built as "Peerless" for H. L. Maxwell, she was named "Pleione" and owned by C. C. Rumrill and E. T. Irvin during her first year.

The Fifties were raced very hotly the first two years but had few protests and no serious collisions. The author raced on "Barbara" many races the first two years and can say that under their original rig they were fine, comfortable racing yachts when they had a crew of four or more professionals, but after World War I they were too expensive to run even if good crews had been available so several were changed to yawls or schooners, or leg-o'-mutton sloops. However, the Astor Cup for sloops has been won by one or another of them about nine times, and "Pleione," under a schooner rig designed by the author, has won the Astor Cup for schooners four times for her owner, J. V. Santry. Mr. Frederick F. Brewster, with two different yachts named "Elmina," has won it some seven times, and the sloop "Avenger" has won it four times with three different owners, but as "Pleione" won it once as a sloop there must be five Astor Cups, each worth one thousand dollars, with her name on them.

"Pleione" today seems as sound as when built, and when I examine her below I am amazed at the fine materials which are in her: some of her deck beams have the grain nearly parallel with the crown of deck from side to side. When "Pleione" was changed to a schooner she had the first box section spars to be used on a yacht of that size, together with shrouds attached with tangs instead of being spliced around the spar, and many other features now universally used.

If the winter of 1912–13 had been a busy one for the wood-workers of the Herreshoff Company the winter of 1913-14 was a busier one for all hands, for that winter, besides building the one hundred and sixty-two feet O.A. steel schooner "Katoura," they built the cup boat "Resolute," the Newport twenty-nine-footers, the first of the numerous class of twelve-and-one-half-footers, and also some power yachts. At that time the Herreshoff Company had bought some heavy machinery for the steel construction shop, the principal machines being plate rollers for bending and forming plating, and a plate planing machine for planing the edges of plates after they were sheered out. These machines saved a lot of hard work which had previously been done mostly by hand.

"Katoura," was the largest yacht the Herreshoff Company ever built and she just about filled up the south construction shop with little to spare endwise, sidewise, or overhead. Her tonnage was so great that Captain Nat did not think the ways strong enough for her so that she was designed to have only about three quarters of her lead on the outside, the rest of her ballast being made up of cast lead blocks which were put into her after she was launched. Her foremast was the hollow steel mast that had been made for "Constitution," and her mainmast was the mainmast of "Reliance." These spars the Herreshoff Company had bought when these two cup boats were broken up. Her model was similar to "Westward" and "Elena" but if anything prettier: she was one hundred and sixty-two feet L.O.A., one hundred and fifteen feet L.W.L., thirty feet beam, and eighteen feet draft, and her gross tonnage was three hundred and thirteen. She was built under Lloyds inspection and classed as a 100-A1 vessel. It is probable that "Katoura" was, all around, the finest yacht that Captain Nat designed, but Captain Nat made a mistake in designing such a racy yacht for that particular owner, for he had been used to heavier and more seagoing types of yachts. Her owner, Mr. Robert E. Tod, was a very capable seaman but the large sail area and light but scientific rigging of "Katoura" really needed a man like Charlie Barr to manage it, and a yacht of this type definitely needed a captain who could stay with her all the time she was in commission. But Mr. Tod decided to act as captain himself and had as sailing master a Russian Finn who did not understand her light wire rigging and many winches, nor apparently could he get along with the crew, so it might be said "Katoura" never went for a real sail with everything used as designed. On the contrary, after having difficulty with managing her, her rig was soon reduced. I have said Captain Nat made a mistake in making "Katoura" so racy, but Mr. Tod had intimated that he wanted to make some records between ports and over the Cape May and Brentons Reef race courses. Nevertheless, "Katoura" could have been designed less racy and still easily beaten the other schooners in Class A, for at the time "Atlantic" was about the fastest of them and she was logy in anything but a strong beam wind, and even dull in short tacking to windward in light airs.

I do not know the cost of "Katoura" but it probably was around three hundred and fifty thousand dollars as she had numerous winches, quite a lot of fine cabinetwork below decks, the taste of which might be questioned, but all of the finest workmanship. "Katoura" also was built as an auxiliary with a six cylinder Winton engine, special reduction gear, and folding propeller which naturally added to her first cost. I only mention this as all previous large sailboats built at Bristol, with the exception of the second "Vagrant," were without auxiliary power although some of them, like "Elena," had power installed later.

"Katoura," however, won the Brentons Reef Cup three times and the Cape May Cup twice, but both of these cups were forfeited to her in 1914 because of lack of competition. In May, 1915, "Katoura" cruised to Bermuda in company with Harold Vanderbilt's steel schooner "Vagrant," and as the latter was much smaller she ran her auxiliary motor part of the time so they both arrived at Bermuda within a few hours of each other. On the return trip "Katoura" 's best day's run was two hundred and fifty-three miles while "Vagrant" made two hundred and seventeen on the same day, which was probably in proportion to the rating of the two yachts. They both took a little over three days to make the six hundred and sixty-mile run back.

On the day that they made the best run the conditions were not particularly favorable as they consisted of varying breezes from light easterly to strong southwest winds. One is tempted to imagine what "Katoura" would have done if she had had a steady beam wind, her original rig, and Charlie Barr at the helm. My guess would be well over three hundred miles for I believe she was the fastest schooner ever built anywhere at any time. We know "Westward" and "Elena" were fast, but in "Katoura" we had an enlarged sister of these yachts which was nineteen feet longer on the water line and had many other speed-giving qualities, including steel masts and numerous sheet-trimming winches. "Katoura" was laid up at New London during World War I, but after the war Mr. Tod thought that there would be difficulty in securing a crew for such a large and racy yacht so she was sold to Mr. Russell Alger who installed a large diesel engine in her and I believe cut about twenty feet off of the foot of her masts so that she was a rather queer-looking craft with her mainmasts appearing very short in comparison with her topmasts which were not altered. Mr. Alger used her for cruising one or two years, and then she was sold to English owners. I do not know her later history. But I do think she was kind of a heart-breaker to Captain Nat who had hoped she would have a great racing career.

It might be said that "Katoura" was the only racy type of schooner built for Class A as the others, such as "Atlantic," "Karina," "Vergemere," etc. were heavy duty yachts that could hardly get going in light weather on short courses, so it is unfortunate that "Katoura" 's racing life was cut short by World War I.

It is too bad that she had to be cut down and never had a sail with a capable crew under her original rig, for she probably will be the last large sailer, or perhaps the only large sailboat of nice model, light rigging, and racing sails, folding propeller, etc. It would have been interesting to know what she was capable of.

In the case of "Resolute," she too in the end was pretty much of a heartbreaker for she was a victim of strange circumstances that Fate had lined up to keep her at a disadvantage throughout her life. When Lipton challenged for the cup in 1913 it was requested that the races should be for yachts of under seventy-five feet water line, but before the New York Yacht Club would accept the challenge, considerable time was used for making agreements. In the meantime there had been quite a lot of talk on both sides of the Atlantic about the desirability of having smaller cup boats on account of the cost of such yachts as "Reliance" and "Shamrock III." No doubt Lipton and others had been visualizing yachts proportioned like "Reliance" in which case they would have been large and expensive although only seventy-five feet W.L. The deed of gift under which the cup was held stated that the competing yachts must be measured under the rules then in use by the club holding the cup, and as the New York Yacht Club had adopted the Universal Rule since the cup races of 1903 this allowed or compelled a very different model of yacht than those used in the last four series of cup races. In other words, the sail area and over-all length as well as the draft had to be considerably less as compared to the length on water line, but under the Universal Rule it is possible to build yachts of quite different rating with the same water-line length. Because of much talk about the cost of larger yachts Captain Nat chose to design the new cup boat "Resolute" of small rating, and so she was smaller than "Vanitie" and "Shamrock IV," and we will see how this later counted against her.

At any rate soon after Lipton's challenge was accepted in 1913 the New York Yacht Club formed a syndicate to build a yacht for the defense of the cup, and although Captain Nat was getting along in years, being then sixty-five and at the time far from well, the syndicate entrusted him with the order for the yacht that was later named "Resolute." At the time Mr. Alexander Smith Cochran, who had owned "Westward," was having the large three-masted schooner "Sea Call" built, designed by William Gardner and built at the George Lawley & Son Corporation. He decided to build also a cup candidate designed and built by the same firms, which made one of the greatest outlays that an individual has made for sailboats in one year. While I do not know the combined cost of these two yachts I do suppose it was over half a million, and I doubt if they could be duplicated today for one and a half million. This new cup candidate was a very handsome vessel and, when new and throughout her first year, was polished bronze from keel to rail cap; she was most appropriately named "Vanitie" in remembrance of the poem of the "Golden Vanitie," for her polished bronze plating glistened like gold.

At about the same time George M. Pynchon and E. Walter Clark ordered another cup candidate from Mr. George Owen who at the time was designing very successful racing yachts for the smaller classes. Mr. Owen had acquired some of his training while working under Captain Nat, and, although a very talented man, was under the great disadvantage that his yacht was built by five or six different concerns. She was of composite construction, the metal framing being built by the Bath Iron Works; the planking and other woodwork by Hodgdon Brothers; the spars, fittings, rigging, and sails being furnished by four other companies. This yacht was named "Defiance" and as might be expected had so much trouble with rig and fittings that she only raced in about half the trial races in 1914, and then retired from racing altogether. She, too, was considerably smaller than "Vanitie," and if I remember right, rated even lower than "Resolute." The general dimensions of these three cup candidates follow:

	L.O.A.	L.W.L.	Beam	Draft
"Vanitie"	118'	75'	22' 6"	13' 8"
"Reliance"	100'	75'	21' 2"	13'
"Defiance"	115'	75'	22'	13' 9"

In the first part of the season of 1914 "Vanitie" was managed mostly by Bill Dennis who had much experience with large racing yachts and could train a crew, but "Resolute," which was under the management of R. W. Emmons with C. F. Adams as helmsman and Chris Christensen as sailing master, was somewhat hamstrung for these three men, though all experienced sailors and seamen, were all peculiarly lacking in mechanical sense so never could quite understand or take advantage of the many mechanical contrivances on "Resolute." To be sure both Mr. Emmons and Mr. Adams were natural helmsmen who could sail small- and medium-sized yachts as well as anyone by some instinct, as you will occasionally find a remarkably good female automobile driver, but they, as well as Chris Christensen, had no understanding of the mechanics of "Resolute." "Resolute" was therefore a very different proposition for Captain Nat compared to his last four cup boats. In the place of a very affable, appreciative, and quick to understand man like E. D. Morgan with whom he could talk things over sensibly, or the very keen and capable Mr. Iselin, he had on "Resolute" men who could neither understand his work nor with whom he could talk intelligently.

In the first race between "Vanitie" and "Resolute" the "Vanitie" came in about quarter of an hour ahead, but after a few races "Resolute" improved in speed so much that Captain Bill Dennis, who I believe was not very well, decided to retire. After this, "Resolute" generally beat "Vanitie" boat to boat although on a thirty-mile course "Vanitie" had to allow her more than three minutes. At the end of the first season the score of the three yachts was as follows:

	Firsts	Seconds	Thirds	Others	Total
"Resolute"	15	2	0	1	18
"Vanitie"	5	14	1	0	20
"Defiance"	0	4	3	3	10

In other words "Resolute" beat "Vanitie" fifteen times, and "Vanitie" beat "Resolute" three times, and in one of the races "Resolute" withdrew on account of fog, so the first year's score between "Vanitie" and "Resolute" was something like five to one in favor of "Resolute." Two of "Vanitie"'s wins were over "Defiance" when "Resolute" did not race.

In the meantime war had started in Europe, but in spite of this "Vanitie" and "Resolute" went at it again in 1915. This time "Vanitie" was better managed for she had been chartered for the season by ex-commodore Cornelius Vanderbilt who, besides being an experienced helmsman on yachts of this size, was a capable manager. He had money of his own and could make decisions as to changes in sails and all without consulting anyone. Besides this Chris Christensen, who had the season before been sailing master of "Resolute," went with Commodore Vanderbilt on "Vanitie," and I imagine Christensen was happy to get back under the commodore for whom he had been captain on "Aurora," and thus get away from the indecisions on board "Resolute." This gave "Vanitie" quite an advantage for, of course, Christensen knew all the tricks of the "Resolute" afterguard and could generally tell what they would do under various circumstances. And, too, Butler Duncan, who had been the manager of both "Defender" and "Constitution," was in the afterguard of "Vanitie."

That year "Resolute" did much experimenting with rigs, one of which had a rather small fore triangle, which has since proved to be a disadvantage, and probably the year before had been the principal defect of "Defiance." With these changes "Vanitie" made some improvement and the score at the end of the second season was:

	Firsts	Seconds	Others	Total
"Resolute"	12	2	2	16
"Vanitie"	4	11	1	16

The "Shamrock IV" had sailed over, but as the war in Europe had become serious the cup races were indefinitely postponed. "Shamrock" was stored at City Island while "Resolute" and her gear were stored in a building especially built for her at Bristol. Thus these yachts rested during the next five years until things quieted down after World War I.

Now I must say something about "Shamrock IV." In his fourth attempt at the cup, Lipton had gone to Charles E. Nicholson of the firm of Camper and Nicholsons Ltd. at Gosport, England. This concern was located in sight of the most popular yacht racing courses in England, and nearly opposite the ancient navy yard at Portsmouth. I think Mr. Charles Nicholson was of the third generation of yacht designers and yacht builders, and his company had been building yachts for some hundred years.

However, it is interesting that all but one of the cup challengers since "Galatea" in 1886 had been built in Scotland, so this shift to England is interesting for certainly Mr. Nicholson had been producing many of the most successful yachts for several years, and he was to design the next four in a row which made the most number of challengers designed by one man.

"Shamrock IV" was Mr. Nicholson's first attempt at a Universal Rule yacht, and while he had been designing quite normal shapes under the various Y.R.A. rules he seemed to think some sort of abnormal model would have the best chance to lift the cup. While "Shamrock IV" was the same water-line length as "Resolute," she rated considerably higher. Her low full ends made her take a penalty in quarter beam measurement, and she was slightly deeper than the draft limit for her L.W.L. I, myself, did not like her model and considered that her topsides were shaped for higher speed than the full lines below the water line would allow. The full lines below water, of course, were necessary to acquire the proportion of displacement required by the rule. However, this "Shamrock" was of very scientific construction with deep wooden web frames and probably the first, and perhaps the last, large racer to use much laminated wood in her construction. I say this because later yachts did and probably will use metal in many places where laminated wood was used on this "Shamrock," but all later cup boats were built to Lloyds rules for construction. Nevertheless, many features in the construction of "Shamrock IV" have since been used in airplane construction. "Shamrock"'s spars and rigging were all very ingenious and scientific, and her sail plan high and narrow. Some people have said she was the homeliest yacht that had ever raced for the cup.

Although "Shamrock IV"'s rating was not definitely known some people over here thought that it would be so great that she would have to allow "Resolute" some ten minutes over a thirty-mile course. While this later proved to be an exaggeration still the cup defense committee were in a panic believing that if the defender won all her races with time allowance, while being beaten boat to boat, the public both here and abroad would be dissatisfied, in which assumption they were undoubtedly right for the public both in England and over here were heartily tired of our holding the cup so continuously. So now the hue and cry was to increase the rating of "Resolute," or at least bring it up to that of "Vanitie," and that caused Captain Nat much annoyance. You see it is easy to increase the rating of a yacht under the Universal Rule by simply increasing her sail area, but the increase in speed will be much less in proportion. While "Resolute" had beaten "Vanitie" quite regularly, it had usually been with handicap, or, in other words, "Vanitie" several times beat her boat to boat, and the competition was unusually close. Also, a few years before, Captain Nat had been talked into increasing the sail area and rating of the fifty-seven-footers so that they rated sixty-five feet, and he knew from experience that this change had made them less potential winners.

In the meantime World War I was raging, and Captain Nat had been in very poor health. He had gone to a hospital in New York to have his teeth extracted and to have other treatment, which did eventually improve his condition, particularly his rheumatism which had been very painful for many years. Captain Nat's brother, John Brown Herreshoff, whom we have been calling J. B., died on July 20, 1915, and this threw the work of managing the plant on Captain Nat's shoulders and forced him to do work he disliked for he did not like to be financially responsible for his brother's holdings in the plant. So soon after J. B.'s holdings and some of Captain Nat's were taken over by a syndicate of yachtsmen. They ran the plant through the war and a few years after until it was liquidated by auction in August, 1924.

In 1915, at the age of sixty-seven, Captain Nat, having been a widower for ten years, was married to Ann Roebuck who had been a close friend to the family for many years, and it was she who nursed him back to health and undoubtedly made it possible for him to live to the age of ninety.

We must get back to "Resolute" again. In August, 1919, it was decided that the international races, which had been postponed on account of the war, would be run off in July, 1920. At that time Mr. Cochran, who was failing in health, presented "Vanitie" to the Flag Officers Syndicate which owned "Resolute." He presented her under the condition that she was to be raced as a contender for the honor of defending the cup. Mr. George Nichols, who had been in the afterguard of "Resolute" and was the navigator on her in the 1914–15 races, was chosen to manage her and promptly secured the services of W. Starling Burgess, his old schoolmate at Milton Academy, to rerig and recondition her. Starling had been about the best yacht designer east of Cape Cod and for some years had been in the aeronautical business designing heavier than air craft before the war and working on dirigibles during the war. He was the son of Edward Burgess, who had designed "Puritan," "Mayflower," and "Volunteer." Thus, not only did he have a yacht designing background, but, thanks to his work in aeronautics, was well versed in the mathematics of light structural design. Under his direction the pine deck of "Vanitie" was removed and a thin plywood canvas covered deck laid in its place. Her bronze bulwarks, which were an extension of her bronze plating, were cut down to deck level excepting for a short section where the bowsprit was housed. Her sail plan was altered by cutting two feet off the bowsprit and main boom: her mainmast lengthened two feet, and her topmast lengthened six feet. Her whole rig was lightened and improved and one of the most important improvements was due to the fact that Mr. Nichols had persuaded Captain Nat to build for the "Vanitie" a duplicate set of the winches used on "Resolute" for handling sails and backstays and which saved much time in maneuvering.

By doing this Captain Nat was partly cutting his own throat for apparently Gardner and Burgess could not design these special fittings. After these changes, inside lead ballast was added to compensate for the weight saved. Although "Vanitie"'s potential speed was increased her rating was reduced. Ratsey also made "Vanitie" an almost perfect suit of sails for that season. The afterguard of "Vanitie" was Mr. George Nichols, Mr. C. Sherman Hoyt, Mr. W. Starling Burgess, and Mr. Charles G. Nourse. Mr. Cochran became very much interested in her again and contributed generously to her expenses, while Mr. Addison G. Hanan followed the races to act as observer and critic, so that on the whole "Vanitie" had a remarkably well-balanced afterguard, and in Sherman Hoyt perhaps the best helmsman on the Sound.

In the meantime much pressure was brought to bear to have Captain Nat increase the sail plan and rating of "Resolute," which of course was a mistake as she had originally been built too small to be driven fast enough to make up for an increase in rating. However, in an endeavor to accomplish this, "Resolute" was given a light, hollow, built-up mast, which included the top-mast in one piece, and her sail plan slightly increased and made higher, but unfortunately in the first race of 1920, off New Haven, "Resolute" carried away this new light mast. This writer was quite close to leeward when the accident occurred, and it happened like this. The race had been in moderate weather, but as "Resolute," which had a good lead, bore off to round the mark at the north end of the course a very heavy squall came off the shore and struck her. Her main sheet was slacked away, but unfortunately her backstays, which were controlled from below deck, were not, so that the sail and gaff bore very heavily on the backstays. In fact it looked as if the topmast backstay would almost cut the sail. At the time I was much excited for I knew what would happen with this terrific additional compression put on the mast. All of a sudden the mast seemed to explode and become splinters, which were strewn for some distance over the water. The mast must have broken in several pieces at once for it almost instantly changed from a spar to a hundred or more slivers. It was a beautiful example of a nearly perfectly proportioned spar becoming overloaded.

It would have been very interesting to see how "Resolute" would have fared with this lighter mast and increased area, but instead she had to hurry back to Bristol and have one of her steel masts with a topmast stepped, with the usual consequences of a forced change in rig. Besides this her crew was jumpy the rest of the season.

While there was not time for many trial races that year I believe there were twelve starts in which "Resolute" won seven firsts and "Vanitie" four firsts, showing the great improvement that Burgess had made in "Vanitie." Even then the score for the three years that they raced with gaff mainsails stands, "Resolute" first thirty-four times, "Vanitie" first thirteen times, though two of "Vanitie"'s firsts were when she defeated "Defiance" and "Resolute" was not in the races. Thus the score works out about three to one in favor of "Resolute," and as Herb Stone says in his excellent book, *The American Cup Races*: "In the three seasons they had met, the Herreshoff sloop had had overwhelmingly the best of it. . . . She was a much 'surer bet' than 'Vanitie,' no matter what one thought of the capabilities of the bronze Gardner boat."

While these races between "Vanitie" and "Resolute" were taking place, "Shamrock IV" was tuning up under the skillful care of Captain Albert Turner, one of the best English professionals, and her trial horse was the twenty-three-meter "Shamrock," which Lipton had sent over for that purpose. In these races "Shamrock IV" was reported to be exceptionally fast, but it would be hard to compare them for the new "Shamrock" was larger and built to a different measurement rule, but she had to be fast for, although changes had been made to decrease the "Shamrock" 's rating and increase the rating of "Resolute," still "Shamrock IV" had to allow "Resolute" some seven minutes over the cup course, although it turned out in the end that "Resolute" could beat her boat to boat when they were in the same conditions.

The first race started at noon, July 15, 1920, in light and fluky weather. On the first leg when close hauled "Resolute" pointed higher and seemed to foot nearly as fast, but the racers encountered a rather heavy thunder shower without much wind and very foolishly the afterguard of "Resolute," who I have said before were not mechanically bright, had her throat halyard slacked away, believing that the shower of rain they had passed through would have shrunk her halyards and luff rope making an unnatural strain on things. As her halyards and luff ropes were of wire, of course the rain had no effect on them. Well, on "Resolute" the halyard jig winch was below deck. Although word had been passed down to slack out, no word had been later given to belay or stop slacking, so the sailor man paid out until he came to the bitter end where the wire was not securely attached for it was designed to be used with a few turns around the drum. Consequently, the end of the throat halyard went aloft and the throat of "Resolute" 's sail came down. Although "Resolute" had been leading at the time, she now lowered her mainsail and withdrew giving the first race to "Shamrock IV."

Another attempt to race was made on July 17, but both yachts were only about two thirds around the course when the time limit expired. In this light weather "Resolute" was much the faster and had a lead of about two miles.

In the race of July 20 "Shamrock IV" did some remarkably good sailing. It was a triangular race, and because the wind shifted, the second leg was a close reach instead of being to windward; it was a reach most all around the course and this was "Shamrock"'s best point of sailing. She won the race in spite of the handicap she had to allow, beating "Resolute" two minutes and thirty-nine seconds. This made "Shamrock" two up, and if she had won another race the cup would have gone to England. There was certainly much interest shown by the public who, by and large, wanted to see "Resolute" beaten as she had never been a popular boat, perhaps because she had a Boston afterguard but was New York owned, and thus was not a thoroughbred but rather some sort of mongrel, or worse.

The third race, July 21, was postponed until one o'clock for lack of wind. It was a windward and leeward race sailed in a moderate breeze, which probably did not favor either yacht, for they kept very close together most of the way around the course. If the spectators wanted an interesting race they certainly saw one this day. "Resolute" did slightly the better on the first leg, which was to windward, and beat "Shamrock" boat to boat, but on the run home the green challenger overhauled her in a freshening breeze and finished nineteen seconds ahead of "Resolute," which, strange to say, was the exact amount of time that "Shamrock" had started ahead of "Resolute," so that both yachts covered the course in exactly the same amount of time. Thus "Resolute" won by exactly the amount of her time allowance— seven minutes and one second.

The next day "Shamrock" went to drydock to have her bottom polished, and on July 23, when they came to the line again in a triangular race which was expected to favor "Shamrock," the interest was intense and the yachts made a very close start. However, "Resolute" went better on the windward leg and nearly held her own on the reach in a good breeze. On the last leg there was a thunder squall with rain and both yachts took in some sail as conditions looked dangerous, but the squall, after it passed, killed the wind and the wind shifted to the northwest for a while and then swung back to the southwest. During much of this time "Resolute" managed to keep a ballooner drawing while "Shamrock," under various headsails, dropped back, so that "Resolute" finished three minutes and forty-one seconds ahead of the green challenger in one of the most trying races imaginable for the afterguards of both yachts. Thunder squalls and shifting winds are terrifying on racers of that type when racing for such an important cup.

The fifth and deciding race was to be sailed the next day but when they got out to the light ship there was a puffy or squally southwester blowing with a short steep sea running, and as conditions looked as if the weather would be worse during the afternoon, the committee boat signaled the racers to inquire if they would consent to calling off the race, which both readily agreed to. While the general public has criticized this action, it is the opinion of experienced yachtsmen that it is both foolish, dangerous, and expensive to race yachts of that size and type in bad weather, particularly as some of the crew are apt to be washed overboard.

And in relation to this incident I will say that many yachtsmen had hoped that the races of that time would have been held with schooners like "Westward" and "Elena." They would not have cost any more but would have been able to race in rough water and heavy winds if the public had wanted such a race; it would have been quite difficult to make restrictions that would insure such strong, safe boats. And what is more, they would have been able to race on some days when the spectator fleet could not follow them comfortably, which in itself is not practical.

The last and final race of July 27 I was lucky to see. It was a windward and leeward race with the start postponed until 2:15 P.M. on account of lack of wind. Then a light southwest wind began to show under the Jersey shore. Both yachts were very even in the first of the windward leg, but for some reason in the latter part of the leg "Resolute" went much the better and rounded the weather mark four minutes ahead of her adversary. It was very light weather to be sure; the windward leg alone took over three hours, and "Shamrock" was admittedly poor in a drift. The last of the race was a procession with "Shamrock" miles astern and "Resolute" winning by twenty minutes and fifteen seconds corrected time. This concluded the races of 1920 and made the sixth consecutive time that one of Captain Nat's yachts defended the America's Cup.

Now I shall say something about the helmsmen in this international race for this was the first time that the cup boats had been handled by amateurs. "Shamrock IV" was handled by Sir William P. Burton, and "Resolute" by Charles Francis Adams. They were both counted among the best helmsmen of their respective countries, and both were peculiarly alike in having absolutely upright characters. They arranged a meeting before the races and talked over the difference in the racing rules of their respective countries and acquainted each other with the way they understood the rules that affect certain maneuvers at the start. Both of these men sailed their yachts almost perfectly in one of the most trying set of races ever sailed, and brought down no criticism from the press, which was quite different from the treatment most of the previous professionals had had. They proved definitely that amateurs could handle yachts of this size in an international race, for there were no protests or even suggested infringement of rules. They both should have felt considerable satisfaction in knowing they had represented their countries in the best possible way to promote good sportsmanship and good feeling.

In 1925 "Resolute" was purchased by Mr. E. Walter Clark and "Vanitie" by Mr. Robert E. Tod, neither of whom was particularly a racing man, but both had owned large schooners so both yachts were rerigged as staysail schooners. In the meantime some change in Mr. Tod's plans made it inconvenient for him to race "Vanitie" so she was sold to Harry Payne Whitney who had Robert W. Emmons manage her. As C. F. Adams often acted as helmsman, strange to say, "Vanitie" was sailed by the previous afterguard of "Resolute." This you might say gave "Vanitie" a crack racing crew and "Resolute" a cruising crew. Also Starling Burgess, whose firm had previously designed the first staysail-rigged schooner "Advance," designed the new rig for "Vanitie" while Captain Nat, who was then some seventy-seven years old, tried to convert "Resolute." It would have been much cheaper and better if they had been rerigged as yawls with a moderate sail plan, but the staysail schooner was the rage at that time so staysail schooners they were. The result of the racing was a foregone conclusion with "Vanitie" getting much the better of it, "Vanitie" winning twenty-six firsts and "Resolute" thirteen firsts when both were schooner rigged.

For the season of 1929 "Resolute" and "Vanitie" were again rerigged. This time the leg-o'-mutton sloop rig was chosen and they had the conventional three headsail rig. Mr. Whitney sold "Vanitie" to Mr. Gerald B. Lambert who had Starling Burgess design the new rig, which was up-to-date with the shrouds attached with tangs instead of looping the mast, a feature that had been developed six years before in the firm of Burgess and Paine, the first yacht rigged that way being Frank Paine's "Gypsy." The mainmast of "Vanitie" was said to be the longest single stick used in a yacht, and the area of her leg-o'-mutton mainsail probably the greatest of any such sail made in this country. Mr. Adams, who was then Secretary of the Navy, sailed her whenever he could get away from Washington: at other times she was handled by Mr. George Nichols. Captain Nat, though now in his eightieth year, did much of the designing on "Resolute"'s new rig but stuck to the shrouds looped around the mast.

This time the two yachts rated a little closer with "Vanitie" allowing "Resolute" approximately one minute in ten miles. Partly by being better handled "Vanitie" proved the faster now, and during the next few years quite regularly beat "Resolute." As last impressions are often the strongest, the average person now considered that "Vanitie" was the faster yacht of the two, but this was far from being so under their original rigs. Because "Resolute" did so well the first two years their final scores of first places are not so different although "Vanitie" was sailed one year longer. Their scores against all comers are as follows: "Vanitie" won seventy-three firsts in 164 races in ten years; "Resolute" won fifty-three firsts in 142 races in nine years. Therefore "Vanitie" won something like 44½ per cent of her races while "Resolute" won some 37 per cent of hers. It would take too much research to tell just how many times one beat the other for in most of their later races there were many competitors. Of course they both often raced against smaller boats at times, and the author's "Istalena" beat them both in the Astor Cup Race in 1931. In the little book called "*Vanitie*," written by George Nichols and William U. Swan, there are listed sixty-one different yachts that have raced against "Vanitie." At any rate "Vanitie" and "Resolute" probably raced more times than any other large American yachts, but it is claimed that "Britannia" in England competed in 539 races during the twenty-one seasons she was in commission.

"Vanitie," with her longer lines, was better proportioned than "Resolute" for the higher speeds that a leg-o'-mutton mainsail produced. In my opinion "Resolute" was a little full at the water line below the chain plate. I do not remember another one of Captain Nat's models that had a similar hardness at this point, and this peculiarity probably retarded "Resolute" when close hauled in light weather and there was a ground swell running. Gardner had produced a beautiful model in "Vanitie" and her finely modeled long overhangs always made her popular with the public, but it was not until Burgess redesigned her that she began to hold "Resolute," and not until Burgess had designed the third sail plan for her that she more than held "Resolute," so it would be hard to tell how to divide the honors between Gardner and Burgess.

If "Vanitie" and "Resolute" had raced all nine years as they had been designed originally, it is likely that the score would have continued to remain something like four to one in favor of "Resolute." After "Resolute" 's rating was increased she was at a disadvantage; she definitely had too short lines for the increased driving power of the leg-o'-mutton mainsail she raced under in later life.

The "J" boats of 1930 showed the great increase in water-line length that was appropriate with modern rigs. It is somewhat astonishing that "Resolute" did so well in her later years with a cruising crew. So "Resolute" had always been the victim of circumstances that Fate had lined up against her.

Although I have gone up until 1931 with "Resolute," we must go back again to 1916 for others of Captain Nat's designs.

CHAPTER THIRTEEN

Captain Nat's Later Designs

ALTHOUGH the Herreshoff Company built few yachts of interest in 1915 the schooner "Haswell" of composite construction and some power yachts were built that year. "Haswell," with a length overall of sixty feet, water line forty-six feet nine inches, beam, fourteen feet two inches, and draft eight feet one inch, was a fine little vessel though when new she did not appear very rakish or sporting. She was higher freeboard than was then customary, but, like several others of Captain Nat's designs, after ten or fifteen years, she became very desirable, and some people who have known her will say she was one of the best all-around small cruisers ever built. She later had the name "Diabolo" and became a famous racer on the Pacific Coast. I regret I do not have a picture of her to show you for even today she would seem a modern design. "Haswell" was originally built for Mr. H. L. Tiffany of New Bedford, and later under the name of "Diabolo" was owned by Mr. W. W. Pedder of Los Angeles.

In 1916 the one-design class of New York Yacht Club forty-footers was built. They were in some ways rather homely craft because the committee who ordered them originally told Captain Nat they wanted sort of sailing houseboats that could be run with a small crew. The New York Yacht Club Fifties a few years before had turned out to be too expensive to run for the yachtsman who wanted a yacht on which he could live comfortably; Harry Maxwell had figured out that in those days it even cost about three thousand dollars a season per man of crew to run a yacht of that type. In other words, a yacht with a crew of four, like the Fifties, seemed to cost twelve thousand dollars a year to race, but as a matter of fact the wages of the crew alone were a small part of this sum. The Forties were originally designed, however, to be cruisers with good accommodations, which could be run with a small crew and racing was expected to be a secondary consideration, so the Forties at first had rather small sail area. After the first year their sail area was increased. They were the hottest racing class of their time, and were called The Fighting Forties and The Roaring Forties. It is said that they never reefed in a race, which I can well believe, having seen them hard pressed many times. So the Forties were used for hard, hot racing instead of sailing houseboats, and I mention this as many will not know why a racing class was built so wide, high sided, and tubby. The Forties were well-built yachts, nevertheless, and have turned out to be able, useful yachts, perhaps a little lively or corky in a seaway, but several of them are still in use and much liked. Two of them under yawl rigs have won the Bermuda race, and it is believed they were the last one-design class of yachts built that were that large or were built in any considerable number by the same builder. There were about fourteen of them built altogether—twelve the first year, and their dimensions, their names, and owners are listed below.

Original Name	Original Owner	Later Name	Later Owner
"Black Duck"	A. K. Brown	"Memory"	Bancroft Bavier
"Dolly Bowen"	A. S. Cochran	"Cockatoo"	A. Coolidge
"Jessica"	Wilson Marshall	"Jessica"	E. D. Morgan, Jr.
"Katherine"	Arthur F. Luke	"Katherine"	T. H. Shepard
"Maisie"	Morton F. Plant	"Typhoon"	Mr. Leslie
"Mistral"	Geo. M. Pynchon	"Mistral"	Wm. B. Bell
"Pamparo"	Dr. Jas. Bishop	"Pamparo"	Chandler Hovey
"Pauline"	O. G. Jennings	"Banshee"	H. L. Maxwell
'Rowdy"	H. S. Duell		
"Shawara"	Harold Wesson	"Shawara"	Wm. B. Bell
"Squaw"	John S. Lawrence	"Squaw"	F. R. Kellogg
"Zilph"	Edgar Palmer	"Marjee"	Ed. W. Goss
"Marilee"	E. I. Cudahy		

These yachts were fifty-nine feet overall, forty feet six inches on the water line, fourteen feet six inches beam, and eight feet draft, and they rated forty under the Universal Rule.

From the list of owners you can see that many of the Forties have been owned by very famous yachtsmen, and probably that is the reason they were raced so actively, and, in spite of being sailing houseboats, were considered quite fast. Although Captain Nat made them rather homely and tubby some people have said that no one else could have developed such speed with as wide and roomy a model, and certainly this has not been done since, but Frank Paine's "Gypsy" could be cited as a modern yacht of much room for her water-line length which has shown high average speed.

It is interesting to note that many people criticize the Forties as being too deep for cruising, while some of the racers have felt they lacked draft enough to prevent them from making leeway in a sea and strong breeze, and I imagine all future cruising racers will be criticized for these reasons if they do not have centerboards. Although the Forties raced hard their first year the war in Europe was becoming serious, and the following year, 1917, we entered the war which put a stop to yachting for the next few years.

Captain Nat was not very active during World War I and there were several reasons why: In the first place he was nearing seventy and realized that he was not up to date on the naval requirements of that time. Also by that time the Herreshoff Manufacturing Company was owned by a syndicate of yachtsmen and managed by Mr. James Swan who had been the general manager of the New York Shipbuilding Company. Captain Nat was an ardent pacifist and very much disliked war, and this caused some people to think that he might have had German sympathies, coupled with the fact that his name was of Prussian derivation. But that very definitely was not so as he had very strong feelings against the German policy of using submarines to attack and sink unprotected merchant vessels. He considered this kind of warfare as the lowest form of piracy that had ever been practiced on the high seas, and as a matter of fact seven eighths of his ancestors were English. Unfortunately during World War I the Herreshoff Company was looked upon as a Republican concern and so never received desirable contracts but rather were handed the jobs others did not want. Among these were building hulls for seaplanes, which included two of the N C class, the first type of craft to fly the Atlantic, although they did land to be refueled on the way. The company also built several V-bottom steel floats to carry seaplanes when towed at high speed behind destroyers. These craft were complicated and had requirements which were nearly impossible to meet, being built to be partly submersible by flooding various compartments, which were arranged to be blown free of water by compressed air. They built two steel twin screw patrol boats of about one hundred and ten feet length, and two smaller wood steamers for the same service, besides several gasoline patrol boats and torpedo retrieving craft, but as these craft were principally designed by Captain Nat's oldest son, A. Sidney DeW. Herreshoff, they are now only spoken of briefly.

It was partly because the company did not come up to the stockholders' expectations in making money during the war that the board of directors decided to liquidate the concern shortly after the war. However, right after the war much of their work was reconditioning several yachts that had been in naval use, and this apparently was not very remunerative so it might be said the Herreshoff Company never got on its feet again after World War I. Of course the principal reason for this was that the death of J. B. Herreshoff had removed their only real business executive. The Herreshoff Company and Captain Nat, however, were very busy soon after the war making changes in "Resolute" and preparing her for the races of 1920 which I have told of. Also the power yachts "Mary Ann," 1919, and "Vasanta," 1920, were built, but in some ways the most interesting product of 1919 was the one-design class of "S" boats, which came out early that spring.

While there were few of them built the first year, perhaps twenty, the company continued building them off and on for the next eight or nine years so that eventually there were perhaps a hundred and fifty or more of them, and besides being good little cruisers they have furnished active racing up to the present time in widely separated districts. If I remember right these little yachts cost less than two thousand dollars the first few years, so they have been a good investment for some owners for they were built well enough to last for years if handled carefully. Perhaps the "S" boats would even have been more popular if they had been a little better looking but that defect should not be wholly blamed on Captain Nat for it was the request of the original sponsors of the class that they have short overhangs and full bows and sterns. This feature has made them rather queer-looking Universal Rule boats, and consequently they are not particularly fast for their rating. But there have been few all-around better boats for afternoon sailing, cruising, and racing, and perhaps also the last one-design class that was somewhat comfortable.

In 1921 the Herreshoff Manufacturing Company built the first yacht that was not designed by Captain Nat. This was the six-meter yacht "Sheila," designed for Paul Hammond by Starling Burgess. "Sheila" was on the first American team of six-meter boats to race in England. After that the company occasionally built yachts designed by others.

During these years the class that is usually spoken of as the Fishers Island thirty-one-footers was slowly developing, but as there were not many of them built at once and because there was some variation in them, I do not speak of them as a one-design class. The first of them were straight sailboats with a gaff rig but the later ones were usually auxiliary with leg-o'-mutton rig.

While these yachts were not first designed for racing they have often done well in some of the ocean races and are well-built little ships that have been particularly liked by their owners; and some were built up to about 1935.

Two interesting yachts that were built in 1922 were the houseboat "Mariette" and the shallow draft cruiser "Ventura." "Mariette" was built for J. F. Brown who had previously had the steel schooner "Mariette" that we have spoken of, but this "Mariette" was a twin screw houseboat driven by gasoline engines and was eighty-nine feet nine inches long, twenty feet five inches beam, and only three feet nine inches draft. Mr. Brown lived aboard her much in the next ten years or so.

"Ventura," was designed and built for George F. Baker, Jr., for cruising and shooting in southern and shallow waters. She was sixty feet seven inches overall, forty-five feet water line, fourteen feet beam, and four feet draft, and she is still in good condition and a remarkably comfortable cruiser with considerable speed on a reach.

In 1923 Captain Nat designed the thirty foot water line sloop "Grayling" for J. P. Morgan, Jr. Mr. Morgan had always been much interested in the New York Yacht Club Thirties and had owned and sailed "Phryne" for several years, but by 1923 he thought the Thirties were getting old-fashioned and tried to start interest in a new class to take their place. He had "Grayling" built as a sample boat for this purpose. She was an all-around nice boat and very well built with principal dimensions as follows: forty-six feet three inches O.A.; thirty feet seven inches L.W.L.; nine feet one inch beam, and six feet draft. If this class had been built it would have been a good investment for the owners, for this was just before the prices of yachts increased greatly and while there were still many fine workmen at the Herreshoff Company. But somehow the class did not "take." After a year or two "Grayling" was sold to J. V. Santry of Marblehead and raced in the "Q" class under the name of "Spindrift," a name that was later changed to "Mary." She was somewhat smaller than the other yachts of that class and usually finished in the middle of the class.

The failure in starting this new class was a blow to the Herreshoff Manufacturing Company for they had little work at that time and the future of yachting looked rather disappointing in 1923. But Mr. Morgan was to have another disappointment. About 1927 he had the New York Yacht Club Thirty "Phryne" rerigged with a leg-o'-mutton sail. He only did this to demonstrate to the other owners how this change would improve the Thirties, but most of the owners seemed to resent this and said that "Phryne" had no right to race in the class, which probably was so, for she should have arranged special match races instead to prove her merits. However, in the first race which she entered in the class, one of the other Thirties ran into her, although "Phryne" had the right of way, but the helmsman of the other Thirty maintained "Phryne" was not of the class and thus should not have been on the race course. This is about the only disagreeable incident that happened in the long history of the New York Yacht

Club Thirties, and it seemed a shame for Mr. Morgan had a great deal of sentiment for the class and was only trying to rejuvenate the class with "Phryne's" changes.

I must also say that J. P. Morgan took quite a little interest in the Herreshoff Manufacturing Company and was much disappointed that they were not doing well financially for he wanted the company to continue under its then present management.

In 1923 Captain Nat designed the steel schooner "Wildfire," a sixty-eight footer, for C. L. Harding of Boston. She first came out with a gaff foresail, and I believe she would have been a very successful yacht if she had continued with that rig and experimented with the use of a vang to hold the foregaff from swinging to leeward. But she was handled in her first few years by helmsmen who had been successful with small light yachts. Upon not doing as well as they had expected they had her sail area increased and the rig changed to that of a staysail schooner, but it is probable that the increase in sail area and consequent increase in rating made her less apt to win. "Wildfire," in my opinion, was not as handsome as most of Captain Nat's previous yachts, but this was because he had been persuaded that the yachtsmen wanted short, full ends more like the so-called fisherman-type yachts, which were popular at that time. "Wildfire" was the last steel schooner that Captain Nat designed—in other words his ninth steel schooner—but as two of his metal sloops, "Colonia" and "Resolute," were changed to schooners, there were eleven altogether which raced in the larger classes.

Captain Nat was seventy-five years old when he designed "Wildfire" and, as I have said before, the future of yachting did not look very bright in 1923. Thomas P. Brightman was running the executive end of the business and doing as well as anyone could under the trying conditions of a rather large plant with little work, but by 1924 the directors of the Herreshoff Manufacturing Company voted to liquidate the plant and property at a public auction held on August 21 and 22, 1924. Captain Nat certainly was a sorry sight as he wandered around during this auction and saw the buildings and machinery that he and his brother had struggled to acquire go at a fraction of their cost, but I have told of this change in ownership and management in Chapter IX. After this Captain Nat was practically an independent designer, as most yacht designers are who are not builders. But it must be mentioned that all the rest of his life the men in the shop looked upon him as the real superintendent, for there were still some of them who had worked many years under his eagle eye and liked it. His advice was still sought in all matters of importance, although his son, A. Sidney DeW. Herreshoff, was taking his place when he was away on his winter vacations in Florida. However, some of the old clients took interest in the company after its reformation, and some of them even held stock in it.

At this time the "R" class under the Universal Rule was much in vogue, and in 1925 Captain Nat designed the "R" boat "Game Cock" for George Nichols and Junius S. Morgan. George Nichols was commodore of the New York Yacht Club at that time and his interest very much forwarded the class: the New York Yacht Club cup was put up for competition in the "R" class for 1926. This cup is usually given for a series of races in the class the flag officers of the club have decided is the most hotly contested class of the year, and it is rather surprising that the cup was given for such small yachts as "R" boats. I am sorry I do not have a picture of "Game Cock." She was a nice all-around sailboat with very moderate overhangs, and although shorter overall, she was wider than most "R" boats of her time. She was forty feet overall, twenty-six feet water line, seven feet eight inches beam, and five feet nine inches draft.

In 1926 Captain Nat designed the "R" boat also named "Grayling" for Junius S. Morgan, with dimensions as follows: L.O.A., forty-three feet; L.W.L., twenty-seven feet; beam, seven feet nine inches; draft, six feet. Although these two "R"'s were remarkably well built and beautifully modeled, perhaps they were too wide and had rather small fore triangles in their sail plan. Though they were undoubtedly well sailed, strange to say, the "R" boat "Yankee," designed by the present author beat them in every race that they came together, and Captain Nat did not know whether to be mad or glad at this result but he never spoke to me of these races.

The next year, 1927, he designed another "R" for Junius Morgan. This one was named "Puffin" and had these dimensions: L.O.A., thirty-eight feet three inches; L.W.L., twenty-six feet six inches; beam, six feet six inches; draft, five feet eleven inches; and with her smaller beam was a good all-around boat though perhaps not in the class with some of the "R's" that had improved sail plans, box section masts, and neat rigging.

The most important yacht built by the Herreshoff Manufacturing Company in 1927 was the steel twenty-three-meter yacht designed by W. Starling Burgess for Robert E. Tod. She was launched on May 2 and christened by Miss Katherine K. Tod, the owner's daughter. This is a yacht that has had many names. While she was christened "Katoura" as were several of Mr. Tod's yachts, she has since had the names of "Blackshear," "Artemis," and "Manxman." She was built to the International Rule as a twenty-three-meter yacht and had the general dimensions of L.O.A., one hundred and twelve feet; L.W.L., seventy-five feet; beam, twenty feet; draft, thirteen feet seven inches. While this yacht perhaps should not be spoken of as being much connected with Captain Nat, still it is interesting that she was the first of Starling Burgess' metal racers and it was through the methods of building that Captain Nat had developed that Burgess, with this yacht, acquired his first knowledge and practice of high-grade metal construction which was to enable him to design the later cup defenders.

Another yacht designed by Burgess that was built at Bristol that winter was the "M" boat "Prestige" for Harold Vanderbilt, and this combination of Vanderbilt, Burgess, and Herreshoff were to produce the next two cup defenders.

Mr. Tod had planned to take "Katoura" to England to race, but other plans interfered, and for some reason or other he did not like this twenty-three-meter boat. The following year, 1928, he had Captain Nat design him the bronze yacht "Thistle.

Altogether, Mr. Tod probably has spent as much money on sailboats as any American for he had a great many of them through some thirty-five years, and they were all quite large. "Thistle," I believe, was about the largest yacht, other than cup defenders, built of bronze. She was L.O.A., one hundred and two feet; L.W.L., seventy-four feet three inches; beam, twenty-one feet six inches; draft, thirteen feet. She is, I believe, still in very good condition and has had few changes made in her. She was Captain Nat's last metal yacht, and he was eighty when he designed her. These two yachts, the twenty-three-meter "Katoura" and "Thistle" built for Mr. Tod, were to be the last yachts to race in the larger classes.

After sailing "Thistle" for two years Mr. Tod got it into his head that he was too old for sailing so he had Captain Nat design him a power yacht, ninety-three feet long. This yacht was also named "Katoura," and I think was the third yacht of that name he had had. She was ninety-two feet on the water line, with a beam of sixteen feet five inches and draft of five feet. She was driven by two large six-cylinder Sterling engines, and the most remarkable feature of this yacht was that she was planked with teak and was perhaps the longest vessel built in America planked with teak, though many large sailing ships had been built in England of copper-sheathed teak between 1775 and 1875 when teak was more plentiful. So it might be said that Mr. Tod had the largest straight pleasure yacht that was plated with bronze and the largest American built yacht with teak planking, and these two yachts with normal care should last many years.

In 1930 the Herreshoff Manufacturing Company also built the cup defender "Enterprise," designed by Starling Burgess and managed by Harold Vanderbilt, as well as the cup candidate "Weetamoe," designed by Clinton Crane and managed by George Nichols. While these yachts were not closely connected with Captain Nat, still they used many features of construction he had developed and were equipped almost entirely with winches, steering gears, and deck fittings he had designed for former cup boats. "Enterprise" was Starling Burgess' second metal yacht, and the personnel of the drafting department of the Herreshoff Manufacturing Company was of great assistance to him. Of course Mr. Crane had designed many metal yachts before and on the whole he possibly produced the best design of the "J's" built that year, but the "Weetamoe" was somewhat hamstrung with sails and possibly not sailed as intently and cleverly as "Enterprise."

The years between 1928 and 1930 had been profitable ones for the company as they had for most all other American yacht yards, but it is my opinion that the Herreshoff Manufacturing Company would have been more successful during the next few years if they had been contented with less profit, but they seemed to want to kill the goose that laid the golden eggs. Of course Captain Nat was now getting too old to do much work, but he did design a class of small sailboats for the shallow waters of Florida. He was much interested in the Development Class of small sailboats, the rule for which was gotten up by Bill Atkin, and he designed four or five for this class. Some of these boats had different rigs of the same area, and this made them unusually interesting to race, for the rigs could be changed in a few minutes. A few of these little boats are still in existence, but they were a little delicate and required careful handling although when in the water were fast and lively, and, if properly handled, were remarkably good sea boats. It is interesting that Captain Nat at his advanced age took such interest in these light boats, and he wrote several enthusiastic letters to me about them when he was eighty-five or so.

The last yacht of any size that Captain Nat designed was the auxiliary yawl "Belisarius," built in 1935 when Captain Nat was eighty-seven years old, and as he had modeled "Violet" in 1864 this made a span of seventy-one years of yacht designing, and undoubtedly he had spent more years at the art than any one else. Mr. C. E. Nicholson is making a close approach to this and may equal it for he made his first design, a ten-ton cruiser sixty-five years ago and is still at it, but I do not think anyone else has even approached these two, and few, if any, in number of yachts designed or quality of the designs, although Watson may have produced more tons or dollars' worth of yachts in the comparatively few years he was active since many of his steam yachts were very large.

Although it is now inpossible to check on the number of boats and yachts Captain Nat designed, some people think it is in the neighborhood of two thousand, including the individual boats in one-design classes, dinghies, launches, and all. Altogether their tonnage and dollars' worth must have been considerable for the steel schooners, torpedo boats, and cup boats were neither small nor inexpensive.

To get back to "Belisarius," she was designed for Charles B. Rockwell, a neighbor of Captain Nat at Bristol, who as a young man had cruised on some of Mr. Herreshoff's steam yachts and was a close friend of the family. The "Belisarius" was designed partly to fit the Cruising Club of America's measurement rule so she was modeled with somewhat of a clipper bow to reduce one of the length measurements. As her rig was inboard in the modern way without a bowsprit this left her stemhead or figure-head rather unprotected, so that her stemhead is somewhat larger than is compatible with grace in this type of bow. Otherwise she is a remarkably able and fast sailing yacht. She was particularly well built and expensive for she has several bronze floor timbers which support the frames abreast of the centerboard box, so she should have a very long life and always be a most desirable cruiser with her moderate draft of five feet eight inches, which is less than the usual ocean racer of her size. "Belisarius" is fifty-two feet two inches O.A., forty-one feet W.L., fourteen feet beam. She has an auxiliary engine which drives her at good speed with unusual economy.

Even after "Belisarius," Captain Nat made imaginary designs and worked on models besides helping many people with his great store of nautical knowledge, which I will tell about in the next chapter.

CHAPTER FOURTEEN

Mr. Herreshoff's Later Life and Friends

IN HIS LATER YEARS, between 1910 and 1915, Captain Nat went south nearly every winter to Bermuda where he had the two sailboats "Oleander" and "Alerion" which he had designed especially for sailing at Bermuda and which were spoken of in a previous chapter. For a few years he cruised south to Florida in one or the other of his two power yachts "Helianthus II" and "Helianthus III." The "Helianthus II" was sixty-five feet long and seventeen feet beam and very shallow draft, and he went south in her in the winters of 1918 and 1919. At first she was powered with two gasoline engines but Captain Nat thought them noisy and not economical so he replaced them with two of the steam launch engines built by the Herreshoff Manufacturing Company, and designed a new boiler for her which was fired by a Stanley automobile burner that used kerosene for fuel and had Stanley automatic controls for controlling steam pressure and water level. He went to Florida with the steam power plant in the winter of 1919 and said it worked very well and gave him the cruising speed of eight and one half knots, or nearly ten miles an hour, but he sold this "Helianthus" in the spring of 1920, and in 1921 had "Helianthus III" built— sixty-two and one half feet long and twelve feet nine inches beam. Captain Nat went back to the gasoline engine again with this yacht, apparently because the steam plant in the previous "Helianthus" required an engineer most of the time. He cruised to Florida in "Helianthus III" in the winters of 1921, 1922, 1923, and 1924, and one or two winters towed his fifteen-foot sailboat "Lantana," but this was quite an undertaking for a man of his age and sometimes required long hours at the wheel. However, "Helianthus III" was a very comfortable, able craft, and Captain Nat and Mrs. Herreshoff enjoyed cruising in her. But in 1924 he thought he was getting too old for cruising, being then seventy-six, so he sold her to a Mr. Peters of Boston.

While Captain Nat could have cruised many years more if he had been willing to let someone else take some of the responsibility and management, he had all of his life handled and navigated his yachts and so could not relax when under way. He certainly was a skillful navigator and clever helmsman for in some fifty years of handling yachts of all sizes never had he had a serious accident or grounding; in fact he was the most careful sailing master and navigator that I have ever known, but he took the management of a yacht so seriously that it generally detracted from the pleasure of cruising, and long trips finally became too much for him. Nevertheless, he did prove that yachting and cruising may be done without any injury, or even depreciation to the yacht, if utmost care is taken. On his last trip north the late Commodore George Nichols went along with him and acted as helmsman on the long runs, and it is doubtful if Captain Nat would have had confidence in a less capable man for I believe they had some strong winds and unpleasant weather on the trip.

In these cruises south Captain Nat had several times called on Commodore R. M. Munroe at Coconut Grove, and one winter at least spent much time anchored near the commodore's home. These two gentlemen became very friendly and seemed to greatly enjoy each other's company. Mr. Munroe was of about the same age as Captain Nat, perhaps a year or two younger, and had spent his younger years on Staten Island, New York, where he had become very much interested in yachting and shipping in the eighteen-sixties. He had been one of the earliest photographers to take instantaneous exposures, or snapshots, of nautical subjects and had a fine collection of photographs taken by himself and others of the yachts that had been famous when he and Captain Nat were young men. I think their first attachment came through looking at and talking of these yachts of their youth. In many cases they helped each other in patching up the history of these craft, for the commodore and Captain Nat both had most excellent memories and could identify almost every yacht shown in the background of a picture as well as telling some interesting incident of her origin and later history.

Commodore Munroe had been one of the early settlers at Coconut Grove and in about 1880 had taken a Connecticut Sharpie there for the shallow waters. This sharpie proved so useful that the Commodore developed from her a type of sailboat that had a flat floor and slightly flaring sides like a sharpie, but was built round bottomed, as we say, or had no chines. These boats proved so remarkably useful in Florida waters that the commodore designed approximately fifty of them, and, although they were nearly all shallow centerboarders, many of the early ones were of about the same beam-length ratio as a sharpie. These boats were used for all purposes from wrecking and beachcombing to ocean cruising, and were remarkably good sea boats. The later and larger ones, however, were of more beam for the length, and two of them, "Carib" and "Alice," spent an unusual amount of time at sea. The life of Commodore Munroe and something of a description of his most famous boats is charmingly told in the book *The Commodore's Story* by Ralph M. Munroe and Vincent Gilpin, and should be read by all who are interested in small craft or the history of Florida.

At any rate the commodore and Captain Nat became very intimate and after Captain Nat sold his last power yacht and had given up long distance cruising Commodore Munroe let him occupy a cottage on his land at Coconut Grove, and here Captain Nat spent the last active winters of his life and seemed to be very happy. Perhaps there had been just enough difference in the type of yachts that these two had produced to make each other's work interesting and avoid rivalry, which often exists between men who have devoted their lives to similar work. There is no doubt but that the commodore had a mellowing effect on Captain Nat, for in his middle life he was not a pleasant conversationalist and seemed to dislike talking to anyone, while in his last years he was much more human and even might be said to be a pleasant conversationalist had he not by that time become slightly deaf in one ear. Captain Nat was much impressed with the shallow draft boats the commodore had developed, and several of Captain Nat's last designs were comparatively shallow centerboarders that were rather long and lean like "Aida," shown in the illustrations. But it is doubtful if anyone but Commodore Munroe ever influenced him.

Captain Nat's lifelong habits of work, or we may say pleasure of designing and seeing yachts built, would not allow him to remain idle, so in his winters at Coconut Grove he spent much of his time in building model yachts. These little models were framed out and planked up just as larger yachts are built, and their stems, keels, deadwood, floor timbers and all were just as they would have been on one of his full-size yachts. Most of these models were equipped with what is called a vane steering gear, a method of steering a model, which I believe he first used in about 1870, and consists of a vane or weathervane connected to the rudder through various connections according to where the vane is mounted.

Some of his earlier models used a feather at masthead for this purpose, and, while this is the lightest sort of vane that is not easily damaged, it was difficult to get feathers as straight as he desired. He experimented quite a bit with the wishbone rig on models and liked it very much for that purpose.

This model-making activity with him was at its height between about 1929 and 1931 when he was between eighty-one and eighty-three, and it is amazing what fine work he was capable of at that age.

Captain Nat, of course, had sailboats at Coconut Grove and even cruised some in company with Commodore Munroe in his narrow, shallow draft yachts, but as I do not know much about this late activity of Captain Nat in Florida I will quote from some notes of his about the yachts that he owned.

1924–25   "Pleasure"   #907

After selling "Helianthus 3d" and expecting to go to Coconut Grove, Fla. to pass winters I decided to have a sailing boat so in fall of 1924

I designed "Pleasure" and had her built by the H. Mfg. Co. She was shipped to Florida by rail, arriving about 1st of February 1925. She is 30′ O.A., 24½′ W.L., 8′ 4″ beam, 31″ draft with outside lead ballast and knockabout rig that was changed to yawl rig the next year. She proved a very satisfactory boat. The spring of 1928, realizing I was getting unreliable to get around on deck and to handle so large a boat, I decided to sell her, and had her shipped to New York and there sold to Burgess, Riggs & Morgan. She afterward became the property of Harry Maxwell.

1928   "Water Lily"

After selling "Pleasure" I still had a longing to sail. In the fall of 1928 I bought the boat "Limited" from the H. M. Co. that I designed a few years before for a proposed class for Biscayne Bay and had this boat built as a sample, but the class did not mature. I made many changes in "Limited," renamed to "Water Lily," and so she could be entirely handled without getting out of the cockpit (except to hook on the mooring after sailing). I always made it a rule to lower jib before coming to the mooring or dock. I used this boat at Coconut Grove in winters of 1928 and 1929. In the following fall I was not reliable on my feet and decided to give up using boats entirely. So I turned over "Water Lily" to Miss Pattie Munroe who still has her.

The End.

While he has finished up with the words "The End," I believe he did sail a little after this in his twenty-six foot sloop "Alerion" which he kept at Bristol for sailing in the summer. "Alerion" was kept in a sheltered spot beside a stone dock in front of his home at Bristol, and he had moored her and arranged her rig so that she could be gotten under way with little exertion, but one day when sailing alone he had a fainting spell so never went singlehanded again. I think he was about eighty-one then, but he went on the water with others perhaps until he was about eighty-six. Although Captain Nat did not have any organic trouble he did have low blood pressure and, as he said, this made him "unsteady on his pins." After he gave up going to Florida he realized that old age was creeping up on him and that he might soon be bedridden so he busied himself in his workshop, making several arrangements for his convenience when in bed. One of these was a drawing board which could be wheeled in place and somewhat similar to the stands for dining trays used in some hospitals although the one he made was mostly of wood.

Captain Nat always had been methodical, and so he continued, arranging things, so that he could keep himself busy to the last, and putting in order all his affairs as best he could. Among other things he made a very long and complicated will which filled twenty long typewritten pages with most of his holdings mathematically divided into hundredths, and giving the mathematical distribution that should be used in case various ones of the benefactors died. By the time he was eighty-seven he began staying in bed more hours than usual, but carried on a very large correspondence with several people, most all of which he wrote himself. His writings to W. P. Stephens on the past history of yachting in itself would have been more than most younger men could have accomplished, and, although much of his later writings were done in bed on the drawing board he had made for that purpose, his mind and memory were as sharp and clear as ever. Although physically very weak, he interested himself in the affairs of others and he carefully followed the latest trends in engineering and yachting.

It was about this time that the Roosevelt dynasty started, and while Captain Nat had never been interested in politics, he did very much object to some of the doings of the democrats. He was scandalized when they talked of shorter working hours and retiring men from working at about the age he had thought a man's work was the most valuable. He said, "The reason this country has advanced so rapidly is because we worked more hours than other countries," and that "if we ever get out of the habit of working it will be mighty hard to get back into good habits." He thought there were too many automobiles and too many people riding around in them who should be home working to make some money to live on when they grew old. He thought that "if everyone worked hard, used his head, and saved he would be all right and the whole country would be prosperous." When I said to him, "How about the poor?" he replied, "The only way to do away with the poor is to prevent the poor from having children."

I mention these things to show that Captain Nat thought that work was the most important thing in this world and that every one should like it, and I must say that if everyone did like his work he would be happy and successful, for in Captain Nat's case he had always liked his work and could not understand why everyone else did not.

In spite of gradually growing weaker he continued to work occasionally in his model room until he was eighty-eight years old and delighted in making small things for his sons and others. Among other things, at that time he made several small drawing boards about nine and one half inches by thirteen inches, which are most convenient for sketching and drawing when sitting in a chair: he also made several small "T" squares for small drawing boards, and in 1936 made two small special drafting scales for me that were machine divided on his Rivett lathe, and these are remarkably nice work for a man that old. About this time he had a fainting spell when taking his morning bath, and this seemed to make him lose confidence so that he stayed in bed most of the time after that.

In 1937 when "Endeavor II" and "Ranger" were being conditioned at the Herreshoff Manufacturing Company, he had a mirror arranged so that he could see something of what was going on while lying in bed, and one day when Harold Vanderbilt called on him, Captain Nat intimated that he would like to meet Mr. C. E. Nicholson, the designer of "Endeavor II" and the previous three challengers, so Mr. Vanderbilt brought Mr. Nicholson to call. Captain Nat was pretty weak by that time and so much affected with meeting Mr. Nicholson that about all he could do was to hold his hand for a minute or so, but we can well imagine the respect and affection he tried to convey to Mr. Nicholson even if he was then too weak to talk much, for Captain Nat thought Mr. Nicholson had done a very great deal for British yachting.

Some time after that Starling Burgess called on Captain Nat and, as they had been close friends ever since Starling was a boy, they talked on several subjects. One of the things that had always interested Starling particularly was the possibility of an after life, or perhaps what is generally called the resurrection of the dead, but when Starling asked Captain Nat what he thought about it

Captain Nat said he had been so busy all of his life that he had not had time to think about such matters, but it was his opinion that when man died he went out like a candle. I fear Captain Nat did not like to talk about these matters for the next time I called on him he said, "Sometimes I think Starling talks a little foolish."

It is an interesting thing that when Captain Nat grew weak and his blood pressure dropped lower and his pulse was very weak the principal drug that seemed to have a beneficial effect on him was nicotine. Of course the doctor never let him know that he was taking nicotine but it is the irony of fate that a man who detested tobacco in all forms was kept alive in his last months with a little stimulant from nicotine.

The last time I saw Captain Nat was on his ninetieth birthday. He was propped up in bed and seemed very happy. He had received several cards and letters of congratulation from friends, and what seemed to please him most, a large bouquet of flowers which the Town Council of Bristol had sent him with, if I remember right, a note of thanks for the employment and publicity he had given the town for some sixty years. We had a nice chat that day, and he said he had never expected to live to an old age since he had never been very robust, and he had had both pneumonia and typhoid fever in middle life. When I left him he said I might never see him again, and while this proved true I had thought that he seemed so bright and was so mentally alert that he might last some time, but there came a time when he could no longer even get out of bed, and then he said that he would rather die than to become such a care and nuisance, and, like some other old people who are very weak, when he lost the desire to live he passed away in a few days, his wife, Ann Roebuck Herreshoff having given him the most loving and expert care that was possible. The doctors said that he had no organic trouble but that low blood pressure, weak pulse, low temperature were the causes of death. So, like one of his torpedo boats that had outrun its usefulness in a long life and whose fires were drawn for the last time, there passed away a very vital spirit. He died on June 2, 1938, at the age of ninety years and two months.

In some ways it was fortunate that he did not live to see the

1938 hurricane which came a few months after his death and swept away the boathouse in front of his home, destroying several small craft which he had been fond of, one of which was the "Riviera" in which he had toured Europe in 1874, sixty-four years before.

CHAPTER FIFTEEN

Some of Captain Nat's Accomplishments

1. He designed the first light steam power plants.
2. He designed the first U.S. Navy torpedo boats.
3. He developed nearly all of the methods of constructing light wooden hulls that are in use today, and introduced screw fastenings for the planking in this country.
4. He invented the web frame and longitudinal system of framing a metal vessel: the first one so built was the cup boat "Constitution" built in 1901.
5. He invented the crosscut sail with cloths running at right angles to the leach.
6. He developed light hollow steel spars, combined with scientific rigging.
7. He designed the first flat sterned steam launches and steam yachts that could be driven at high-speed length ratios without squatting.
8. He developed the overhangs on sailing yachts to allow longer lines and greater stability.
9. He invented the type of sail track and sail slides which are in common use throughout the world today.
10. He designed the first full-size successful fin-keel yacht.
11. He was one of the principal developers of the bulb keel for sailing yachts.
12. Perhaps his greatest feat was to have designed yachts that successfully defended the America's Cup six times.

13. It is said he designed more models of steam engines than anyone else.

14. At the time of his death there were approximately eighteen thousand drawings in the files of the Herreshoff Manufacturing Company that to a great extent had been laid out or drawn in pencil by Captain Nat although they had been inked in or traced by others. Some of these drawings, like the construction plans of the cup defenders and the power plants of the torpedo boats, required great skill and concentrated scientific work, not to mention much research and mathematics.

15. It is not known how many models he made but, including the duplicates for yacht clubs, possibly a thousand, many of which were very important because of being new developments in both steam and sailing craft, and because since some of these models were made, there have been no later improvements in the types that they represented.

It would be very difficult to make up a list of the winnings of his yachts, but it is likely that in the important classes they outnumber the winnings of all other designers between 1890 and until the time of his death in 1938.

In the Astor Cup races, and this has been our most important annual race, his yachts in the schooner class between 1890 and 1938 won seventeen out of thirty-five; in the sloop class between the same years he won nineteen out of thirty-five.

In the King's Cup races up to the time of his death his yachts won fifteen out of twenty-eight. Between 1912 and 1925 one of Captain Nat's yachts won the King's Cup each year but one, that was in 1923 when "Enchantress," designed by Cary Smith, won, but in these thirteen years neither Gardner nor any other than Herreshoff and Cary Smith won a race.

In the Eastern Yacht Club's annual classic, the Puritan Cup Race between 1890 and 1938, Captain Nat's yachts won eighteen out of forty-two.

To have designed more winners than anyone else in these races would have been quite a feat, but to have designed more winners than all other designers put together seems amazing.

Partial List of Herreshoff-Built Boats

Name	Type	Owner	Year
"Acis"	18' cat	F. L. Franke	
"Actinia"	42' steamer	Alexander Agassiz	1871
"Acushla"	50' sloop	G. M. Heckscher	1913
"Adelaide"	21' fin keeler	C. O. Iselin	1894
"Adelaide II"	30' 1" sloop	G. A. Adee	1905
A class of	14'	Adirondack-Florida School	
"Adolar"	66' gas launch	August Heckscher	1920
"Adrienne"	49' 5" gas launch	A. Iselin	1903
"Adventuress"	45' 6" cutter	Chester C. Rumrill	1909
"Alarm"	20' sonder boat	Max Agassiz	1909
"Albatross"	26' 3" steam	U. S. Fish Commission	
"Alera"	30' 1" sloop	A. H. Alker	1905
"Alerion I"	32' 5" fin keeler	N. G. Herreshoff	1894
"Alerion II"	27' 3" fin keeler	N. G. Herreshoff	1894-5
"Alerion III"	21' 9" sloop	N. G. Herreshoff	1912
"Alert"	140' steam	Chas. A. Stone	1920
"Alert"	28' 3" sloop	A. H. Alker	1902
"Alert"	15' J & M	W. Barklie Henry	
"Alfreda"	21' sloop	F. P. Wright	1898
"Alice II"	45' cutter	P. M. Warburg	
"Alice"	28' 6" catyawl	C. F. Herreshoff	
"Alice"	21.1 cabin cat	Sharpe Brothers	1880
"Aloha"	32' gasoline tender for steamer "Aloha"	Arthur Curtiss James	
"Aloha"	32' gas 2d tender for steamer "Aloha"	Arthur Curtiss James	1932
"Alpha"	15' cat	C. M. Baker	
"Alpha"	21' sloop	John F. Brown	1892
"Altair"	45' cutter	Cord Meyer	1900
"Althea"	15' J & M	M. C. Robinson	
"Andy Gump"	16' J & M	Malcolm E. Read	
"Anemone"	15' 5" cat	Geo. E. Savage	
"Anemone"	38' steam	J. B. Herreshoff	1879
"Anemone II"	30'	J. Murray Mitchell	1905
"Anita"	33' cutter	R. T. Crane 3d	1902
"Anita"	15' Buzzards Bay	Chas. E. Hellier	1907
"Anita"	"S" boat	Chas. Fletcher	1929
"Ann"	15' J & M	G. W. Mitton	
"Annie Morse"	60' steam, the first steamer built by Herreshoff Co.	J. B. Herreshoff	1868

Name	*Type*	*Owner*	*Year*
"Anoatok"	30' 3" fin keeler	George Owens	1895
"Antonette"	48' steam	Edward A. Hopkins	
"Apache"	62' 4" gas launch	Robert F. Herrick	
"Aquila"	48' steam	Wm. Randolph Hearst	
"Ara"	165' diesel	Ernest B. Dane	1922
"Arabian"	30' cutter	Robert Winsor	1902
"Arethusa"	21' sloop	C. M. Baker	1902
"Aria"	30' J & M	W. G. Cotton	
"Ariel II"	46' 9" gas commuter	W. E. Woodward	1931
"Ariel"	33' 5" sloop	C. A. Locke	1886
"Ariel"	33' 5" sloop		1877
"Ariel"	30' 6" sloop	D. C. Anderson	1882
"Ariel"	23' sail area boat	Chas. E. Hodges	1931
"Arria"	30' cutter	Walter G. Cotton	1902
"Arrow"	20' 6" sloop	Demarest Lloyd, Jr.	
"Asahi"	28' 10" fin keel sloop	E. V. R. Thayer	1896
"Astrild"	31' 6" cutter	Henry L. Eno	1903
"Atair"	N.Y. Thirty	Cord Meyer	1905
"Athene"	70' cutter	Wm. O. Gay	1899
"Atlanta"	33' steam	U.S. Navy	
"Augusta"	141' 7" steam	I. L. Elwood	1889
"Augusta"	55' steam	Charles Kellogg	
"Augusta"	93' steamer	J. B. Herreshoff	
"Aumbere"	62' 4" gas. Given to Navy for scout patrol	Henry M. Sears	1914 (?)
"Aunt Eppie"	16' J & M	Chas. N. Smith III and E. R. Trowbridge	
"Au Revoir"	38' aux. cutter	L. A. Scott	1908
"Aurora"	62' 8" cutter	Cornelius Vanderbilt	1907
"Avenger"	53' cutter	Robert W. Emmons	1907
"Avocet"	20' 6" J & M	D. B. C. Catherwood	
"Azura"	32' 5" aux. sloop	Geo. H. Field	1929
"Azor"	34' cutter	J. Malcolm Forbes	1902
"Bacera"	45' 6" steam	Herreshoff Mfg. Co.	
"Bagatelle"	25' sloop	Geo. B. Dabney	1914
"Ballymena"	148' steamer	Alexander Brown	1888
"Bambino"	30' cutter	Lawrence Grinnell	1904
"Banzai"	30' sloop	N. D. Lawton	1905
"Barbara"	50' sloop	Harry Payne Whitney	1913
"Barracuda"	16' J & M	DeF. Hicks	
"Barracuda V"	20' 6" "S" boat	Lawrence F. Percival	1929
"Bat"	31' cutter	Edgar T. Scott	1903
"Bee"	17' 6" J & M	C. P. Bun	
"Bellemere"	20' electric launch	S. T. Shaw	
"Belisarius"	41' aux. yawl	Charles B. Rockwell	1935
"Ben"	31' cutter	A. Y. & P. C. Stewart	1903
"Beze B"	20' 6" "S" boat	Robert B. Bowler	
"Bibelot"	19' 6" sonder boat	Harry Payne Whitney	
"Black Duck"	40' sloop	Arthur K. Bourne	1916
"Blazing Star"	25' J & M	C. M. Baker	
"Bluebell"	16' 6" cat	F. Stoddard	1872
"Bobtail"	28' 4" sloop	Edgar Scott	1902
"Bogey"	28' 4" J & M	Henry M. Sears	
"Bonita"	16' J & M	C. R. Crane	
"Bonnie Doon"	30' sloop	J. W. Gibb	1893
"Breeze"	15' J & M	W. G. Roelker	
"Breeze"	30' sloop fin keeler	Capt. L. Miller	1896
"Brownie"	16' J & M	John G. Brown	
"Bubble"	18' 3" J & M	Baron van Tuck	

Name	Type	Owner	Year
"Bubble"	25' 10" gas launch	A. Sidney Herreshoff	
"Budda"	45' knockabout J & M	Pembroke Jones	
"Caloola"	40' gasoline	Richard Croker, Jr.	
"Calypso"	16' 6" cat	J. A. Oldenberg	1872
"Camilla"	60' steam	Dr. J. G. Holland	1881
"Canvasback"	59' 11" gasoline launch	Frederic G. Bourne	1909
"Caprice"	16' 4" to carry on steamer	J. J. Astor	
"Cara Mia"	30' 1" sloop	Stuyvesant Wainwright	1905
"Carlita"	30' sloop	Oliver Harriman	1905
"Carola"	115' power using oil	Leonard Richards	1919
"Carolina"	29' 5" sloop	H. Walters	1896
"Carolina"	50' sloop	Pembroke Jones	1913
"Cassandra"	34' steam tender for steam yacht "Cassandra"	Roy A. Rainey	
"Cat's Paw"	15' J & M	S. D. Warner	
"Celia"	21' fin keel sloop	C. A. Gould	1894
"Chance"	31' 8" aux. sloop	Arthur E. Whitney	1927
"Charlotte"	37' 9" sloop	Goddard Brothers and William Binney	1868
"Chewink IV"	29' 5" sloop	F. G. Macomber	1904
"Chewink VI"	22' 9" sonder boat	F. G. Macomber	1906
"Clara"	140' steam	Spanish Naval Commission	
"Clara"	29' 4" catyawl	N. G. Herreshoff	1887
"Clara"	97' steamer	Charles Kellogg	1887
"Clara"	64' 5" steamer	H. H. Westinghouse	1899
"Clio"	21' cat	W. F. Gillings	1871
"Clytie"	33' sloop	J. B. Herreshoff	1867
"Cockatoo"	21' J & M	C. F. Eaton	
"Cockle"	16' J & M	G. C. MacKinsie	
"Cock Robin"	21' sloop	Charles S. Eaton	1896
"Cock Robin II"	40' cutter	Charles S. Eaton	1904
"Cod"	16' J & M	H. S. Shonnard	
"Colonia"	85' 4" steel cutter	Archibald Rogers, et al.	1893
"Columbia"	89' 9" cutter	J. P. Morgan	1899
"Comet"	29' sloop	Cornelius Vanderbilt	1914
"Constitution"	90' cutter	August Belmont, et al.	1901
"Consuelo"	28' 6" catyawl	N. G. Herreshoff	1883
"Coquina"	16' 6" catyawl	N. G. Herreshoff	1889
"Coquina II"	16' catyawl	W. G. Hollis	
"Corinthian"	34' 3" sloop	Seawanaka Corinthian Y. C.	1911
"Corsair"	30' 6" launch for steam yacht "Corsair"	J. P. Morgan	
"Corsair"	35' gas launch for steam yacht "Corsair"	J. P. Morgan	
"Cosetts"	97' steamer	C. F. Chickering	1884
"Countess"	32' sloop	O. Sanderson	1900
"Cricket"	32' 2" cutter	F. G. Ladd	1903
"Curlew"	17' J & M	H. S. Forbes	
"Curlew"	31' cutter	R. H. Gallatin	1903
"Cushing"	138' steam torpedo boat	U.S. Navy	
"Cygnet"	30' sloop, 6-meter	Paul Hammond	1929
"Cyrilla"	21' sloop	R. W. Emmons	1899
"Cyrilla II"	31' 8" aux. sloop	W. Barklie Henry	1927
"Dacotah"	35' 2" fin keeler	Henry Allen, Scotland	1892
"Dad"	15' 9" J & M	Morton F. Plant	
"Dahinda"	34' sloop	W. Butler Duncan	1905

Name	Type	Owner	Year
"Daiguire"	62' 4" gasoline	Henry A. Morse	1917-8
"Danae"	30' 6" sloop	Miss Draper	1927
"Dandelion"	16' 10" cat	Chas. F. Adams, 2d.	1875
"Dawn"	48' steamer	T. H. Newberry	1888
"Dawn"	81' steamer	J. S. Newberry	1901
"Dawn"	58' launch	Gas. Engine & Power Co.	1889
"Defender"	89' sloop	W. K. Vanderbilt, E. D. Morgan and C. O. Iselin	1895
"Delaware, Jr."	28' steam tender	W. K. Vanderbilt	
"Delight"	19' 5" sloop	N. G. Herreshoff	1908
"Diana"	35' gas	J. B. Herreshoff	
"Dianthus"	65' gas	J. B. Herreshoff	1913
"Dido"	60' steamer	Dr. T. V. Roe	1881
"Dilemma"	26' 6" sloop	N. G. Herreshoff	1891
	The first bulb fin keeler built and now in museum at Newport News.		
"Dolly Bowen"	40' sloop	A. S. Cochran	1916
"Dolphin"	42' steam	Robert L. Kennedy	1879
"Dolphin"	28' steam cutter for the "Dolphin"	U.S. Navy	
"Dolphin"	29' sloop	O. G. Jennings	1914
"Doodah"	20' 6" J & M	F. B. Crowninshield	
"Doris"	56' 10" cutter	S. Reed Anthony	1905
"Dorothea"	28' steam tender	Wm. Cramp & Sons	
"Dorothy"	21' sloop	F. P. Boynton	1916
"Dorothy"	21' J & M	Harry Payne Whitney	
"Dorothy"	26' 6" sloop	Hollis Burgess	1889
"Dorothy II"	30' J & M, fin keel	Harry Payne Whitney	
"Dorothy Q"	25' sloop	Hollis Burgess	1907
"Drusilla"	34' 9" fin keel sloop	E. D. Morgan	1892
"Dude"	13' 6" spritsail	H. E. Hebbard	
"DuPont"	175' 6" steam torpedo boat	U.S. Navy	
"Duquesne"	131' steamer	T. R. Hostetter	1895
"Eagle"	28' steam	U.S. Coast Survey	
"Eaglet"	15" knockabout	R. W. Emmons	
"Eaglet"	15' Newport J & M	W. Grossinor	
"Echo"	15' Newport J & M	E. D. Morgan	
"Edith"	30' open sloop	J. D. Masury	1892
"Edith"	20' 11" sloop	C. M. Baker	1897
"Edith"	17' J & M	C. M. Baker	
"Edith"	60' steam	William Woodward, Jr.	1880
"Eel"	16' J & M	C. P. Stewart	
"Effort"	31' 6" sloop	F. M. Smith	1900
"Effort I"	36' 6" sloop	F. M. Smith	1901
"Eight Bells"	25' aux. sloop	Dr. O. S. Lowsley	
"El Chico"	25' fin keeler	H. M. Kersey	1892
"Eleanor"	26' 3" "Q" boat	F. W. Fabyn	1907
"Electra Jr."	26' gasoline	Elbridge T. Gerry	
"Electra"	22' 6" steam	Elbridge T. Gerry	
"Electra I"	31' 2" cutter	H. O. Havemeyer	1900
"Electra II"	27' 5" sloop	H. O. Havemeyer	1902
"Elena"	96' schooner	Morton F. Plant	1911
"Elf"	15' J & M	Elisha Flagg	
"Ellen"	20' 6" "S" boat	Ralph Ellis	1920
"Ellen"	40' schooner	Charles H. Noxon	1888

Name	Type	Owner	Year
"Ellen"	62' 4" power U.S. Navy Scout Patrol boat	Charles P. Curtis	1917
"Elsie"	16' 2" cat	C. F. Hardwick	1879
"Elva"	20' 6" J & M	C. M. and T. B. Bleecker	
"Enaj III"	89' 4" steamer	Thomas G. Bennett	1909
"Endeavor"	15' J & M	G. H. Fish	
"Enterprise"	80' sloop	Winthrop Aldrich, et al.	1920
"Esloma"	99' gasoline	W. H. Van Dervoort	1932
"Esperanza"	30' sloop	A. S. Van Winkle	1986
"Estelle"	120' steam	Cuban Insurgents Government	1877
"Esther"	18' sloop	E. M. Farnsworth, Jr.	1895
"Eugenia"	78' 6" steam	J. B. Herreshoff	
"Eugenia"	113' steam	J. B. Herreshoff	1904
"Evangeline"	23' sloop	Hollis Burgess	1901
"Evelyn"	30' cutter	John Hitchcock	1902
"Express"	89' steamer	Morton F. Plant	1902
"Express"	51' gas launch	Morton F. Plant	1903
"Fad"	40' gasoline	F. L. Dunne	
"Fair American"	"S" boat	T. Roosevelt, Jr.	
"Falcon"	31' 3" sloop	E. M. Abbott	1926
"Fandee II"	"S" boat	Mrs. Elizabeth A. Chalifoux	
"Fanny"	23' 10" cat		1866
"Fannie"	21'	Captain Gibbs	1865
"Fannie II"	21' 7"	Captain Gibbs	1867
"Fannie"	30' steamer		1882
"Faustine"	79' 6" steamer Built as schooner & lengthened at Cowes, 1878	G. P. Russell	1873
"Felix"	16' J & M	Wm. C. Huntoon & John C. Washburn	
"Fin"	19' 11" fin keel	L. M. & H. Stockton	1892
"Fish Hawk"	24' steamer	Capt. Z. L. Tanner	
"Flicker"	15' J & M	W. G. Ladd	
"Flickerman"	15' J & M	Mr. Lathrop	
"Flight"	25' sloop	Horace Havemeyer	1903
"Flight"	31' cutter	Edward deV. Morrell	1903
"Flo"	32' yawl	J. B. Cornwall	
"Florence"	98' steamer	A. H. Alker	1900
"Fly"	16' sloop	R. Watts	1916
"Fly"	21' knockabout	Wm. O. Gay	
Flying Boat Hulls (10)	F-5	U.S. Navy	
Flying Boat Hulls (10)	H-16	U.S. Navy	
"Flying Cloud"	44' cutter	F. B. & L. Grinnell	1911
"Foraminifer"	20' 3" sloop	D. L. Whittemore	
"Frances"	35' launch	E. M. Slocum	1905
"Friday"	35' gas tow boat	Herreshoff Mfg. Co.	
"Frolic"	16' 8" cat	W. R. Blaney	1871
"Gadfly"	21' sloop	A. C. Harrison	1899
"Gadget"	26' gasoline	Robert W. Goellet	
"Gamecock"	30' cutter	Louis Bacon	1902
"Gamecock"	"R" boat	J. S. Morgan, Jr. & George Nichols	1925
"Gannet"	29' 6" catyawl	E. D. Morgan	1891

Name	Type	Owner	Year
"Gee"	12¼' spritsail	Mr. Hinckley	
"Gee Whiz"	27' yawl	Edward Mallinckrodt, Jr.	
"Ghost"	29' 6" sloop	A. H. Flint	1881
"Ginty"	15' sloop	E. G. Bourne	
"Gleam"	25' 6" cat	F. A. Gower	1877
"Gleam"	134' steamer	W. H. Grahm	1880
"Gloria"	19' 2" catboat	A. J. Drexel	
	Sailing tender for		
	"Mayflower"		
"Gloriana"	45' 3" cutter	E. D. Morgan	1891
"Gnome"	Half-rater	F. M. Hoyt	
"Gov. Hamilton"	96' steamer	State of Maryland	1883
"Grayling"	30' sloop	J. P. Morgan	1923
"Grayling"	"R" boat	J. S. Morgan, Jr.	1926
"Grayling"	50' sloop	J. P. Morgan	1913
"Grunt"	16' J & M	S. T. Shay	
"Gwynn"	100' steam torpedo	U.S. Navy	
"Gymnotus"	30' steam	Geo. R. Dunnell, England	
"Haida"	26' steam	M. C. Fluschman	
"Haidie"	25' sloop	Dr. S. Powell	1864
"Haidee II"		Dr. S. Powell	1866
"Haidee"	34' 6" sloop	A. Withers	1875
"Handsel"	30' fin keel	James R. Hooper	1892
"Happy Princess"	27' 5" cat	John P. Crozer	1905
"Harlequin"	39' aux. schooner	Geo. B. Knowles	1925
"Haswell"	44' schooner	Henry L. Tiffany	1915
"Haulray, Jr."	27' steam	Bath Iron Works	
"Hawk"	15' J & M	W. Jannell	
"Hazard"	21' keel sloop	Henry M. Sears	1897
"Hebe"	18' 9" cat	G. A. Goddard	1869
"Helianthus"	64' gasoline	N. G. Herreshoff	1912
"Helianthus II"	65' gasoline	N. G. Herreshoff	1917
"Helianthus III"	64' 5" gasoline		1921
"Helvetia II"	49' 6" launch	C. O'D. Iselin	1903
"Henrietta"	16' cat	Mr. Holden	1865
"Henrietta"	48' steam	Norman L. Monroe	1866
"Hera"	30' fin keel	Ralph Ellis	1896
Herreshoff	59' steam	George R. Dunell for the	
Torpedo boat		English Navy	1878
"Hindoo"	18' J & M	R. W. Emmons	
"Hist"	27' steam	David Dorris, Jr.	
"Hope"	15' J & M	C. O. Iselin	
"Houri"	20' 5" fin keel sloop	Butler Duncan	1894
"Humma"	44' cutter	J. Rogers Maxwell	1901
"Hyassa"	15' J & M	E. Moras	
"Hyepus"	33' aux. sloop	J. B. Whitherill	1910
"Ianthe"	49' schooner	Charles L. Davenport	1870
"Ibis"	30' sloop	O'Donnell Iselin	1905
"Ibis, Jr."	30' steam	J. F. Brown, Jr.	
"Idle Hour"	41' 3" gasoline	E. W. Sparrows	
"Idle Hour"	60' steam	B. F. Carver	1879
"Illusion"	21' J & M	C. M. Baker	
"Inca"	100' steam	U.S. Navy	
"Inca"	62' 4" gasoline	Frank B. McQuesten	1917
"Indian"	31' cutter	W. C. Allison	1903
"Ingomar"	87' 3" schooner	Morton F. Plant	1903
"Intrepid"	25' 1" tender	Lloyd Phoenix	
"Iona"	82' power	Frank R. Rice	1910

Name	Type	Owner	Year
"Iris"	"S" boat	G. H. Chisholm	
"Iris"	22' 6" catyawl	George Owen	
"Iris"		W. A. W. Stewart	1924
"Irolita"	50' cutter	E. W. Clark	1903
"Irolita"	66' schooner	E. W. Clark	1906
"Iroquois II"	50' sloop	Ralph Ellis	1913
"Isabelle"	30' 3" gasoline	Com. L. C. Ledyard	
"Isis"	26' steam	J. B. Webb	
"Isolde"	45' fin keel cutter	Baron vonZedwitz	
"Isolde"	45' aux. yawl		1895
"Istalena"	62' 8" cutter	George M. Pynchon	1907
"Istalena"	54' cutter	George M. Pynchon	1929
"Itala"	28' steam	H. J. Grosbeck	1906
"Item"	57' 6" steamer	Herreshoff Mfg. Co.	1896
"Jap"	18' J & M	G. P. Gardiner	
"Javelin"	54' 3" steam	U.S. Navy	
"Javelin"	97' 10" steam	E. D. Morgan	1891
"Jean"	77' 6" steam	T. A. Gillespie	1897
"Jersey Lily"	65' steam	Norman L. Monroe	1888
"Jessica"	40' sloop	Wilson Marshall	1916
"Jilt"	21' sloop	W. O. Gay	1899
"John Gilpin"	31' catamaran	A. Panich	1878
"Joker"	31' cutter	Henry M. Sears	1903
"Josephine"	15' J & M	F. L. Jenks	
"Joy"	20' 6" sloop	O. L. St. John	1925
"Joyant"	36' sloop	Wm. H. Childs	1911
"Judy"	102' 3" steamer	F. T. Howard	1890
"Judy"	31' 8" aux. sloop	Morton N. Buckner	1927
"Juliet"	45' steamer	A. Newbold Morris	1881
"Kalolah"	99' 6" steamer	Charles H. Hayden	1893
"Kamaulipua"	20' 6" sloop	Robert W. Atkinson	1929
"Kanawa"	45' steam	U.S. Army	
"Kangaroo"	62' 4" power	C. F. Ayer, given to Navy	1917
"Katherine"	40' sloop	Arthur F. Luke	1916
"Katoura"	115' schooner	Robert E. Tod	1914
"Katoura, Jr."	12' 8" tender for "Katoura"	Robert E. Tod	
"Katoura"	26' gasoline tender for "Katoura"	Robert E. Tod	
"Katoura"	75' sloop cutter, 22-meter boat	Robert E. Tod	1927
"Katoura"	93' power	Robert E. Tod	1930
"Katrina"	99' 2" steam	H. F. Noyes	1897
"Katrina"	73' launch	Charles L. Hubbard	1890
"Katrinka"	16' J & M	Roderick F. Makepeace & Emerson P. Smith	
"Katydid"	23' sloop	Thos. W. Russell	1932
"Katydid"	27' steam	E. D. Morgan	1891
"Kelpie"	47' steam	William H. Grahm	
"Kelpie II"	29' 5" sloop	J. B. Herreshoff	1865
"Kelpie"	31' 8" aux. sloop	Henry L. Maxwell	1930
"Kelpie"	26' 9"	J. B. Herreshoff	1862
"Kelpie"	39' 3" sloop	H. Howard	1891
"Kestrel"	31' 8" aux. sloop	Dudley F. Wolfe	1928
"Kewana"	30' 8" J & M	J. B. Trevor	
"Kid"	22' steam	W. S. Webb	
"Kid"	17' sloop		1904
"Kildee"	18' sloop	Miss Florence DeWolf	1895

Name	Type	Owner	Year
"Kim"	21' sloop	Charles E. Hellier	1911
"King Phillip"	31' J & M	R. F. Haffenreffer	
"Kite"	22' 9" sloop	W. H. Dunwood	
"Kittatinny"	60' steam	J. D. & H. Brodhead	
"Kittie S"	17' 10" sloop	H. H. Stilling	1876
"Kooyong"	80' power	W. E. S. Dyer	1918
"Kotic"	30' sloop	Richard M. Hoe and Edw. K. Dunham	1905
"Kotick"	20' 6" sloop	Henry S. Morgan	1926
"Kuwana"	31' cutter	John B. Trevor	1903
"Ladoga"	39' 5" steam launch for ship "Chicago"	U.S. Navy	
"Ladoga"	97' steam	George S. Brown	1865
"Lady Gay"	58' power	Mrs. J. B. Lippincott	1917
"Lagofa"	19' 6" J & M	Sir A. C. Jarvis and H. B. Webb	
"Lang Syne"	46' gasoline	Herman Dock	
"Lanthe"	49' schooner	Charles L. Davenport	1870
"Larikin"	30' cutter	Robert Bacon	1902
"Latona"	61' schooner	B. F. Carver	1872
"Leila"	100' power-steam	Walter Langton	1881
"Lightning"	57' steam	U.S. Navy	
"Linnet"	30' sloop	Amos T. French	1905
"Little Robin"	16' sloop	C. S. Eaton	1902
"Little Sovereign"	112' power	M. C. D. Borden	1904
"Lodolo"	30' catamaran	N. G. Herreshoff	1879
"Loon"	62' steam	Robert M. Riddle	1893
"Lotus Seeker"	48' steam	Norman L. Monroe	1887
"Lotus Seeker"	72' 11" steam	E. R. Holden	1892
"Louanna"	15' J & M	Frazer Jelke	
"Louise"	102' steamer	Charles H. Hayden	1893
"Louise"	22' sloop	Henry L. Tiffany	1908
"Lucile"	69' steam launch	George Vanderbilt	1884
"Lucile"	94' steam	U.S. Navy	
"Lucile"	90' steam	Charles Kellogg	1885
"Lucy"	42' 5" steam	Frank S. Birch	1880
"Lynx II"	58' gasoline	Nathaniel F. Ayer	1917
"Mab"	15' 9" open cat	John Shaw	1891
"Mab"	20' 6" J & M	George C. McMurtry	
"Mackabaro"	21' J & M	C. L. Stone	1909
"Madge"	48' steam	J. A. Drake	1888
"Magic"	25' sloop	J. P. Gardner	1877
"Maggie"	first rigged as cat, bowsprit & jib added later when mast was stepped back	J. B. Herreshoff	1863
"Maggie"	16' J & M	Byron A. Waterman	
"Magistrate"	63' gasoline	Harold S. Vanderbilt	1916
"Magnet"	35' power launch for "Corsair"	Junius S. Morgan, Jr.	1924
"Magnolia"	99' steam	Fairman Rogers	1883
"Mai"	30' fin sloop	O. G. Jennings	1896
"Maid of Mendon"	30' sloop	W. D. Guthrie	1905
"Maisie"	40' sloop	Morton F. Plant	1916
"Mameena"	31' 6" aux. sloop	George E. Watson	1927
"Manatee"	16' sloop	Albert Strauss	1916
"Marchioness"	47' sloop	John P. Crozer	1900
"Margaret"	39' J & M	George C. Tuttle	1904

Name	Type	Owner	Year
"Margaret"	18' sloop	William O. Taylor	1904
"Margaret"	40' power	William O. Taylor	1907
"Maribee"	15' J & M	D. P. Robinson	
"Mariette"	80' aux. schooner, later known as "Cleopatra's Barge"	Jacob F. Brown	1916
"Mariette"	85' power	Jacob F. Brown	1922
"Mariette"	23' sloop	Franklin M. Haines	1932
"Marilee"	40' sloop	Edward I. Cudahy	1926
"Maroposa"	24' 10" sloop	O. F. Coe	1882
"Marjorie"	16' J & M	J. G. Gould	
"Mary Ann"	66' power	Henry F. Lippitt	1919
"Mary Rose"	47' 8" aux. schooner	Harold W. Brooks	1926
"Mashnee"	30' cutter	R. W. Emmons	1902
"Masie"	20' electric launch	Charles A. Starbuck	
"Maud"	20' steamer	H. H. Warner	
"Maud"	18' 6" cat	H. A. Nash, Jr.	1871
"Maude"	18' 6" sloop	W. A. Howard	1871
"Maude"	21' 9" sloop	G. H. Richards	1876
"Maude"	21' 9" sloop	F. W. Sargent	1879
"Maureen"	15' J & M	Edward I. Cudahy	
"May Fly"	15' J & M	Robert Goelet	
"May Queen"	25' sloop	C. Whittemore	1899
"Mecca"	31' 6" steamer	Jason P. Whittier	1889
"Meg"	20' 6" sloop		1910
"Meneen"	24' 4" J & M	A. H. Jackson	
"Merry Thought"	26' cat	John P. Crozer	1901
"Meteor"	12' centerboard	The first boat that J. B. Herreshoff built	1856
"Mickey"	16' J & M	F. S. Parsons	
"Mimosa III"	30' 11" J & M	C. S. Eaton	1904
"Mineola II"	70' cutter	August Belmont	1900
"Mink"	25' sloop	Howard Stockton	1914
"Minnow"	16' J & M	F. S. Williams	
"Minvon"	15' J & M	Henry F. Lippitt	
"Mirage"	81' steamer	E. D. Morgan	1900
"Mirwena"	18' 3" J & M	Miss Sutton	
"Mische Nahma"	20' 6" fin cutter, sailing tender for steam yacht "Nahma"	Robert W. Goelet	1900
"Mischief"	29' sloop	Mrs. Hugh D. Auchincloss	1914
"Mischief"	18' 6" sloop	Dr. H. C. Bradley	1926
"Missisquoi"	48' 6" steamer	W. S. Webb	1890
"Miss Q"	15' J & M	T. Thatcher	
"Mist"	27' fin keeler	A. S. Van Winkle	1899
"Mist"	59' launch	Edward deV. Morrell	1904
"Mistral"	15' J & M	A. C. Bostwick	
"Mistral"	40' cutter	George M. Pynchon	1916
"Mojave"	20' cat	William N. Murray	1893
"Monsoon"	15' J & M	S. Wylie Wakeman	
"More Joy"	26' 5" sloop	William H. Childs	1909
"Morris"	140' steam torpedo boat	U.S. Navy	
"Moya"	15' J & M	W. Butler Duncan	
"Muame"	30' J & M	J. M. MacDonough	
"Muriel"	15' J & M	Herman Oelrich	
"Murmur"	15' sloop	Frederic Cunningham	1907
"Musme"	29' 6" J & M	J. M. MacDonough	1896
"Nahma"	16' J & M	W. Butler Duncan	
"Nancy"	15' J & M	S. C. Reigster	

Name	Type	Owner	Year
"Nassau"	21' J & M	John P. Wilson	
"Natella"	15' J & M	M. A. Whitney	
"Naulahka"	32' sloop "P" boat	J. M. MacDonough	1909
"Nautilus"	24' steam	Johns Hopkins University	
"Nautilus"	30' sloop	L. Delano	1905
"Navahoe"	84' cutter	R. Phelps Carroll	1893
"Navette"	114' power	J. P. Morgan	1917
"Neckan"	109' steamer	H. C. Baxter	1894
"Neith"	38' 6" cutter	Dr. E. K. Dunham	1907
"Nellie"	33' steam	Charles Hallett	1882
"Nellie"	36' cutter	Morton F. Plant	1903
"Neola II"	30' sloop	George M. Pynchon	1905
"Nepenthe"	42' aux. sloop	George P. Slade	1868
"Nereid"	76' steam	Col. I. J. Gray	1882
"Nettie"	12½'-footer	Charles Francis Adams	
"Next"	15' Buzzards Bay	R. W. Emmons	1899
"Niagara"	45' cutter	Howard Gould	1895
"Niagara III"	81' power	Howard Gould	1901
"Nimbus"	33' 3" sloop	J. J. Souther	1866
"Nina"	99' steamer	Charles G. Emery	1897
"Noanet"	15' J & M	G. C. Lee	
"Nora"	16' 2" cat	G. B. Dennie	1871
"Norma"	30' 3" steam tender for yacht "Nourmahal"	Vincent Astor	1916
"North Star"	28' steam launch	Com. F. G. Bourne	1907
"Notos"	30' cutter	C. H. Taylor, Jr.	1902
"Nova"	15' J & M	C. O. Iselin	1887
"Now Then"	88' steam	Norman L. Munroe	1887
"Ogeechee"	50' steam	George Appleton	
"Ohonkara"	79' 1" aux. schooner	Carll Tucker	1920
"Oiseau"	25' knockabout	J. Rogers Maxwell	1899
"Oleander"	20' J & M	N. G. Herreshoff	1911
"Olita"	15' J & M	H. C. Rouse	
"Olive"	20' 6" J & M	Charles S. Whitman	
"Omega"	14' cat	S. A. King	
"Oonagh"	32' fin keel sloop	T. J. Pirie	1901
"Opossum"	16' 4" sloop	R. W. Emmons	1898
"Orienta"	125' steam	J. A. Bostwick	1882
"Oriole"	30' sloop	Lyman Delano	1905
"Orion"	49' 2" sloop	C. W. & G. C. Cooper	1869
"Osprey"	14' 5" J & M	T. Yznaga	
"Ossabaw"	64' steam schooner	Percy R. Pyne, Jr.	1883
"Our Mary"	65' steam	Norman L. Munroe	
"Paddy"	29' 3" sloop	Wm. K. Vanderbilt	1925
"Padick"	33' sloop	E. E. Dickinson, Jr.	1932
"Pamparo"	40' sloop	Dr. James Bishop	1916
"Pandora"	20' 6" sloop	H. M. Curtis	1922
"Panini"	21' sloop	Earl M. Thacker	1928
"Papoose"	31' cutter	Victor E. Macy	1903
"Parthenia"	131' steamer	Morton F. Plant	1903
"Pastime"	30' sloop	George N. Tower	
"Patterson"	27' steam	U.S. Coast & Geodeitc Survey	
"Pauline"	40' sloop	Oliver G. Jennings	1916
"Peerless"	27' steam	William Cramp & Sons	
"Peg"	19' sloop, sonder	Galen L. Stone	1910
"Peggy"	20' 6" sloop	Percy Chubb 2d	1926
"Pelican"	26' 6" catyawl	E. D. Morgan	1890

Name	Type	Owner	Year
"Peri"	18' 6" cat	Henry Parkman	1873
"Permelia"	95' steam	Mark Hopkins	1883
"Pernab"	20' 6" "S" boat		1922
"Periwinkle"	16' J & M	H. R. Hayes	
"Periwinkle"	20' 6" "S" boat	Phoebe Ayer & Mildred McCormack	
"Petrel"	56' yawl	H. VanR. Kennedy	1899
"Petunia"	58' gasoline	H. L. Tiffany	1920
"Phosie"	20' cat	E. C. Palmer, Jr.	1874
"Phryne"	30' sloop	H. L. Maxwell	1905
"Piltoris"	15' J & M	F. A. Cabot	
"Pink"	12' 7" cat	C. A. Fry	1872
"Pintail"	30'	August Belmont	1905
"Pixie"	15' J & M	J. M. Goetchius	
"Pleasure"	24' 6" aux. yawl	N. G. Herreshoff	1925
"Pleasure"	45' cutter	O. H. Havemeyer	1900
"Pleione"	50' sloop	E. T. Irvin & Chester C. Rumrill	1913
"Pluckermin II"	20' 6" J & M	William Woodward	
"Polliwog"	21' sloop	Frederic C. Hood	1911
"Polly"	69' steam	Gen. C. A. Whittier	1885
"Polly"	21' 2" sloop	Homer W. Hervey	1867
"Polly"	15' sloop	C. L. Harding	1908
"Pollyanna"	35' gasoline	E. Mallinckrodt, Jr.	
"Pollywag"	21' J & M	F. C. Woon	
"Polyanthus"	86' steamer	J. B. Herreshoff	1895
"Pompano"	16' J & M	W. H. Appleton	
"Pontiac"	30' sloop	J. Arthur Beebe	1902
"Porpoise"	16' J & M	R. T. Crane	
"Porter"	175' 6" steam torpedo boat	U.S. Navy	
"Praxilla"	30' cutter	John Parkinson, Jr.	1902
"Premier"	34' gasoline	J. B. Herreshoff	
"Prestige"	54' cutter	Harrold S. Vanderbilt	1927
"Pronto"	20' 6" "S" boat	Mrs. Elizabeth Beale	
"Psyche"	49' 11" sloop	J. J. Murphy	1866
"Puck"	45' steam	Ernest Edwards	1878
"Puck"	29' 5" sloop	E. D. Morgan	1896
"Puffin"	"R" boat	Junius S. Morgan, Jr.	1927
"Quakeress"	21' 6" sloop	A. C. Harrison	
"Quakeress II"	30' cutter	W. F. Harrison	1902
"Quakeress III"	21' sloop	A. C. Harrison	1906
"Queen"	92' 6" schooner	J. Rogers Maxwell	1906
"Quickstep"	124' steam	Russell & Frederick Grinnell	1902
"Qui Vive II"	39' 8" sloop	Thomas Clapham	1863
"Qutee"	31' 8" aux. sloop	Jos. H. Holmes	1930
"Raccoon"	30' bulb fin sloop	T. R. Hostetter	1896
"Radiant"	20' 5" sloop	C. M. Baker	1901
"Rainbow"	70' cutter	Cornelius Vanderbilt	1900
"Reaper"	20' 9" sloop	Henry P. Benson	1892
"Rebekah"	15' sloop	Franklin W. Hobbs	1906
"Red Jacket"	"S" boat	Paul Whitin	1920
"Redwing"	31' sloop	F. G. Congdon	1903
"Reliance"	89' 7" cutter	C. O. Iselin, et al.	1903
"Rena"	18' 5" cat	H. L. Soule	1870
"Reposo"	75' steamer	Bradford McGregor	1890
"Republic"	22' steam	Wright Whitney	

Name	Type	Owner	Year
"Rescue Boat"	40'	U.S. Navy	
"Resolute"	75' sloop	N.Y. Yacht Club Syndicate	1914
"Riviera"	17' sloop	N. G. Herreshoff	1874
"Roamer"	93' 7" steamer	N. G. Herreshoff	1902
"Roamer"	18' 2" gas tender for "Roamer"	John K. Robinson, Jr.	1913
"Robin"	12' 2" J & M	S. Duncan	
"Rofa"	39' aux. schooner	Henry L. Tiffany	1926
"Rogue"	21' sloop	E. T. Bedford	1901
"Romp"	26' 6" catyawl	Geo. A. Thayer	1883
"Rose"	15' 6" cat	T. H. Cabot	1872
"Rowdy"	40' 5" sloop	Holland S. Duell	1916
"Ruby"	19' cat	A Boston owner	1872
"Rugosa"	28' 10" sloop	Russell Grinnell	1903
"Rugosa II"	40' yawl	Russell Grinnell	1926
"Sabalo"	16' J & M	A. R. Whitney	
"Sadie"	59' sloop	J. B. Herreshoff	1868
"Sadie"	21' 9" J & M	E. C. Benedict	
"Sally III"	21' J & M	D. C. Percival	
"Sally"	17' J & M	A. P. Loring	
"Samuri"	50' sloop	William Earl Dodge	1913
"Sandfly"	16' cat	R. H. Coleman	1878
"Sandust"	"S" boat	Gifford K. Simonds	1935
"Sandpiper"	knockabout	August Belmont	
"Saracen"	21' J & M	Robert Winsor	
"Sarah Webb"	50' gasoline	George H. Webb	1908
"Sardine"	16' J & M	B. G. Work	
"Sassy Sally"	16' J & M	E. R. Bancroft and Francis M. Smith	
"Satan"	50' steamer	W. O. Cutter	1884
"Savage"	31' 8" aux. sloop	T. W. Russell	1930
"Sayonara"	25' 3" cat	E. H. Williams	1892
"Say When"	138' steamer	Norman L. Munroe	1888
"Scapa"	22' 8" sloop	Harry Payne Whitney	1920
"Schlern"	17' 2½" J & M	Mr. Kirsten	
"Scout"	81' steamer	A. Belmont	1900
"Scoot"	15' J & M	W. O. Taylor	
"Scud"	31' cutter	A. J. Cassatt	1902
"Sea Farer"	20' 6" "S" boat	Parker Corning	
"Sea Hawk"	62' 4" gasoline	Arthur Winslow	
"Sea Hawk"	15' J & M	Clarence W. Dolan	
"Seaplane"	N-C 1	U.S. Navy	
"Sea Robin"	16' sloop	Junius S. Morgan	1916
"Sea Urchin"	61' steamer	Robert M. Riddle	1905
"Secret"	21' 5" cat	S. M. Weld	1864
"Seeps"	15' J & M	S. B. Warner	
"Seneca"	32' sloop	M. P. Pembroke	1907
"Senta"	25' aux. sloop	J. M. Whitehall	1910
"Seven Brothers"	65' steam, first steam pogie boat in America built for the seven brothers named Church		1879
"Shadow III"	48' 10" power	Dr. J. C. Ayer	1916
"Shadow"	33' 5" sloop	Dr. Sisson	1871
"Shaneondoa"	15' J & M	M. N. Buckner	
"Shark"	16' J & M	H. C. Smith	
"Shark"	45' cutter	F. Lothrop Ames	1900
"Shawara"	40' sloop	Harold Wesson	1916

Name	Type	Owner	Year
"Sheerness"	54' 8" aux. sloop	Marshall Sheppey	1928
"Shelldrake"	12½'-footer	A. Adams	
"Shimna"	53' cutter	Morton F. Plant	1910
"Shrimp"	16' J & M	W. A. W. Stewart	
"Shuttle"	70' power	Junius S. Morgan	1928
"Siesta"	98' steamer	H. H. Warner	1882
"Signet"	6-meter	Paul Hammond	
"Sinbad"	42' steam	Philip Schuyler	1879
"Sintram"	21' sloop	W. P. Fowle	1898
"Sis"	21' 11" sloop	E. T. Bedford	1899
"Sisilina"	94' 6" power	Nathan Strauss	1906
"Skate"	16' J & M	H. L. Smith	
"Skiddoo"	20' sloop, sonder boat	Henry M. Sears	1906
"Skip"	30' 6" sloop	Albert R. Pierce, Jr.	1925
"Snapper"	16' J & M	W. E. Roosevelt	
"Snipe"	15' J & M	I. M. Whitehall	
"Sonya"	47' cutter	Mrs. T. G. Farley, England	1906
"S P"	83' 2" steam Scout Patrol given to U.S. Navy	R. S. Russell	1917
"S P 118"	83' 2" steam Scout Patrol given to U.S. Navy	W. W. Aldrich	1917
"Spalpeen"	56' ketch	R. M. Riddle	1897
"Spartan"	50' sloop	Edmund Randolph	1913
"Speedwell"	45' steamer	Archibald Rogers	1876
"Spinster"	20' sloop "S" boat	Paul Hammond	1920
"Splash"	15' J & M	C. H. Thorn	
"Spook"	16' J & M	Francis Lee Herreshoff	
"Sport"	45' steam	C. R. Flint	1880
"Spray"	42' open steam launch	U.S. Navy	
"Sprite"	20' the second boat J. B. built	J. B. Herreshoff	1860
"Spritsail"	11' 7" spritsail	W. H. Buffington	
"Squaw"	40' sloop	John S. Lawrence	1916
"Squib"	65' steamer	N. G. Herreshoff	1898
"Squid"	16' J & M	F. Remington	
"Starling"	16' J & M	C. B. Rockwell	
"Step'n Fetchit"	16' J & M	C. W. Haffenreffer	
"Sterling"	39' 10" gasoline	L. J. Knowles	
"Stiletto"	35' steam	Jay Gould	
"Stiletto"	94' steamer	Herreshoff Co.	1885
"Stroller"	46' 9" power	C. D. Rafferty	1929
"Stroller"	81' steamer	G. T. Rafferty	1901
"Sunbeam"	60' power launch	J. L. Hutchinson	1903
"Sunflower"	72' gasoline	John P. Crozer	1919
"Surf"	21' 9" sloop	W. C. Loring	1872
"Surinam"	20' 6" sloop	Philip J. Roosevelt	1922
"Surprise"	31' 6" aux. sloop	E. H. Cooper	1930
"Suzetta III"	41' 7" sloop	C. A. Herter	1905
"Swanhild II"	25' J & M	Robert Loesner	
"Swiftsure"	51' 8" power	N. G. Herreshoff	1904
"Sylph"	16' 9" cat	Augustus Hemenway	1872
"Tabasco"	15' J & M	J. B. Nichols	
"Tabasco"	30' 1" sloop	H. F. Lippitt	1905
"Tahena"	21' 9" sloop	C. E. Williams	1871
"Talbot"	100' steam torpedo boat	U.S. Navy	
"Tarantula"	19' 4½" gasoline	W. K. Vanderbilt	
"Tarpon"	16' J & M	L. F. Bishop	

Name	Type	Owner	Year
"Tarpon II"	16' J & M	Halsey DeWolf	
"Tautog"	40' gasoline	Robert F. Herrick	1908
"Terrapin"	20' 9" sloop	L. S. Dabney	1902
"The Bird"	15' 11" open cat	William Peet, Jr.	1890
"Thistle"	15' J & M	R. Barry	
"Thistle"	103' aux. yawl	Robert E. Tod	1928
"Tinavire"	32' Sloop	Elihu Root, Jr.	1927
"Tinker"	15' sloop	Mrs. R. W. Emmons	1905
"Toboggan"	19' sonder boat	R. W. Emmons	
"Toddy Wax"	59' 8" steam	W. P. Hinszey	
"Tom Boy"	16' J & M	Chas. E. Trowbridge	
Torpedo retrieving launches (5)	gasoline	U.S. Navy	
"Tramp"	82' steamer tender for "Athene"	William O. Gay	1901
"Tranquilo"	68' 8" steam	E. D. Morgan	1892
"Triton"	61' schooner	Edward Pomeroy	1872
"Trivia"	33' 5" cutter	Harold Vanderbilt	1902
"Truant"	132' steamer Her engine is in the Ford Museum.	Helen H. Newberry	1892
"Trust Me"	16' J & M	W. Longden	
"Try"	15' J & M	M. Williams	
"Tulip"	16' 4" cat	Gordon Dexter	1872
"Tuna"	16' J & M	T. Scudder	
"Tuza"	40' 3" gasoline	Herreshoff Company	
"Twinkle"	15' sloop	A. Hemingway	
"Tyara"	34' 9" aux. yawl	S. S. Pierce	1919
"Typhoon"	21' J & M	E. V. R. Thayer	
"Uarda"	15' sloop	R. W. Emmons	1899
"Undine"	33' 4" sloop	J. N. Bourne	1872
"Vacuna"	84' 6" steam	Selah R. Van Duzer	1896
"Vagrant"	56' schooner	Harold S. Vanderbilt	1910
"Vagrant"	79' schooner	Harold S. Vanderbilt	1913
"Vamoose"	112' steamer	W. R. Hearst	1891
"Vanessa"	20' 10" sloop	A. Bigelow, Jr.	1892
"Vanish"	48' steam	J. A. Aspinwall	1893
"Vant"	"S" boat	H. P. Benson	
"Vaquero I"	21' fin keeler	Herman B. Duryea	1894
"Vaquero III"	29' 6" fin keeler	H. B. Duryea	1896
"Vara"	150' power	Harold S. Vanderbilt	1928
"Vara"	22' owner's launch	Harold S. Vanderbilt	
"Vara"	22' crew's launch	Harold S. Vanderbilt	
"Vasanta"	81' gasoline	George M. Pynchon	1920
"Veda"	29' 6" sloop	Cornelius Vanderbilt	1896
"Ventura"	45' aux. sloop	George F. Baker, Jr.	1922
"Ventura"	50'	George F. Baker, Jr.	1913
"Viero"	17' J & M	W. H. Forbes	
"Vigilant"	86' 3" cutter	C. O. Iselin syndicate	1893
"Viking"	33' 9" sloop	F. C. Swan	1870
"Viking"	15' J & M	Mr. Bailihme	
"Viola"	17' cat	H. Marston	
"Violet"	15' cat	H. Marston	
"Violet"	35' sloop	Eben Denton	1865
"Virginia"	16' sloop	C. H. Plympton	1871
"Virginia"	70' cutter	W. K. Vanderbilt, Jr.	1900
"Vitessa"	25' sloop	Galen L. Stone	1914
"Vixen II"	"S" boat	Mrs. Anne Archbold	

Name	Type	Owner	Year
"Vixen"	30' steam	U.S. Navy	
"Volader"	16' J & M	Daniel Baker	
"Vortex"	150' power	Harold S. Vanderbilt	1928
"Wacona"	15' J & M	H. C. Pierce	
"Wahtawah"	30' cutter	Archibald Rogers	1902
"Waif"	30' steam	A. E. Oatman	
"Wana"	132' steam	S. R. Van Duzer	1903
"Wanda"	23' cat	E. T. Bedford	1898
"Wanderer, Jr."	27' 11" steam	H. A. C. Taylor	
"Waneche"	40' 3" gasoline	W. Butler Duncan	1906
"Warbug"	62' 4" gasoline	Felix Warbug	
"Wasaka"	27' 10" sloop	S. P. Anthony	1904
"Wasp"	45' 6" cutter	Archibald Rogers	1892
"Wasp"	23' steam	U.S. Coast Survey tender	
"Water Witch"	24' steam	C. T. and C. R. Flint	
"Waturus"	15' J & M	R. Morgan	
"Wave"	83' steam ferry boat	U.S. Navy	
"Wave"	24' 6" cat	F. H. Baldwin	1875
"Wawa"	29' 6" bulb fin	James A. Stillman	1896
"Wayfarer"	31' 10" starboard launch	Alfred G. Vanderbilt	
"Wayfarer"	30' 3" port launch	Alfred G. Vanderbilt	
"Weetamoe"	83' sloop	Geo. Nichols et al.	1930
"Wee Winn"	fin keel half rater	Blair Cochran	
"Westward"	96' schooner	Alexander S. Cochran	
"Westward"	35' gasoline tender for schooner	Alexander S. Cochran	
"Whisper"	15' J & M	E. D. Morgan	
"White Bait"	16' J & M	A. M. White	
"Whitecap"	15' J & M	L. Minot	
"Wildfire"	68' aux. schooner	C. L. Harding	1923
"Wild Goose"	31' 8" aux. sloop	Charles B. Rockwell	1930
"Wink"	19' 9" sloop	D. G. Whittock	1911
"Winona"	25' fin keeler	Henry Allen	1892
"Winsome"	62' 8" cutter	Henry F. Lippitt	1907
"Wiz"	12' spritsail	A. C. Harrison	
"Wizard"	18' J & M	F. Sargent	
"Wraith"	23' catyawl	Charles Fletcher	1892
"Xantho"	45' steamer	J. B. Watkins	1884
"Xpdnc"	43' gasoline launch	Frank H. Croker	1904
"Xiphies"	16' J & M	F. G. Hinsdale	
"Yacona"	30' steam	H. C. Pierce	
"Yalu"	15' J & M	R. Codman	
"Yankee"	70' cutter	Herman B. Duryea and Harry Payne Whitney	1900
"Yankton"	23' steam	U.S. Coast Survey	
"Yawlcat"	40' 6" aux. yawl	E. E. Mallinckrodt, Jr.	1932
"Yosemite"	28' steam	U.S. Coast Survey	
"Young Miss"	30' cutter	C. Whittemore	1902
"Zaidee"	28' 6" schooner	Rev. R. L. Greene	1870
"Zara"	31' cutter	Joshua M. Sears	1903
"Zinganee"	81' steamer	Wm. H. Moore	1902
"Zingara"	30' cutter	E. M. Farnsworth	1902
10	58' steel barges	U.S. Navy	
No. 308	112' steam patrol boat	Robert E. Tod, given to U.S. Navy	1917

Miscellaneous

Name	Type	Owner	Year
"Prudence"	36'		
"Patience"	36'	Fishing boats for	
"Hope"	28'	Narragansett Bay	1864
"Faith"	28'		
No name	11' 7" J & M	William O. Gay	
	Two 13' tenders	Herreshoff Company	
	17' J & M	Herreshoff Company	
	16' J & M	Herreshoff Company	
	14' J & M	Herreshoff Company	
	23' steam	Spanish Naval Commission	
	Two 14' J & M	A. H. Sweetland	
	15' J & M	Ogden Mills	
	14' sailing dinghy	I. B. Merriman	
	14' J & M	Charles F. Ludington	
	28' steamer	W. Hopkins	
"Flickamoro"	15' J & M	Robert W. Emmons	
	14' 5" J & M	A. J. Drexel	
	14' J & M	E. B. Douglas	
	11' 6"	Mr. Darlington	
	First "S" boat built	Nathaniel F. Ayer	
	"S"	Walter Ayer	
No. 149	48' steam Vedette	British Navy	1888
150	" " "	" "	
No name	14' J & M	H. M. Matheson	
	14' J & M	W. J. Matheson	
	14' J & M	Fred H. Pollard	
	15' 6" sailing dinghy	George M. Pynchon	
	14' J & M	F. L. Seely	
	15' J & M	E. D. Thayer	
	27' steam	J. E. Ward	
	16' J & M	H. E. Warner	
	15' J & M	W. C. Whitney	
	Five boats for 14' J & M	Biscayne Bay Yacht Club	
	27' steam launch for "Atlanta"	Jay Gould	
	35' steam launch for same		
No. 5.	30' steam	New York Coast Survey	
"Go Bye"	15' Buzzards Bay	R. W. Emmons	
"Mongoose"	15' Buzzards Bay	R. W. Emmons	
"Peacock"	15' Buzzards Bay	R. W. Emmons	
"Teaser"	15' Buzzards Bay	R. W. Emmons	
"Toby"	15' Buzzards Bay	H. O. Havemeyer	
"Jilt"	21' sloop	W. O. Gay	1899
"Jack"	15' Buzzards Bay	Robert F. Herrick	
"Venture"	15' Buzzards Bay	M. J. Hitchcock	
"Mecoh"	15' Buzzards Bay	Osborn Howes	
"How Come"	15' Buzzards Bay	E. B. Knowlton	
"Tricoon"	15' Buzzards Bay	J. L. Stackpole	
"Peasant"	15' Buzzards Bay	Robert Winsor	
No name	15' Buzzards Bay	R. Bigelow	
No Name	15' Buzzards Bay	L. Brooks	
"Surprise"	"S" boat	R. B. Lanier	

Name	Type	Owner	Year
"Widgeon"	"S" boat	R. A. Leeson	
No name	"S" boat	J. R. McBeath	
"Sea Dog"	"S" boat	W. L. Marston	
No name	"S" boat	Geo. H. MacFadden	
"Bobby"	"S" boat	E. Bruce Merriman	
No name	"S" boat	Wm. S. Moore	
"Bridget"	"S" boat	John J. O'Brien	
No name	"S" boat	Stanley Clark	
"Danea"	"S" boat	Gano Dunne	
"Priscilla"	"S" boat	Wendell H. Endicott	
"Rocket"	"S" boat	Henry M. Faxon	
"Jacks"	"S" boat	A. Y. Gowan	
"Raggedy Ann"	"S" boat	R. F. Haffenreffer III	
"Whoopee"	"S" boat	Wm. H. Hand, Jr.	
"Dolphin"	"S" boat	F. G. Hinsdale	
"Dilemma"	"S" boat	E. C. Janeway	
"Fano"	"S" boat	B. Jennings	
"Koshare"	"S" boat	Mrs. Mary G. Ogden	
"Elfrida"	"S" boat	L. P. Ordway	
"Barracuda"	"S" boat	Lawrence F. Percival	
"Skip"	"S" boat	Albert Pierce	
"Eleanor"	"S" boat	Joseph Pulitzer	
"Spray"	"S" boat	Fulton J. Redman	
"Firefly"	"S" boat	John S. Rogers	
"Rowena"	"S" boat	J. M. Rothwell	
"Artemis"	"S" boat	Warwick P. Scott	
"Stella II"	"S" boat	Henry M. Sears	
"Shrimp"	"S" boat	P. L. Spaulding	
"Spindrift"	"S" boat	F. O. Spedden	
No name	"S" boat	Harry H. Thorndike	
"Lulworth"	"S" boat	Francis M. Weld	
"Teaticket"	"S" boat	H. D. Whitten	
"Dolphin"	"S" boat	Holden P. Williams	
No name	"S" boat	M. Williams	
"Mary Bud"	"S" boat	Alex Winsor	
"Wren"	"S" boat	J. M. Witall	
"Doughboy"	"S" boat	O. G. Wood	
"Nightmare"	"S" boat	A. S. Brown, Jr.	

12½-footers

Name	Owner	Name	Owner
"Buddy"	Franklin M. Haynes		George A. Ratsey
"Granny"	J. W. Hollowell	"Katy"	Mrs. J. S. Redman
"Flit"	Paul D. Howe	"Sally"	Philip L. Reed
"Gloria II"	Mrs. Frank P. Howe	"Sambo"	Mrs. Sarah Reed
	Mrs. Hope Howland	"Whiz"	C. F. Richmond
	Richard F. Hoyt		Alpheus Reybne
"Spider"	William H. Hubbard	"Phantom"	C. B. Rockwell
"Comet"	Paul Hurst		Dorothy C. Rogers
"Mischief"	Guy Hutchinson	"Chemo"	D. L. Rogers
"Gallogog"	O'D. Iselin	"Fanny"	Henry A. Ross
"Blue Fish"	James Jackson	"Beetle"	Thomas W. Russell
"Duckling"	Walter C. Jenney		E. C. Rust
"Pirate"	Harold C. Keith		Mrs. Nora B. Ryerson
"Hatasu"	John W. Knowles	"Junco"	R. Saltonstall
"Daphne"	W. Huston Lillard	"Sparklet"	S. P. Shaw, Jr.
"Mummy Chug"			Mrs. John B. Sheller
	Ruth Lionberger	"Osprey"	Philip B. Stanley
"Bandit"	Charles D. Rafferty	"Kelpie"	John W. Stedman

12½-footers

Boat	Owner	Boat	Owner
——	A. G. B. Stell	"Dreadnought"	Paul Dudley Dean
"Tern"	R. G. Stewart	R. I. Red	Mrs. H. DeWolfe
"Bullet"	Galen Stone	"Woozlie"	W. Barton Eddison
"Betty"	Robert Stone	"Isabelle V"	Dean Emory
"Anne"	Hosmer L. Sweetster	"Papillon"	H. Wendell Endicott
"Windego"	E. Kent Swift	"Breeze"	W. G. Roelker
"Peggy"	W. O. Taylor	"Shelldrake"	Arthur Adams
"Tern"	H. L. Tiffany	"Doris"	S. R. Anthony
"Sea Lion"	Charles Tiffany	"Weetamoe"	Eugene Ashley
"Little Rhody, Jr."	Charles Tillinghast	"Spotty"	Perley Barbour
"A A 1"	B. W. Trafford	"Kingfisher"	August Belmont, Jr.
"Wee Wonder"	Douglas Van Dyke	"Perro"	F. H. Bennett
"Swish"	Harriet T. Verry	"Hope"	Dr. Thomas L. Bennett
"Dodo"	George T. Walker	No name	Lewis F. Bishop
"Kido"	George T. Walker	"Betty"	F. A. Bowman
"Black Maria"	Mrs. A. T. Wall, Jr.	"Butterball"	G. Brooks
——	Rodman Wanamaker	"Oriole"	Donaldson M. Brown
"Rhodera"	R. S. Webster	No name	Donaldson M. Brown
"Blue Bill"	Myles W. Weeks	No name	W. Stephen Carey, Jr.
"Sampan"	Mr. Whittall	No name	George B. Massey
"Onwego"	P. H. Lombard	No name	H. L. Maxwell
"Skipper"	Caleb Loring	No name	H. L. Maxwell
"Rab"	Arthur Lyman	No name	H. L. Maxwell
"Tar Baby"	Arthur Lyman	"Kittiwake"	Max Ginlay
"Oval"	A. A. McDonald	"Comet Jr."	I. B. Merriman
"Fidget"	Mary Louise McIlerney	"Elf"	G. H. Monks
"Felix"	Roger Millick	"Katydid"	H. A. Newberry
"Pigmy"	G. H. Monks	"Sachuest"	F. B. Nourse
"Dormouse"	A. H. Newman	"Black Jack"	H. C. Osburn
"Falcon"	J. A. Noyes	"Gray Gull"	C. B. Prayns
"Widgeon"	John S. Palmer	"Buzzard"	W. Y. Peters
"Thistle"	T. N. Perkins	"Winka"	S. H. Prouty
No name	Mrs. Benjamin Pitman	"Cricket"	H. B. Farnum
No name	Francis M. Rackeman	"Barbakins III"	Crawford R. Ferguson
"Flying Fish"	Alfred L. Ferguson	"Wanderer Jr."	D. W. Flint
No name	Henry L. Ferguson	"Ringlet"	W. C. Forbes
"Clethra"	W. C. Forbes	No name	James B. Ford
"Doodlebug"	M. Forbes	"Thistle"	Frederick Foster
"Merganser"	Noble Foss	"Bumble"	Dwight E. Fullerton
"Whiffus"	Reginald Foster	"Shrimpo"	Geo. P. Gardiner, Jr.
"Moro"	G. P. Gardiner, Jr.	"Rosinante"	C. A. Goodwin
"Jeff"	Jerome R. George	No name	Geo. N. Gregory
"Beverly Hills"	Jerome R. George	"Porpoise"	R. H. Hallowell
"Juno"	Russell Grinnell	"Cinch"	F. A. Harding
"Malolo"	Wm. H. Hand, Jr.	No name	Albert E. Carroll
"Sizzle"	Harry G. Haskell	"Schipperke"	Mrs. J. W. Chapman
"Ojai"	G. Hartley Chamberlain	No name	Herman F. Clark
No name	Mrs. W. H. Claflin	"Puffin"	Dorothy A. T. Coggswell
No name	Mr. Clifford	"Widgeon"	W. C. Coleman
No name	Francis W. Cole	"Ding Hao"	Chas. A. Coolidge
Nancy Bell	Mrs. G. M. Congdon	No name	Courtney Crocker
Scamp	W. Murray Crane	"Gnome"	E. I. Cudahy
"Duck"	G. Crompton	No name	Donald F. Cutler
"Wender"	Robert W. Cummings	"Quickstep"	Paul Dudley Dean
"Empress"	Mrs. Murray S. Danforth	"Crow"	Robt. L. DeNormandie
		"Bandit"	Mary C. Draper
		"Spindrift"	John P. Elton
		"Chub"	R. W. Emmons

12½-footers

No name	K. R. Albers	Matrema	Marion Bigelow
"Nettie"		"O Kay"	W. McBlair
"Gurgle"	Scofield Andrews	No name	Elmer H. Bright
No name	Pierce Archer	No name	Walter D. Brooks
"Bonita"	E. W. Atkinson	No name	J. Herbert Brown
"Lindy"	F. B. Barden	No name	W. Starling Burgess
No name	F. B. Barden	"Juanita"	W. C. Carpenter, Jr.
No name	F. B. Barden		

Index

Index